15.—

ESSAYS IN
ELIZABETHAN HISTORY

By the same author

QUEEN ELIZABETH I

THE AGE OF CATHERINE DE MEDICI

THE ELIZABETHAN HOUSE OF COMMONS

ELIZABETH I AND HER PARLIAMENTS
1559-1581 · 1584-1601
[2 VOLS.]

ESSAYS IN ELIZABETHAN HISTORY

BY

J. E. NEALE

JONATHAN CAPE
THIRTY BEDFORD SQUARE
LONDON

FIRST PUBLISHED 1958

PRINTED IN GREAT BRITAIN IN THE CITY OF OXFORD
AT THE ALDEN PRESS
ON PAPER MADE BY JOHN DICKINSON & CO. LTD
BOUND BY A. W. BAIN & CO. LTD, LONDON

CONTENTS

ESSAYS IN ELIZABETHAN HISTORY

NOVEMBER 17TH

OVER the years I have written many short historical studies in articles, lectures and reviews. Most of them served an immediate purpose and are best left unresurrected; some were on themes that I have subsequently traversed in my books. A few, however, escape these two vetoes and I hope that I have not erred in deciding to make them available to a wider public.

I do not know how long a certain diffidence about reliving my past would have delayed the appearance of this volume, had it not been for the approach of a date which this country of ours has good reason to salute. I refer to November 17th, 1958, the fourth centenary of Queen Elizabeth I's accession to the throne: a day now forgotten, but once celebrated by generations of Englishmen. When I was young, I cherished the thought of one day writing the posthumous history of Good Queen Bess, tracing through the centuries a legend which became part of our folklore and which is not yet dead, though much of its vitality has ebbed away. Time and temperament have quietly disposed of my youthful ambition, and in consequence the posthumous history of Queen Elizabeth must remain a subject in search of an author: a fascinating and far from insignificant subject.

Had I written my dream-book, a central thread, running through most of the story, would have been that day, November 17th, whose fourth centenary this volume is meant to commemorate. For Protestant Englishmen who saw the first Elizabethan Accession Day, it had much of the quality of Bastille Day for Frenchmen or November 7th for present-day Russians. It was a Thursday, and they called the day before, when rumour spread that Mary Tudor was dying, Hope Wednesday. As its first and later anniversaries came round, many minds must have recalled the event and hearts warmed in devout thankfulness. But it was not then the custom to mark the years of a monarch's reign by special celebrations: after all, in Catholic England there had been saints' days galore to provide the people with Holy Days and fortify parish bell-ringers with practice, refreshment and fees. Protestant England cut down the number of saints and thereby deprived the people and their bell-ringers of much traditional festivity.

The diminution in saints' days, we may presume, produced favourable conditions for the more or less spontaneous appearance of a new type of Holy Day – a holiday as Protestant as the compulsory fish-day instituted by Parliament in 1563 and dubbed by the Papists 'Cecil's Fast'. At any rate, the inspiration that made a national Holyday of November 17th – the Queen's Day, Accession Day, or, as it was often erroneously called, Coronation Day – was the revolutionary spirit of November 1558, revived by Catholic threats at home and abroad and personified in a Queen, whose life, to ardent Protestants, was the most precious thing on earth. The contemporary historian, William Camden, tells us: 'The twelfth year of the reign of Queen Elizabeth being now happily expired, wherein some credulous Papists expected, according to the prediction of certain wizards, their Golden day – as they termed it – all good men through England joyfully triumphed, and with thanksgivings, sermons in churches, multiplied prayers, joyful ringing of bells, running at tilt, and festival mirth began to celebrate the seventeenth day of November, being the anniversary day of the beginning of her reign; which, in testimony of their affectionate love towards her, they never ceased to observe as long as she lived.' Camden was perhaps a year or two late in his dating. In some places church bells seem to have been rung as early as 1568; but the general celebration of Accession Day probably followed the successful weathering of the first great crisis of the reign – the Rebellion of the North in November and December 1569, and the promulgation, just after, of the Papal Bull deposing Elizabeth.

As the pattern of this annual festival became settled, its central attraction was at Court, where in the tiltyard at Westminster courtiers displayed their prowess, and, aided by professional writers, let fantasy riot in more and more elaborate and costly devices, pageantry and masking. At Cambridge, and presumably at Oxford, there were orations in College halls and bonfires in the quadrangles, while, throughout the land, in village and town, all the church bells were rung. In churchwardens' and borough-chamberlains' accounts we can still see recorded the cost of repairing the bells in preparation for the day and the rewards given to the bell-ringers. At Bridgnorth, for example, there is the following entry in 1585: '3s. 4d. to the clerk of the Castle church for ringing of the Queen's Holiday; 7s. to the clerk of St Leonard's church for ringing at the same time.' In 1601 the cost is noted of felling, preparing and carting wood for the bonfire customarily lit on that day. Bells and bonfires: they were long to remain features of popular rejoicing on November 17th.

A search of local records would probably reveal many pleasing variations in the celebration of this day. At Ipswich in 1583 the town's schoolmaster presented 'certain pageants in joy of the Queen's coronation', and was paid forty shillings 'for his pains and charges'. In 1584, the London parish of St Andrew, Holborn, began a new practice by converting into a sort of Maundy occasion each of 'the two memorable feasts of our gracious sovereign lady, Queen Elizabeth' — her birthday on September 7th, and her 'coronation day' on November 17th. On the birthday, 'fifty-two old women of the greatest age in the parish' received at a maid's hands a spice cake, a draft of wine and twopence in money, the total cost being 17s. On 'coronation day' — the Queen then entering the twenty-seventh year of her reign — twenty-seven of the parish's most aged women were assembled in the church, this time with twenty-seven 'young maiden children' attendant. 'After public prayers earnestly made for her Majesty's long and prosperous reign over us', the maids and churchwardens distributed to the old women a spice cake, a draft of burnt claret wine and threepence apiece, while the children received a cake, a draft of claret wine and one penny apiece: superior largesse to that of the birthday. 'And so', adds the worthy churchwarden, who entered this charming note in his account book, 'after prayer and thanksgiving again zealously made for her Majesty, with joyful hearts and thankful and devout minds, they all departed in God's praise home to their houses, expecting (if it so please God) the continuance of so good an exercise, to the glory of God, the parish's credit and their relief; that by this means many prayers and thanksgiving unto God may be continually made of many, for the continuance of His manifold and great blessings, many years to endure, upon His church, our Queen and Realm.'[1]

Writing to Dudley Carleton in 1602, John Chamberlain, the letter writer, described the celebrations in the capital on the last Accession Day of the reign: 'Her day passed with the ordinary solemnity of preaching, singing, shooting, ringing and running. The bishop of Limerick ... made a dull sermon at Paul's Cross. At the tilt were many young runners.' Carleton's fool, Garret, he added, 'had good audience of her Majesty and made her very merry'.

By 1576 the Church had added the day to its select rota of Holy Days, and in that year the royal printer issued 'A Form of Prayer with Thanks Giving, to be used every year, the 17th of November, being the day of the Queen's Majesty's entry to her reign'. To that biblically-minded generation, God seemed to be working in Elizabethan England with the same sure purpose revealed by the scriptures in Israel; and the psalms and lessons for the day were chosen with striking appropriateness:

Lord, thou hast granted to thy land
The favours we implor'd

[1] I am indebted for this item to Mr H. G. Owen, a research student of mine.

And faithful Jacob's captive race
Hast graciously restor'd.

Many a puritan heart, as these opening words of the 85th Psalm were intoned, must have been stirred by thoughts of Catholic Mary's days and the miraculous preservation and triumph of her sister, Elizabeth. That is how John Foxe in his *Book of Martyrs* saw the working of Providence; how Holinshed the chronicler and many a speaker in the House of Commons saw it too. For the first lesson, officiating clergymen were offered a choice of passages from the Old Testament, recalling the godly rulers of Israel – Jehoshaphat, Hezekiah and Josiah, men who 'did that which is right in the sight of the Lord', and whose enemies God confounded. For the second lesson, the thirteenth chapter of St Paul's Epistle to the Romans was prescribed, opening with that famous verse, which was the familiar bulwark of monarchy in those days: 'Let every soul be subject unto the higher power. For there is no power but of God. The powers that be are ordained of God.'

Two years later there were special metrical thanksgivings available in print, to be sung as psalms:

Sound out the trump courageously,
Blow as on solemn days:
Both high and low, come fill the sky
with sweet resounding praise.
For why? when we were bound in thrall,
and eke in grief did stand,
The Lord did set us free from all
by this his servant's hand.

As the cult of the Queen spread and mellowed, ballad-writers were to add other such simple verses to the music of the day.

And so, each year, the people fêted their Eliza, whose boast it was that 'though God hath raised me high, yet this I count the glory of my crown, that I have reigned with your loves'. The like had never before been known in this land, and perhaps has only been repeated since in the unique hold on Englishmen's affections won by Sir Winston Churchill during the late war.

On the Queen's death, her successor, James I, transferred the Accession Day celebrations to his own date, March 24th. The courtly pageantry of the Westminster tiltyard was held on that day; and apparently the villagers rang their bells. But the old spontaneity, rooted in popular affection, could not be sustained. Very soon, the glory of England, which for Elizabethans had been in the present, slipped into the past, and the ghost of Good Queen Bess returned to possess a nation's heart. Bishop Goodman, in his *Memoirs of the Court of King James*, relates that 'after a few years, when we had experience of the Scottish government, then – in disparagement of the Scots and in hate and detestation of them – the Queen [Elizabeth] did seem to revive. Then was her memory much magnified – such ringing of bells, such public joy and sermons in commemoration of her, the picture of her tomb painted in many churches; and in effect, more solemnity and joy in memory of her coronation than was for the coming in of King James'. The posthumous history of Elizabeth I had begun.

To put a precise year or time to the revival seems difficult, but on November 17th, 1620, John Chamberlain indited a letter to his friend, Dudley Carleton: 'From London this 17th of November, the happiest day that ever England had to my remembrance.' He was not the only eminent Englishman to think nostalgically of the past. In a speech in the House of Commons on November 27th, 1621, when Queen Elizabeth's Accession Day was probably in his mind, the unpoetic Sir Edward Coke was moved to say that 'she was the flower of Queens, as the rose [is the] queen of flowers'. And in April 1623 John Chamberlain reported that the St Paul's sermon of a young Magdalen preacher was liked the better because 'he was not long nor immoderate in commendation of the [present] time, but gave Queen Elizabeth her due': a comment that virtually paraphrases a similar appreciation of a Paul's Cross sermon in 1617. Francis Osborne, who wrote his *Traditional Memoirs of the Reign of Queen Elizabeth* in the middle of the century – they were published in 1658, the first centenary of Accession Day – referred to the felicity of her reign, which, he says, 'was never since matched, nor have we had yet any cause to hope it will be'. He mentions 'the bonfires and loud acclamations used still by the people upon the day of her inauguration'.

Discontent and despondency – disgust with the government, dislike of the Scots, fear of Catholicism: these had led Englishmen to recall the memory of Good Queen Bess and honour her day. The fear of Catholicism was to continue for a very long time; and when under Charles II and James II the Protestant faith seemed once more to be in danger, old passions were revived and, in London at least, Queen Elizabeth's Accession Day – now apt to be called her Birthday – acquired something of the significance it possessed in her own lifetime.

A new chapter of our story begins with Titus Oates and the exploitation of his Popish Plot for party ends. For London prentices and the London mob, the seventeenth of November became henceforward a second Guy Fawkes day. In 1678, the first November of the Plot years, 'great solemnities' were planned for 'the birthday of Queen Elizabeth', and we are told that 'a constable brought one lately before a Justice of the Peace for speaking treason against Queen Elizabeth'. The following year, during the agitation over the Exclusion Bill – directed against the succession of James to the throne – London's celebration of November 17th was staged with unparalleled elaboration. Great sums of money are said to have been spent on wine and spirits for 'incredible multitudes' of people and on the tableaux for a fantastic procession: tableaux that included the Pope, with the Devil in attendance as his privy counsellor, Cardinals and Jesuits, and Sir Edmund Berry Godfrey, the people's martyr and Papists' victim. That morning the bells started ringing at 3 a.m. and at 5 a.m. the procession started on its way from Moorgate to Temple Bar, where, before the statue of Queen Elizabeth – adorned for the occasion with a crown of gilded laurel and a golden shield bearing the legend, 'The Protestant Religion and Magna Charta' – the Pope, in all his grandeur, was toppled on to a huge bonfire. Afterwards, this grotesque show, with the doggerel verses written for it, was commemorated in a descriptive pamphlet, entitled *London's Defiance to Rome*.

There were similar celebrations in following years, and when in 1682, at the desire of the Lord Mayor – who feared a tumult – King and Council intervened to prohibit the factious people from burning the Pope, 'they drowned him' instead. In November 1688 William of Orange had just landed in England; and a correspondent then wrote that James II, fearing the London prentices, who were daily committing disorders, deemed it prudent to defer his departure from the city till after 'Queen Elizabeth's birthday'.

In Queen Anne's reign, the celebration of Accession Day once again became an instrument of party politics. 'This being Queen Elizabeth's birthday', wrote Swift in his *Journal to Stella*, on November 17th, 1711, 'we have the d—— and all to do among us.' The Whigs designed to have a mighty torchlight procession at midnight, with effigies of the Pope, the Devil, Cardinals, the high-churchman Sacheverell, etc., which were to be thrown on the bonfire. However, by order of the Secretary of State the effigies were seized, and the public had to be content with a broadside account of the intended mock procession, along with verses written for the occasion:

Let us sing to the memory of glorious Queen Bess,
Who long did the hearts of her subjects possess,
And whose mighty actions did to us secure
Those many great blessings which now do endure:
For then she did lay that solid foundation
On which our religion is fixed in this nation.

It was ironic, and yet it was also apt, to use the name and day and fame of Queen Elizabeth for the crude passions of a Protestant mob. Ironic, because she herself had been high Anglican in outlook and the inflexible opponent of fanaticism and intolerance. Apt, because fate had made her the instrument of revolution, and her accession day, which its commemorators loved to call the Birthday of the Gospel, had indeed been that. She had been engaged in mortal conflict with Catholicism for close on half a century, her own life and the ethos of her country at stake. She boasted of being 'mere English', and, as the Virgin Queen, identified herself with patriotism and the people to the exclusion of all other earthly attachments. She was, she rejoiced to be, England's Eliza; and if her devotees committed many solecisms in her name, she can scarcely be blamed.

The annual salute to Queen Bess's fame continued. When in 1713 Pope Pius V — author of the famous bull of 1570 deposing her — was canonized, there came a counterblast in a tract entitled *A Protestant Memorial for the Seventeenth of November, being the Inauguration Day of Queen Elizabeth.* The author remarks: 'In a grateful remembrance of God's mercy in raising up, continuing, and prospering this most illustrious benefactor of England, the good Protestants of this nation (those especially of London and Westminster) have annually taken notice (and not without some degree of decent and orderly solemnity) of the 17th of November, being the day on which her Majesty Queen Elizabeth began her happy reign. And', continues the author, 'such decent and orderly observation of it seems to me not only warranted by former motives, but also enforced by a new and extraordinary argument', namely, the canonization of Pius V. A volume of *Miscellanies*, published in George I's reign and containing 'Merry Observations' on remarkable days throughout the year, also mentions this day: a day, the author affirms, which 'will prove another protestant Holiday, dedicated to the pious memory of that antipapistical Princess and virgin preserver of the reformed Churches, Queen Elizabeth. This night', he adds, 'will be a great promoter of the tallow-chandler's welfare; for marvellous illuminations will be set forth in every window, as emblems of her shining virtues; and will be stuck in clay, to put the world in mind that grace, wisdom, beauty and virginity were unable to preserve the best of women from mortality'.

In 1718 a periodical, giving an account of public spectacles, linked the ancient and laudable custom of burning the Pope on November 5th with that of commemorating Queen Elizabeth on the 17th; but – and this is the point to note – the author was conscious that decline had set in. 'I am sorry', he comments, 'to see this ceremony is not performed of late years with the usual pomp and triumph.' A few more traces of the day remain. Newbury in Berkshire, we are told, rang its bells every November 17th for Queen Elizabeth's accession, down to 1739. Then, in 1760, a correspondent of the *Gentleman's Magazine* wrote to say that, 'this being the anniversary of Queen Elizabeth's accession', he was reminded of the celebration in 1679. Evidently, the festival had become, or was becoming, little more than a memory. By 1803 even the memory was fading. In that year another correspondent of the *Gentleman's Magazine* quoted a couplet from one of the satires of John Oldham, the late-seventeenth-century poet:

> Louder than on Queen Bess's day the rout
> For Anti-Christ burnt in effigy shout.

He proceeded to ask: When is Queen Bess's day; why was it so called; and when was it discontinued?

The day has its place in John Brand's *Observations on Popular Antiquities*, as re-edited by Sir Henry Ellis in 1813 and often re-published in the nineteenth century; but it is as a defunct anniversary – except that Ellis noted (as he also did in another publication in 1827), that the day was still kept as a holiday at the Exchequer and at Westminster and Merchant-Taylors schools.

Times had changed. The raw emotional appeal of 'the Birthday of the Gospel' could not survive the Age of Reason and the French Revolution. Catholic emancipation was on its way, and England no longer needed her Eliza. In any case, romantic notions about monarchy were out of date. There was little credence in a great Queen, nor was there much sympathy with a Queen who was something of a blue-stocking. Harris Nicolas, writing a biography of Lady Jane Grey in 1825 and listing her linguistic accomplishments, remarked — and presumably would have said much the same of Elizabeth: 'She possessed acquirements now properly deemed neither requisite nor useful in female education.' If William Cobbett had lived a few generations earlier, the odds are that he would have shouted with the lustiest for 'the best of women', on November 17th; but to him Elizabeth was 'Bloody Queen Bess', and by perversity Mary 'Good Queen Mary'. And in the sentimental, civilized age of Victoria, how could the murderer of Mary Queen of Scots be good? Except in folklore, where scores of apocryphal stories about her kept on circulating, the posthumous history of England's Eliza was ended. When the three-hundredth anniversary of Accession Day arrived on November 17th, 1858, neither heart nor mind responded. The leading article in *The Times* that day was on manure.

If today we are inclined to salute an ancient Holyday, it is not because bygone passions have revived. Our historical perspective has changed and our knowledge advanced. We recognize the Elizabethan period as an age strangely like our own, and, understanding its problems, see in the Queen a leader meet for the times: one endowed with wisdom, courage and tolerance, able to inspire the nation, save it from its perils, and conjure immortal glory from its aspirations.

It remains for me to thank those editors and others who

have given permission to reprint the following essays. In my selection I have included two papers that are more technical and closely argued than I could have wished. Apart from their subject matter, which I hope may prove of interest, they seem to me useful as an indication to laymen of the deceptive idiom that so often confronts the historian of remoter times.

THE ELIZABETHAN AGE[1]

It could hardly have been expected of me that I should choose any other subject for this occasion than my Elizabethan period; and the name of Bishop Creighton, whose work as a historian we commemorate, was also an injunction to keep to my last, for, as you all know, Creighton was one of Queen Elizabeth's biographers. There is, or there was, a tradition that this lecture should be broad in its scope (though not necessarily in its chronology); that it should proceed more obviously from reflection than from research. Seeking for a theme in this vein, it occurred to me that I might try to answer the question, What made the Elizabethan period a great age? Can the historian by his process of analysis answer, or at least throw some light on, so subtle and difficult a question? If he can, then he may exceed the purely antiquarian purpose of satisfying man's curiosity about the past, and, in this bewildering, changing society of our own day, may proffer that modicum of understanding which is to be found in historical analogy. The supreme privilege of human beings among God's creatures is that they can garner experience; and history is man's storehouse.

No one is likely to accuse me of begging the question by assuming the greatness of the Elizabethan age. Its own people grew to be conscious of it. The ballad-writers, the chroniclers, the playwrights — in short, the literary voice of Elizabethan England, and voices abroad also, including Pope Sixtus V — proclaimed it. The apocalyptic mood of Mr Churchill's great words — 'This was their finest hour' — possessed many Elizabethans. And after the Queen was dead and the age become a

[1] The Creighton Lecture, University of London, 1950; published by the Athlone Press, 1951.

memory, after the novelty of possessing a male sovereign in the person of James I had worn off — and how quickly this happened! — Englishmen grasped with instinctive certainty that that indeed had been their finest hour. So the tradition remained in this land of ours. While personal monarchy lasted or religion suffused politics the greatness of the age was personified in Elizabeth — 'the Queen whose feast the factious rabble keep', as Dryden wrote.

> Fixt in our hearts thy fame shall live;
> And maugre all the popish spite,
> To honour thee our youth shall strive,
> And yearly celebrate this night.

So ran some verses written in 1679 to celebrate the anniversary of Elizabeth's accession to the throne — 'the Birthday of the Gospel', as it was called.[1] And when such passions died down and personal monarchy went out of fashion, still the age was acclaimed great, though the credit might be transferred from the sovereign to her ministers. In our own lifetime, even the cynics, in the years of disillusion after the first world war, however they bespattered personalities left the tradition about the age free from denigration.

Thus, with the consensus of the centuries behind us, we may proceed with our inquiry: Why did England achieve greatness in this age? If we try to generalize the question and apply it first to the individual, we might agree that in addition to the capacity for greatness there must be the will to achieve it and the opportunity. Many a potential genius must have died after a commonplace life through the lack of a chance to live otherwise; and all of us who have passed our youth must realize that opportunity may be there but ability alone is no guarantee that it will be seized. The same considerations surely hold in a nation's life. The thesis is implied in the passage of

[1] C. H. Firth, 'The Ballad History of the Reigns of the Later Tudors', in *Trans. Royal Hist. Soc.* 3rd ser. iii, 117-18; E. K. Wilson, *England's Eliza*, p. 73.

Mr Churchill's from which I have already quoted. When the stream moves quietly and satisfactorily along, how tempting it is for a nation to rest on its oars!

In the Elizabethan period the waters were far from quiet. That, indeed, may partly explain why Elizabethan history has so manifest an appeal to readers today. Then, as now, Europe was concerned with the clash of two faiths inextricably mingled with politics. Then, as now, the devotees of both sides felt that the truth which was in them was a cause transcending all others. Do not be surprised that I compare the struggle of Catholicism and Protestantism in those days with that of our rival ideologies today. Time has detached religion from politics and emptied it of the old passion and intolerance: but sixteenth-century zealots viewed the rival faith with all the detestation and fear that we see in our world today; and the connection of religion with the state confused international and national politics.

On its doctrinal side the English Reformation may be described as a partisan story down to the accession of Elizabeth. In pre-Nazi and pre-Communist days scholars were prone to make calculations about the number of Catholics in England in 1558 or at later dates. Doubtless there was virtue, although there could be little accuracy, in their labours. Nowadays, however, they strike me as in some ways irrelevant or even naive: irrelevant and naive in the sense that similar calculations about Hitler's Germany or Czechoslovakia would be. Revolutions are not explained by statistics, but by leadership, organization, intensity of conviction, passion and purpose.

The conditions for revolution existed at the end of Mary Tudor's reign: two rival ideologies, one in opposition, with several hundred of its leaders abroad, ready to return and overthrow their opponents. The Protestants possessed certain advantages. They had the sympathy of London and other influential parts of the country. No less important, Mary's reign, by its association of Catholicism with a foreign king and a disastrous pro-Spanish foreign policy, and by the hatred its religious persecution engendered, tended to make patriots anti-Catholic and generally weaken the Catholic cause. We might compare the situation with the Weimar regime in Germany vis-à-vis the nascent party of Hitler.

If a Catholic sovereign had succeeded Mary, the forces of that party would have controlled the machine of government and England would have continued Catholic. Trouble, however, would have come from London and other centres, from Parliament also, perhaps; and the country might well have drifted into civil war. At any rate, the internal stresses of such times must surely have checked the ebullient spirit of the nation. As it was, Elizabeth, a Protestant, came to the throne and, helped by the political bankruptcy of the recent past, was able to make Protestantism the symbol of England. The English Reformation ceased to be a partisan story: it became a national one.

Come over the bo[u]rn, Bessy.

In these words the England of the ballad-writer apostrophized the new Queen in 'A Songe betwene the Quenes Majestie and Englande', published in 1559.

Lady, this long space
Have I loved thy grace,
More than I durste well saye;
Hoping, at the last,
When all stormes were past,
For to see this joyfull daye.[1]

London's welcome of Elizabeth on her accession was an anticipation of revolution. What is more, our latest interpretation of her religious settlement is a study in the tactics of revolution.[2] The Elizabethan Prayer Book and Act of Uni-

[1] Firth, op. cit. p. 71.
[2] Cf. my article, 'The Elizabethan Acts of Supremacy and Uniformity', *Eng. Hist. Rev.* lxv, 304-32.

formity were extorted by the pressure of the Marian exiles, backed by a House of Commons under the leadership of radical Protestant devotees. How misleading, one reflects, is that hackneyed phrase of our text-books which describes the settlement as a *via media*, and starts off the reign on such a note. Valid it may still be in part, but it empties passion from the story and gets the perspective wrong. The Elizabethan age opened with a striking victory for the Protestant revolution; and the subsequent events of the reign – the consolidation of the Catholic Church at the Council of Trent; the French Religious Wars with the infamous blood-bath of the Massacre of St Bartholomew; the flight of Mary Queen of Scots to England, there to become the focus for religious and political discontent, leading almost immediately to the Rebellion of the North; the Papal Bull, releasing Englishmen from their allegiance to the Queen; the Papal plan of an 'Enterprise' against Protestant England; the infiltration of Catholic missionaries from the continent, preparing, as it were, a 'Fifth Column' for the day when the 'Enterprise' would be launched; the recurrent plots against the Queen's throne and life; the unfolding of English policy as anti-Spanish and anti-Catholic – all these happenings, and more, determining the domestic and foreign climate of the next forty years, kept the spirit of revolution constantly alive, and as often as not at white-hot intensity.

Here we must note a paradox. The Queen herself had an instinctive hatred of revolution and its votaries. She did not want to proceed as rapidly as she was forced to do at the beginning of the reign; she modified the revolutionary Protestant programme and injected conservative elements into the service and policy of the Anglican Church; throughout her reign she was the effective obstacle to Puritan activities; and time and again, with her caution and prudence and delays, she was the despair of her statesmen, carried away by the exuberance of the times. Nevertheless, even to the hot-heads – indeed, to the hot-heads most of all – she was the personification of their cause. She was their Judith, their Deborah, their 'Fayre Elisa, Queene of Shepheardes All', their Diana, their Laura, their 'Cynthia, the Ladie of the Sea', their Gloriana and Belphoebe. These were not random extravagances, fashioned by Court sycophants. They voiced a national cult. An American scholar has made a meticulous study of the literature of the age and filled a substantial volume with extracts on such themes.[1] Nor was literature the only expression of the mood. Running through the parliamentary debates of the reign, and reaching lyrical pitch during the period of plots and danger to Elizabeth's throne and life, is the same note. 'If it might prolong her Majesty's life but for one year', said a Member in 1585, 'I protest I would be content to suffer death with the most exquisite torments that might be devised.' 'It makes my heart leap for joy to think we have such a jewel', said another M.P.; 'it makes my joints to tremble for fear, when I consider the loss of such a jewel.'[2] Both rhapsodists belonged to that large Puritan element in the House of Commons which managed to worship the Queen and yet be a never-ending source of trouble.

> Ring out your bels!
> What should yow doe els?
> Stricke up your Drums for joy!
> The Noblest Queene
> that ever was seene
> In England doth Raigne this day.

The quotation is from a ditty, whose title is expressive of its refrain: 'A pleasant newe Ballad, of the most blessed and prosperous Raigne of her Majestye for the space of two and fortye yeeres, and now entring into the three and fortith to the great joy and comfort of all her Ma[jestye's] faythfull subjects.'[3]

[1] E. K. Wilson, *England's Eliza* (Harvard Univ. Press, 1939).
[2] B.M. Lansdowne MS. 43, fols. 168b, 173b.
[3] Wilson, op. cit. p. 52.

Once more let us turn to our contemporary world as a stimulus to imagination. In Italy, Germany, and Russia we have seen a body of doctrine — the *mystique* of a people — linked to the simpler emotions of patriotism and hero-worship. So it was in Elizabethan England. Protestantism was the *mystique*. It fed and was fed by nationalism. The patriotic note runs through the ballads of the reign. It is implicit in the striking development of historical writing and reading: 'an exercise' — Elizabethans held — 'second only to a study of Holy Writ in its power to induce good morality and shape the individual into a worthy member of society'.[1] There was founded in this period the first Society of Antiquaries, to which John Stow and William Camden and many others interested in the antiquities of England belonged. History as the hand-maiden to patriotism: that, too, is familiar in our day.

The cult of Elizabeth has its analogies with the cult of Mussolini, Hitler, and Stalin. It is interesting to reflect that nowadays the revolutionary *mystique* has had to find its personification in an individual, the head of the state, who in varying degrees has been deified by its votaries. There are, however, profound differences to note, as well as analogies. The modern dictator finds the principal psychological basis of power in the cult of himself. He must be the high priest of the *mystique*. In the sixteenth century personal monarchy provided the framework for leadership: power rested in the office of monarch, and therefore it was possible for the Queen to personify the emotion of the nation without necessarily being doctrinaire. Hence the paradox of revolution with moderation at the helm.

Rare personal qualities, great art, and good fortune were needed for the role. It is said that no man can be a hero to his valet; but in this instance those about the sovereign had to be schooled into an instinctive recognition of leadership. A contemptuous, rotten, or merely blasé Court, though it attempted

[1] L. B. Wright, *Middle Class Culture in Elizabethan England*, p. 297. Cf. L. C. Knights, *Drama and Society in the Age of Jonson*, p. 244.

in its own sordid interests to sustain an artificial comedy, would have ruined the play. And there had to be the artistic capacity to draw out and respond to the emotion of the country at large. Elizabeth possessed these qualities *in excelsis*. But, as I have said, she was no revolutionary: she was not, as her sister, Mary Tudor, had been, a *dévote*. Good fortune – which was partly policy – also enters into the argument. If Elizabeth had had a husband and family, the chances are that the ardours of English Puritans would have found a rival focus and their discontents have been directed against the sovereign, thus destroying the spell over the community. In quite another way than that usually thought of, a Virgin Queen may have been essential to the Elizabethan tradition.

Elizabethan England should be regarded as a revolutionary age: that is the point I am anxious to make. Hitler claimed that a nation so inspired is irresistible, except by a like faith. And though Hitler's Germany was overwhelmed, this was accomplished by an opposing faith, stronger for being detached from fanaticism. Indeed, the boast was not an empty one. Inspiration, a sense of purpose, faith, and enthusiasm: though we may sometimes think them misplaced, devilish, or what you will, are they not ingredients of greatness? And surely they are qualities which we perceive in many aspects of the Elizabethan age. They were present in a strange blend of lust for easy riches, piratical impulse, patriotism, and fervid Protestant zeal in the voyages of Elizabethan seamen. 'The too familiar compound of avarice, self-righteousness, and hypocrisy': that is how a finely sensitive and imaginative scholar described these characteristics in 1905.[1] They are words that we too might have used in pre-Hitler days. But we now know the type; and we should not think 'hypocrisy' apt. Listen to the mystical note in the writing of John Davys, the Elizabethan navigator:

[1] Walter Raleigh, 'The English Voyages of the Sixteenth Century', in *R. Hakluyt's Principal Navigations* (Hakluyt Soc. 1905), xii, 32 n. 1.

> There is no doubt but that we of England are this saved people, by the eternal and infallible presence of the Lord predestinated to be sent into these Gentiles in the sea, to those Isles and famous Kingdoms, there to preach the peace of the Lord: for are not we only set upon Mount Zion to give light to all the rest of the world? Have not we the true handmaid of the Lord to rule us, unto whom the eternal majesty of God hath revealed his truth and supreme power of Excellency?... It is only we, therefore, that must be these shining messengers of the Lord, and none but we.[1]

Change the doctrinal and national medium, and such exaltation finds echoes in our own days. 'God's Englishman' was an Elizabethan. As a Tragedy of the 1590s declared:

> Mighty Jove the supreme king of heaven,
> That guides the concourse of the meteors
> And rules the motions of the azure sky,
> Fights always for the Briton's safety.[2]

But behind this *mystique* what was there? Certainly not a propaganda machine, nor a police state. There was a society which politically, socially, and economically had many reasons, if not every reason, to be buoyant. This was the culminating period or phase of a civilization, in which conservative elements from the past were still a vigorous reality, while new forces, having overcome an initial extravagance, had not yet developed their inner weaknesses to the point of gross abuse and social collapse.

In his essay *The Elizabethan World Picture* Dr Tillyard has demonstrated how in its view of the universe and of society the Elizabethan age preserved the medieval idea of order and degree.

[1] Raleigh, op. cit. p. 31.
[2] *The Lamentable Tragedy of Locrine* (c. 1591, by Peele?), quoted by Knights, op. cit. p. 245.

The heavens themselves, the planets, and this centre
Observe degree, priority, and place.

. . . .

O! when degree is shak'd,
Which is the ladder to all high designs,
The enterprise is sick. How could communities,
Degrees in schools, and brotherhoods in cities,
Peaceful commerce from dividable shores,
The primogenitive and due of birth,
Prerogative of age, crowns, sceptres, laurels,
But by degree, stand in authentic place?
Take but degree away, untune that string,
And, hark! what discord follows....[1]

If this philosophy had been too rigidly applied, it might have imposed the paralysis of caste upon society. If it had been utterly ignored, 'the enterprise' would indeed have been sick. Vulgarity, not quality, would have marked the age; and for its gospel we might have had the familiar lines:

The rich man in his castle, the poor man at his gate,
God made them high and lowly, and ordered their estate.

Not unlike the Elizabethan in sentiment, you will note, but how different in implication as well as diction!

In a sense, it is strange to find a philosophy of degree still vigorous in the second half of the sixteenth century, for the Reformation, through the dissolution of the monasteries and chantries and the sale of their vast estates, had threatened social upheaval. It created a prolonged and unprecedented market in land, comparable with a period of great industrial expansion in more modern times: the opportunity for speculators, for new fortunes and new men. Speculators there were:

[1] Shakespeare, *Troilus and Cressida*, act i, sc. 3.

new fortunes and new men as well — in the peerage, the King's Council and elsewhere. The voice of rebellion — of the conservative Pilgrims of Grace — protested against this trend in Henry VIII's reign; and in the brief, unhappy reign of Edward VI discord, as the philosophy prognosticated, did indeed afflict the country. It was the long reign of Elizabeth which ensured that change should proceed in an orderly way and a conservative setting. For all her popular arts, the Queen, both in temperament and policy, was essentially aristocratic. Under her father, the peerage had received a strong and needed injection of new blood. Elizabeth remained satisfied with this and created very few new peers, though aspirants to that dignity were many and clamorous in her later years. Thus by stinting honour she kept it precious, and by insisting on deference to rank she strengthened social stability.

Like the word 'nobleman', 'gentleman' was a term of art in the Elizabethan age, set in the prevailing order of 'degree, priority, and place'. The official view is clearly stated in a commission to Norroy King of Arms: 'no sheriffs, commissaries, archdeacons, officials, scriveners, clerks, writers or others shall call or write in courts and open places or use in writing the addition of esquire or gentleman, unless they can justify the same by the law of arms and the laws of the realm, or ascertain the same in writing from Norroy or his deputies'.[1] Such a theory of nomenclature might seem to indicate a system approaching the social rigidity of France at that time.

However, economic facts, and among them the active land-market, were too strong for an inflexible system. As the purchasers of ecclesiastical estates, like speculators on the modern stock market, sold out and took their profits, ultimate holders of the land benefited from the additional source of wealth. There was prolonged and severe monetary inflation in the second half of the sixteenth century; but — subject to the vagaries of the English climate — rising prices, coupled with

[1] *Cal. Patent Rolls, Eliz.* ii, 92.

an expanding market, brought great prosperity to those landholders who were fortunately situated as regards rent and showed enterprise and ability. This – to borrow the title of Professor Tawney's classical article[1] – was the age which saw the rise of the gentry. Not only did their wealth increase: they were better educated. They sent their sons to the universities, which as a result both of the Reformation and what we call the Renaissance, ceased to be primarily ecclesiastical seminaries. In increasing numbers they also sent them to the Inns of Court to obtain a non-professional knowledge of the law. They invaded the borough seats in parliament and monopolized the House of Commons for their class, as they already dominated local government through the office of Justice of the Peace.[2]

But it was not only the gentleman-born who enjoyed increased wealth and education. Lower classes in the landed hierarchy, and especially yeomen, were beneficiaries. The social distinction between gentleman and yeoman was sharp in theory, and to some extent in practice; but it was not difficult to stride across the barrier. Neither the university student nor the law student had to be *bene natus*. True, a conservative planner at the beginning of Elizabeth's reign, disturbed, like Colonel Blimp, at the prospect of England going to the dogs, wished to impose this restriction on legal training.[3] Like Colonel Blimp he remained a voice ineffective. Though they might be yeomen's sons and be scornfully known as 'gentlemen of the first head', students were by courtesy regarded as gentlemen. Moreover, as Sir Thomas Smith remarked, anyone able and willing to 'bear the port, charge, and countenance of a gentleman' could readily – if at a price – raise himself to that status. Many a yeoman preferred to remain as he was:

[1] *Economic Hist. Rev.* xi, 1-38.
[2] Cf. my *Elizabethan House of Commons*.
[3] *Hist. MSS. Com. Hatfield MSS.* i. 163.

> Then let me live and die a yeoman still.
> So was my father, so must live his son.[1]

But the socially ambitious could climb the ladder; and with class distinction fluid, intermarriage was common. Thus, in agriculture, the chief economic activity of Elizabethan England, there was incentive – plenty of it, social and monetary.

Commerce and trade, for which this was also a period of great expansion, brought similar, and, to a few, much greater rewards. Thomas Wilson, a shrewd social observer, writing about 1600, declared that in his time he had known twenty-four aldermen of the city of Norwich who were esteemed to be worth £20,000 apiece – some much more, and the better sort of citizens the half. 'But', he went on, 'if we should speak of London and some other maritime places, we should find it much exceeding this rate. It is well known that at this time there are in London some merchants worth £100,000; and he is not accounted rich that cannot reach to £50,000 or near it.'[2] If correct, such sums would be most impressive fortunes when translated into present-day values. Wealthy citizens could, and did, buy landed estates for themselves, and, like ambitious yeomen, establish themselves as 'gentlemen'. Moreover, riches were attractive and flexible conventions made intermarriage with the gentry easy. Nor was the flow one way. By the system of primogeniture younger sons of the gentry were driven out to seek a livelihood, and many of them moved into the towns to engage as citizens in trade and commerce. No prejudice existed against this, as in France. There can be no doubt that economically Elizabethan England – especially before the war years – was prosperous. The emphasis was on enterprise and the individual. In the industrial sphere the effect of this was

[1] From the play, *George a Green*, quoted by Knights, op. cit. p. 248 n. 2. For the yeoman, see Mildred Campbell, *The English Yeoman under Elizabeth and the Early Stuarts* (1942).

[2] 'The state of England ...', ed. F. J. Fisher, in *Camden Miscellany*, xvi, 20-1.

so marked that economic historians have found themselves describing an early industrial revolution.[1]

The diffusion of wealth and education and the quickening tempo of economic life had their effect upon the arts and literature. In architecture the home took the place formerly held by the church. It was an age of much building. In contrast with France, where Catherine de Medici spent prodigal sums on palaces, the Queen of England, growing poorer as the nation grew richer, was content with what she inherited. But her courtiers made up for her inactivity, while very many of the gentry and the better-off yeomen rebuilt their homes. 'If ever curious building did flourish in England, it is in these our days', wrote William Harrison in Holinshed's *Chronicles*. And as early as 1562, a bishop remarked: 'Englishmen indulge in pleasures as if they were to die tomorrow, and build as if they were to live for ever.'[2] The furnishings and equipment of the home told of new standards of life. So did personal splendour. The growth of London as a social centre, rivalry at Court, foreign travel, and the goods which merchants, with an eye to business, imported into England — not to mention the example of a Queen whose love for variety in dress was notorious — led, among courtiers and those who aped them, to an emphasis on clothes that was startling: an 'exotic and ostentatious display' such as 'never before nor since has occurred in the history of English costume'.[3] When 'green-headed youths, covered with feathers, and gold and silver lace'[4] bore 'their birth rights proudly on their backs', and an Earl of Oxford helped to bankrupt himself with his finery, the moralist might sharpen his barbs, but charity reflects that the zest of youth leads to much folly.

I do not know whether anyone has attempted to calculate, in the rough manner which alone would be possible, the number

[1] Cf. J. U. Nef, *Industry and Government in France and England, 1540-1640* (1940).
[2] *Zurich Letters* (Parker Soc.), i, 108 (app., p. 64).
[3] Iris Brooke in *Life under the Tudors* (1950), p. 212.
[4] T. Birch, *Memoirs of Queen Elizabeth*, ii, 15.

of books, pamphlets, etc., which were published in the several decades of the Elizabethan period and the decades that went before. The increase, I imagine, would be most striking. And so, in many respects, was the advance in quality. From the early Elizabethan play *Gorboduc* – itself a landmark – to the plays of Shakespeare, what a development! And a point relevant to our argument: the more scholars explore such documents as the records of the Court of Star Chamber, where the behaviour and speech of ordinary Elizabethans are preserved for us, the more Shakespeare becomes understandable as a part of his own age. As for prose: ignoring the euphuistic fashion – which afflicted the Queen, though it had its merits in royal utterances – a good deal of the writing, in historical documents no less than printed books, kept near to the vigour and directness of everyday speech. Metaphors and similes were not limp and lifeless through long and indiscriminate usage. They were freshly invented or gathered in the taverns and the street; and, apart from the natural raciness of an unsophisticated, lively people, we must remember that the ordinary man heard in church each week the verbal music of the Prayer Book. Nowadays, literary critics are becoming enthusiastic about Elizabethan prose: about the primitive muscularity of Nashe, for example, and the vivid invective of Martin Marprelate.[1] In a measure it is due to that change in taste which the best American writing of our generation has done so much to produce. And, incidentally, it seems to me that one might not go far wrong in drawing comparisons between the vitality of American life and that of Elizabethan England.

Within forty years of Elizabeth's death, after almost as many years of increasing political, religious, and social discontent, England was rent by civil war. The political machine had broken down. That fact alone would prompt us to ask how intimate was the connection between the greatness of the age

[1] Cf. Knights, op. cit. pp. 301 seqq.

that was past and its system of government. The answer will be clearer if we first draw a moral or two from the Stuart tragedy. When Elizabeth died, the Tudor political system was doomed. Those economic, educational, and social changes to which I have alluded, made certain of that. The only question was whether there would be imaginative and peaceful adaptation to a new age or whether incompetent leadership would allow the old system to fester and collapse. James I succeeded to an impoverished crown: he cannot be blamed on that count. He was weak in character, and did not know when to say 'No': these are fatal defects in any leader. He subjected Court and government to favourites, and between them they allowed the mercenary instincts of individuals free play. Corruption was rampant, honour cheapened by the sale of peerages and lesser dignities. The political and social evils, evident in the England of 1603, grew like deadly weeds; and, as the dramatists of the time perceived, the decencies of the old order were violated. Charles I completed the disaster. He turned the Puritans and the House of Commons, who had been the most ardent of Queen Elizabeth's votaries, into dangerous critics of the monarchy. Instead of personifying a nation, he led a party.

Control was what the nation needed, and what it got in the reign of Elizabeth; control which, while encouraging the energies of the people and sustaining their gaiety, restrained the cruder promptings of individualism. Government was paternal; and in the economic sphere I fancy we should understand it better if we compared it with the present-day regulated State with its emphasis on the public good. Everything depended from the centre. All aspects of life, from the personal behaviour of individuals to high matters of state came before either the Crown or the Council, or both. And never before and never again was the Privy Council so efficient. Elizabeth kept it small, balancing extremely able commoners with aristocrats; and even the aristocrats were converted by hard work and good training into tolerable and sometimes highly effective statesmen. Unlike James I, she did not blur the distinction between the two elements by rewarding the commoners with peerages. William Cecil was the signal exception to this policy, which maintained the professional outlook of the abler administrators.

But the sovereign was even more important than the Council in determining the quality of government. Under personal monarchy the machinery of government was the ruler's. In theory it was intimately linked with the royal prerogative, while in practice there was a flexibility which permitted and even demanded constant intervention from the centre. If we cast our thoughts back to Hitler's Germany, where the personal influence of the leader and his court in the normal functioning of government shocked our liberal minds, we shall obtain some idea of the picture. Or there is another, and in some respects better, parallel in the peculiar position held by Mr Churchill while England was at war. Those who have read his *Second World War* will remember the appendices of minutes and memoranda which, as a journalist said, 'he fired off unremittingly in all directions'. Though, as this journalist added, the picture is incomplete without the 'come-backs' to some of his 'peremptory rockets', the general effect, one concludes, must have been to keep officials on their toes — as undoubtedly, but by other devices, he kept the nation on its toes. We can readily imagine the effect in the sixteenth century of a Queen, with not a few of Mr Churchill's qualities, on the Whitehall of her day, and beyond that on the country at large. Elizabeth was perfunctory about nothing. Or to be precise, her officials could never rely upon her being perfunctory: which had much the same result. They could never be sure of obtaining her signature to a document without an inquisition, followed sometimes by biting criticism and a stormy refusal. She might interfere in anything. *Mutatis mutandis*, Mr Churchill's notes on the tattered Admiralty flag and on the growing habit among civil servants of addressing each other by their Christian names might have come from the Queen. 'I would to God', wrote Walsingham on one occasion, when she criticized the phrasing and latinity of the commission to try Mary Queen of Scots, 'her Majesty could be content to refer these things to them that can best judge of them, as other princes do.'[1] Perhaps some of our wartime officials, receiving their Churchillian 'rockets', echoed Sir Francis Walsingham's sentiments!

The effect of such a person in such a position was to keep faction, corruption, and other abuses in check, and to maintain that order of 'degree, priority, and place' which was the fragrant essence of society. The able men she chose as her statesmen, and particularly William Cecil, by their vigilance and hard work helped to make a success of paternal government.

It was the Queen herself who kept the nation charged with emotion. The citizens of London and the multitude of visitors there were thrilled by their frequent sight of her. In later life Bishop Goodman described how when a boy in the year 1588, on a dark December evening, they were suddenly told that the Queen was gone to council, 'and if you will see the Queen you must come quickly'. They ran to Whitehall and were admitted to the courtyard, which, lighted by torches, was soon full. After an hour's wait, they saw Elizabeth emerge, 'in great state'.

> Then we cried 'God save your Majesty! God save your Majesty!' Then the Queen turned unto us and said, 'God bless you all, my good people!' Then we cried again 'God save your Majesty! God save your Majesty!' Then the Queen said again unto us, 'You may well have a greater prince, but you shall never have a more loving prince'. And so, looking one upon another awhile, the Queen departed. This wrought such an impression upon us, for shows and pageants are ever best seen by torch-light, that all the way long we did nothing but talk what an admirable queen she

[1] Conyers Read, *Sir Francis Walsingham*, iii, 52 n. 4.

was, and how we would adventure our lives to do her service.[1]

The countryside was given a taste of Londoners' ecstasy in the Queen's annual progresses.

Or take an illustration of the personal touch in quite different style: her treatment of Drake when, at a most delicate and threatening moment in Anglo-Spanish relations, he returned from his voyage round the world. His plunder had to be sequestered in case Elizabeth was compelled to return it; but she sent word that he was to be allowed, in utmost secrecy, to abstract ten thousand pounds' worth of it. She received him at Court, listened with delight to his story, and made her celebrated visit to Deptford to knight him aboard the *Golden Hind*. One might say that she had cocked a snook at Philip of Spain. At such a critical time it was impudent bravura; but it was also political art. As for her skill in handling Parliament — her supreme achievement in patriotic romance — that is a story which would be credible only if fully told.

And now, perhaps, we can assemble our argument. The Elizabethan age was one of rapidly expanding horizons, economic, cultural, and geographical; an age to stir the imagination and incite the energies of the people. At Court, the structure of politics, based on faction and emulation, kept life intense and vigorous.[2] Though sordid in many of its details, it was transformed into romance by the personality of the Queen and disciplined by her masterful character, backed by an acute and highly trained intelligence. In the country the day of the gentry had arrived. It was not simply a matter of inheriting and maintaining old standards of wealth and comfort. Life was in flux: a challenge to enterprise and ability. As at Court, faction and rivalry stirred and invigorated county society. At times and places they revealed their evil

[1] Quoted by Firth, op. cit. p. 106.
[2] On this, cf. my essay, 'The Elizabethan Political Scene', included below.

side, but they were kept within bounds by the aristocratic structure of society — the doctrine of 'degree, priority, and place' — and by the vigilant authority of the Privy Council. In the towns, Fortune could be wooed, and for the ambitious apprentice there were success-stories, such as that of Jack of Newbury, which sober life did not render incredible:[1] stories which might be likened to the proverbial marshal's baton for the Napoleonic soldier, or 'From Log Cabin to White House' for the American of half a century or more ago. Court, county, and town — even London, which, though already a Wen, was still a community — were intimate societies and could respond easily to a prevalent mood. If opportunity beckoned, the will to achieve was quickly diffused; and, with London a national Mecca whose royal and legal courts brought constant pilgrimage from the local communities, the blood coursed through the whole body when the heart of the kingdom throbbed.

Consider the impact on such a society of those voyages whose narratives Hakluyt collected, with their stories and fables of new-found lands and peoples. To a youthful and responsive age, sure of the verbal inspiration of the Bible, conscious of divine intervention in the triumphs and afflictions of everyday life, and believing the many tales of monstrous births and miraculous happenings which honest John Stow recorded in his *Chronicles* and ballad-makers sometimes commemorated in verse — to such an age stories from afar were merely an extension of the wonders in an illimitable world. 'All things became possible; credulity was wiser than experience.' In this mood the poet Spenser rebukes the disbeliever in his 'happy land of Faery':

> But let that man with better sence advize,
> That of the world least part to us is red:
> And dayly how through hardy enterprize,
> Many great Regions are discovered,

[1] Cf. *The Works of Thomas Deloney*, ed. F. O. Mann.

Which to late age were never mentioned.
Who ever heard of th' Indian Peru?
Or who in venturous vessell measured
The Amazons huge river now found trew?
Or fruitfullest Virginia who did ever vew?

Yet all these were, when no man did them know;
Yet have from wisest ages hidden beene:
And later times things more unknowne shall show.
Why then should witlesse man so much misweene
That nothing is, but that which he hath seene?
What if within the Moones faire shining spheare?
What if in every other starre unseene
Of other worldes he happily should heare?
He wonder would much more: yet such to some appeare.[1]

And Marlowe's dying Tamburlaine:

> Give me a map; then let me see how much
> Is left for me to conquer all the world,
> That these, my boys, may finish all my wants.

Reinforcing these reasons for an exuberant national spirit was the dynamic of Protestantism in mortal conflict with the powers of darkness. In his recent volume of *Unpopular Essays* Bertrand Russell has a comforting and, one hopes, a perspicacious passage on the struggle between liberals and fanatics, exposing the inherent weaknesses of a society possessed by what I have called a *mystique*. Now, if Sir Francis Walsingham and his fellow-Puritans — who incidentally dominated nearly every parliament of Elizabeth's reign — had had their way, doubtless we should have been pointing Bertrand Russell's moral with an Elizabethan example. But the secret of that age

[1] *Faerie Queene*, bk. ii, introduction, stanzas 2-3. Cf. Raleigh, op. cit. pp. 101 seqq.

is the unfanatical nature of the Queen. Through her control of foreign and domestic policy England enjoyed the advantages of the liberals coupled with the dynamic of the fanatics.

Government, I am convinced, was a principal, if not the principal, ingredient of national greatness. Would all that energy have been released if the political setting had been different? Professor Nef has written a book to demonstrate the radically different development of industry in contemporary France, due to governmental factors;[1] and I should be inclined to strengthen his thesis with further arguments. Then, it is obvious that the story of voyage and exploration would have been different if Mary Tudor had lived to old age and Philip of Spain remained King of England. Supposing, however, that there had been a regime, similar to the Elizabethan in religious and constitutional complexion but less efficient and less inspiring. What then? Political, religious, and social discontent would have emerged sooner; and even if the friction thus created had not hindered the growth of wealth and enterprise, it would have emptied national life of its spirit. Instead of living in the present, men might have looked to the past — to the days of Bluff King Hal, as Jacobeans looked to the days of Good Queen Bess. Instead of 'a literature of youth and hope', there might have been 'a literature of regret and memory'. England was a small community — four to five millions, knit together socially in many ways, some of which I have described. What wireless has done for our generation, the size, homogeneity, and cohesion of Elizabethan society did for those days. It made romantic leadership of the nation possible. If, in sober historical documents no less than in the literature of the age, the emotional tie of sovereign and people is abundantly clear, then surely it is no illusion to imagine that such leadership enabled the nation to achieve its 'finest hour'. After all, we have lived through a similar period ourselves.

[1] Nef, op. cit.

Of course there were greed and folly, poverty, cruelty, petty tyranny, and injustice in Elizabethan England. And it is right that we should occasionally weep over Jerusalem. But the quality of a society is not to be judged by microscopic examinations here and there, nor assessed without relation to its times. Compared with contemporary France or Spain, or other western countries, the purely social merits of Elizabethan England shine bright. Here, for example, is the comment of a German nobleman, visiting this country in 1584-5.

> It is a very fertile country, producing all sorts of corn.... There are plenty of sheep, cows, and various kinds of meat. The peasants and citizens are on the average rich people, not to speak of the gentlemen and noblemen. They are fond of pomp and splendour, both high and low.... I have seen peasants presenting themselves statelier in manner, and keeping a more sumptuous table than some noblemen do in Germany. That is a poor peasant who has no silver-gilt salt-cellars, silver cups, and spoons.[1]

Professor Tawney has described the Elizabethan age as 'a balanced society'. It was in harmony, politically and socially, with the prevailing philosophy: 'concord within the realm amongst the several members of the same',[2] 'hospitality' as the duty of the gentry. There were individual grievances, but not grievances against the system – at least, to any serious extent. In such circumstances a sense of freedom and social well-being can exist. A civilization attains balance; and if – as was then the situation – political, cultural, social, and economic factors are such as to call for high endeavour on the part of the individual, and the community is knit together by enthusiasm and inspiring leadership, it may achieve great-

[1] G. von Bülow, 'Journey through England and Scotland made by Liupold von Wedel', in *Trans. Royal Hist. Soc.* 2nd ser. ix, 268.

[2] G. de Malynes, *Saint George for England* (1601), quoted by Knights, op. cit. p. 143.

ness. The balance did not last long; and one may doubt whether it could have done so. It was not there in November 1558 when Elizabeth came to the throne, and it was in jeopardy in March 1603 when she died. Like other societies, the Elizabethan age contained the seeds of its own decay.

THE ACCESSION OF QUEEN ELIZABETH I[1]

There are occasions in history when the thoughtful student suspects that much more was going on behind the scene than he is allowed to know. The accession of Elizabeth I is such an occasion. Outwardly everything was peaceable and orderly. It seemed as inevitable and natural a succession as that, say, of Henry VIII after his father, Henry VII. But if we reflect that Elizabeth's Protestant predilections were known to everyone, and that religious differences had been one of the powerful motives in the attempt to supplant Mary Tudor by Lady Jane Grey in 1553, we are prompted to ask why there was no resistance to Elizabeth's accession. Was the sinister precedent of 1553 a cautionary tale, and no more? Another question poses itself: since a change of religion in those days threatened as profound a revolution as the ideological movements in our own time, how was the revolution accomplished? Merely to ask the question is to set the evidence in a new perspective.

Throughout Mary Tudor's reign Elizabeth had been the hope of all Protestants and of the growing body of the discontented. The many plots and intrigues of those years were focused upon her, and sometimes involved those about her. It was a perilous position to be in. It had placed her in danger of death at the time of Wyatt's rebellion and remained a constant threat to her safety. She could not prevent the irresponsible use of her name, nor could she betray any secrets that came to her ears: indeed, her future — if she was to have any — depended on retaining that popular support which might at any time involve her ruin. This trying experience furnished her

[1] Published in *History Today* (Coronation issue), May 1953.

with indelible lessons in statecraft. It may very well explain her extraordinary lenity to Mary Queen of Scots, when in her own reign the presence of this princess in England created, though in reverse, a similar situation. It certainly influenced her in her essentially personal policy of refusing to determine the succession to the throne. In 1566, when the House of Commons was pressing her relentlessly on this subject, she retorted that none of them had been 'a second person' and 'tasted of the practices against her sister'. Some who had then tried to involve her in plots were, she added, in that very Parliament: 'were it not for my honour, their knavery should be known'. 'I stood in danger of my life: my sister was so incensed against me.... So shall never be my successor.'

Mary Tudor, a religious *dévote*, could not bring herself, until very near the end, to acquiesce in the succession of her sister. As late as March 30th, 1558, this pathetic Queen made a will, 'thinking myself to be with child': the child she so ardently desired to guarantee the future of her ideological revolution. On October 28th, when the perils not of childbirth but of disease forced her hand, she added a codicil that referred to her 'next heir and successor by the laws and statutes of this realm'; and some ten days later she yielded to the pressure of her Council, agreeing to send Elizabeth a message that she was content for her to succeed to the crown. She asked her — and how little authority her first request carried, those about Mary must have realized, if she did not — to maintain the old religion and pay her debts.

On November 9th, a special envoy, the Count de Feria, arrived, sent over from the continent by the absent King, Philip. His ostensible purpose was to console the Queen. He found her a dying woman, given up by all her doctors, both English and Spanish. His deeper purpose was to extend Philip's sway over England from the closing to the new reign; and he assembled the Privy Council to tell them how much his King desired the succession of Elizabeth, relying on her friends then present to tell her of this *démarche*. The Councillors, who were already wondering how they would fare under the new dispensation, received him 'as if he brought them the bulls of a dead Pope'.

On November 10th, Feria visited Elizabeth in the country. She had been sweet and agreeable to Philip's ordinary representative, but when the proud Feria started patronizing her and explained that she would owe her throne, not to the Council but to the King, his master, she replied that 'the people' and no one else 'had placed her where she now is'. 'She is very attached to the people', he commented 'and very confident that they take her part: which', he added, 'is true.' Clearly, she was determined to be the puppet of no party and no person, especially no foreign sovereign: she was to be England's Queen. 'She is a woman of much vanity and acumen', Feria remarked; and he noted her admiration for her father, Henry VIII's method of government – a comment of considerable significance.[1]

In thus asserting from the start her personal independence, Elizabeth proved herself profoundly wise and also acutely aware of the way events had played into her hands. Her prospects and latent power sprang from the unpopular character of Mary's rule; and the climax of that unpopularity had come with the national humiliation of losing Calais to the French at the opening of the year 1558. 'I never saw ... England weaker in strength, men, money and riches', wrote the scholar-statesman, Sir Thomas Smith, criticizing this reign in 1560. 'As much affectionate as you note me to be to my country and countrymen, I assure you I was then ashamed of both.' 'They went to the wars hanging down their looks. They came from thence as men dismayed and forlorn. They went about their matters as men amazed, that wist not where to begin or end. And what marvel was it? ... Here [in England] was nothing but fining, heading, hanging, quartering, and burning; taxing,

[1] Kervyn de Lettenhove, *Relations Politiques des Pays-Bas et de l'Angleterre*, i, 279-82.

levying and pulling down of bulwarks at home, and beggaring and losing our strongholds abroad. A few priests, men in white rochets, ruled all; who, with setting up of six-foot roods and rebuilding of rood-lofts, thought to make all cock-sure.' A prejudiced statement, no doubt; but that of a moderate Protestant, not a fanatic, and few Englishmen would have reversed the picture.[1]

No wonder the dying Mary was compelled to acquiesce in the inevitable; no wonder her Councillors and hundreds of others were anxious to salute the rising sun, hastening to Hatfield, where Elizabeth and future fortune lay. But, however propitious the signs, the success of a revolution cannot be taken for granted. At home, the incalculable factor was the action of rabid Catholic leaders. No one could foretell that Cardinal Pole — Archbishop of Canterbury, a man with royal blood in his veins, and a potential focus for resistance — would be stricken with fever and die a few hours after the Queen; nor that four more Catholic bishops would die in the next month or so, and the number of episcopal vacancies thus rise to the debilitating proportion of ten out of a total of twenty-six. Nor, abroad, could the reaction of the irascible Pope Paul IV to Elizabeth's accession be foretold; and certainly it could not be anticipated that his quarrel with Cardinal Pole and Mary Tudor would induce friendly feelings towards Anne Boleyn's daughter. Then, again, England was in a formal state of war with France and Scotland, and the nearest Catholic claimant to the throne, Mary Queen of Scots, had recently married the Dauphin of France. Philip of Spain, zealous Catholic though he was, could not permit the union of France, Scotland and England: that might have been guessed, but it must have been very much in the minds of Elizabeth and her advisers that there was plenty of fuel about if anybody set light to the Catholic tinder at home.

Stray bits of evidence indicate that Elizabeth was taking

[1] Strype, *Life of Sir Thomas Smith*, pp. 249-50.

precautions during Mary's last illness. An original letter of hers survives, dated from Brockett Hall, Hertfordshire, on October 28th, 1558, thanking someone – who for obvious reasons is unnamed – for his readiness 'to do unto us all the pleasure ye can': an offer, she assured him, that she would not forget, 'whensoever time and power may serve'.[1] We may guess that the person concerned was some powerful nobleman. Again, at Longleat there are three letters from her Cofferer, Thomas Parry – an intimate servant – written to Sir John Thynne in October and November, from which we may infer that Thynne, the builder of Longleat, was in close touch with the Princess and Parry, and was acting in her interests, gathering support for her in Wiltshire. The message which Elizabeth willed Parry to send – Blessed is the servant to whom the master, when he comes home, may say, 'I have found thee a faithful and good servant' – conveyed its meaning clearly enough in those weeks when Mary lay dying.[2] Finally, in 1592, in a paper meant to be shown to the Queen, a certain Thomas Markham reminded her that during Mary Tudor's last illness – he being then in charge of a band of three hundred footmen at Berwick – she, through her Cofferer, Mr Parry, signified that with all convenient speed he should repair to Brockett Hall, 'leaving his own band with such other captains as he could trust to be in readiness with their bands likewise to serve for the maintenance of her royal state, title and dignity'. This he did, arriving with signed undertakings from the captains to adventure their lives in Elizabeth's service, along with ten thousand men.[3] If this late reminiscence be substantially correct – and the odds are that it is – then we can assume that in October to November 1558 Elizabeth was organized and ready to fight for her throne, if need arose.

Nor was she without friends in Mary's Privy Council.

[1] B.M. Cotton MS. Vespasian F. III, fol. 27.
[2] Thynne Papers, vol. iii, fols. 21, 23, 24. I owe this information to Professor S. T. Bindoff.
[3] *Hatfield MSS.* iv, 189.

It may have been with the calculated purpose of splitting Catholic ranks, or perhaps out of mutual respect, or even a blend of both: whatever the motive, particular attention seems to have been paid to Nicholas Heath, Archbishop of York and Mary's Lord Chancellor. He was a moderate man, who had been happy under the Henrician Reformation, though unable to accept the Edwardian. Mary's reign, as events were to show, had won him back immovably to Papal Supremacy, but he remained Henrician in his loyalty to the Tudor dynasty. With such a man in such a position, it would have been hard to engineer a Catholic revolt against Elizabeth's accession. From a letter which Heath wrote to Cecil in 1573 it is evident that there were negotiations between him and Elizabeth's representatives when the end of Mary's reign was foreseen. In this letter he recalls inviting Cecil to his house three or four days before Mary's death, when he discussed affairs of state and the subject of religion. He remembers that he begged Cecil to persuade his mistress not to continue him as Lord Chancellor — an office he disliked, but which, judging from Elizabeth's 'gracious and favourable mind' towards him, he was afraid would again be imposed on him. When, on Mary's death, he delivered up the great seal to the new Queen, she spoke so appreciatively of him that his fears were revived.[1] In fact, Elizabeth kept Heath for a month or two on her Council; and it may well be that his last attendance, on January 5th, 1559, represents the critical moment when the Queen allowed the whole Council to know that she intended to break the tie with Rome and he decided that the parting of the ways had come. Heath's loyalty and Cardinal Pole's death were great blessings of fortune.

The nervous atmosphere of the time can also be seen in a document which has recently come to light.[2] It is a long memorandum of advice sent to Elizabeth by her able and

[1] Cotton MS. Vespasian F. XIII, fol. 287.
[2] Printed by me in *Eng. Hist. Rev.* lxv, 91-8.

devoted follower, Sir Nicholas Throckmorton, when rumour reached him that Mary was dead or dying. Perhaps it was written on November 17th, the day of Mary's death; perhaps the day before — 'Hope Wednesday', as it was called[1] — when her death was hourly expected. The news or rumour seems to have caught him when he was in the country; but he was in London by November 18th, acting as Elizabeth's agent and ready to take action on his own initiative. In his memorandum he offered his mistress advice about her first steps as Queen, and included a long list of persons whom she might consider for posts in her government. Throckmorton was a keen Protestant, and it was symptomatic both of the dangers he foresaw and of his faith in Archbishop Heath that this Catholic name headed his list of those 'meet' to be Lord Chancellor. Throckmorton counselled Elizabeth to walk warily: to keep Mary's Privy Council in being for the moment, and not to let those she intended to displace know their fate. Neither 'the old or new should wholly understand what you mean'. It was policy in which Elizabeth needed no instruction; or, at any rate, policy which she carried out with a *finesse* surpassing that of her adviser. 'To succeed happily through a discreet beginning' was the burden of the memorandum. Caution, subtlety, secrecy were required.

The precedent of Lady Jane Grey found no echo at Elizabeth's accession. By sheer good fortune there was no similar person to act as a focus for resistance. No one in his senses would have turned to Mary Queen of Scots, then the enemy of England. Mary Tudor's Council acted unhesitatingly; and two or three hours after the Queen's death, Nicholas Heath, presiding in the upper house of Parliament, addressed the assembled Lords and Commons. 'God this present morning hath called to His mercy our late Sovereign Lady, Queen Mary: which hap, as it is most heavy and grievous unto us, so have we no less cause another way to rejoice with praise to Almighty

[1] Cf. John Foxe, *Acts and Monuments*, ed. Pratt and Stoughton, viii, 677.

God, for that he hath left unto us a true, lawful and right inheritress to the Crown ... which is the Lady Elizabeth ... of whose most lawful right and title ... we need not to doubt.' From Parliament the Lords proceeded to the door of Westminster Hall, where Elizabeth was proclaimed Queen, and from there to the Cross in Cheapside, where, in the presence of the Lord Mayor and Aldermen in their scarlet gowns, the proclamation was repeated. That afternoon, as a simple diarist records, all the church bells of London 'did ring', while at night the citizens 'did make bonfires and set tables in the street, and did eat and drink and make merry for the new Queen, Elizabeth, Queen Mary's sister'. Alas! poor Mary.[1]

Elizabeth herself was at Hatfield: far enough removed from London to be surrounded by her followers and on the defence against any untoward happening. It was there that a delegation of Mary's Council came to announce her accession. Six days of discreet activity followed, and then, on November 23rd, accompanied by a thousand and more lords, knights and gentlemen, ladies and gentlewomen, she came to Lord North's residence, the Charterhouse, outside the walls of London. On the 28th she made a triumphal state entry into the City, and with trumpets blowing rode through crowded streets to the Tower, stopping to hear children make their speeches and waits their music. She was welcomed by citizens, who declared 'their inward rejoicings by gesture, words and countenance'; and 'there was such shooting of guns as never was heard afore'.

It was her first wooing, as Queen, of 'the people', on whose rapturous support and devotion her instinct as an artist, and her experience in the dangerous days now over, led her to rely: as it were, a rehearsal for that matchless Londoners' day, some six weeks later, when once more she came to the Tower in order to pass through the City, now prodigally organized for splendour, pageants, speeches and music, on the way to

[1] Holinshed, *Chronicles*; *Machyn's Diary* (Camden Soc.), p. 178.

her Coronation – the occasion, indeed, for consummate romance and dazzling statecraft.

Lucky Londoners! They saw so much of their heroine. A diarist notes an evening in the following April, when, after supping at Baynard's Castle with the Earl of Pembroke, 'the Queen's Grace rowed up and down Thames, and a hundred boats about her Grace, with trumpets and drums and flutes and guns and squibs [fireworks] hurling on high, to and fro till ten at night ere her Grace departed'. The waterside was thronged with a thousand people. And at the beginning of July the London authorities took their citizens to Greenwich and held their musters there and fought mimic battles before the Queen and the Court, to the blowing of trumpets, banging of drums, and shooting of guns. Elizabeth thanked them heartily, whereupon 'there was the greatest shout that ever was heard, and hurling up of caps'. We are told that above a thousand spectators watched that show.[1]

The pageants and speeches which Londoners prepared for Elizabeth's Coronation progress through the City left no doubt of the role they had cast for her. She was to be their Protestant saviour, their Deborah, to rescue the land from darkness and despair. In that age, when the hand of God was seen in any striking occurrence, her survival from the perils of Mary's reign was assumed to be part of the divine dispensation. John Foxe appended to his story of the martyrs an account of 'the miraculous preservation of the Lady Elizabeth'; and Holinshed borrowed it as a suitable ending to his chronicle of Mary Tudor. The same theme had been in the broadsides of 1559. Thomas Brice published in that year a doggerel 'Register of the Martyrs' from 1555 to 1558, to the refrain 'We wished for our ELIZABETH':

> When raging reign of tyrants stout,
> Causeless, did cruelly conspire

[1] *Machyn's Diary*, pp. 180, 196, 202-3.

To rend and root the Simple out,
With furious force of sword and fire;
When man and wife were put to death:
We wished for our Queen ELIZABETH.[1]

In addition to the Protestant populace of London and other home zealots, there were the Marian *émigrés*, who had fled to Strasburg and the towns of Switzerland, where they had lived a godly life and been actively engaged in propaganda against Mary's regime; longing for the day when they could turn their steps homeward and restore the Gospel to England in the radical simplicity to which they had become accustomed in exile. That day had come. They had received 'the joyful tidings of God's favour and grace, restored unto us'. Now was 'the time for the walls of Jerusalem to be built again in that kingdom, that the blood of the martyrs, so largely shed, may not be in vain'. Among the *émigrés* were the most eminent Protestant divines. They expected the English Church to be handed over to them.

The new Queen was therefore confronted with a revolutionary movement, skilled in the arts of propaganda and organization. By her birth and her role during the troublous reign now ended, as well as by the expectation of thousands at home and hundreds from abroad, she was marked out as its titular head. Her instinct for romantic leadership prompted her to respond to the mood. She desired to lift the nation from dull despair to a glowing pride in the present; 'to do some act' — as she confessed — 'that would make her fame spread abroad in her lifetime, and, after, occasion memorial for ever'. In this instinct of hers lies a clue to the greatness of the new age. But the question which posed itself in 1558-9, and which was to retain its force through the critical decades that followed, was whether she would rule a country or lead a party. Could

1 *Tudor Tracts*, ed. A. F. Pollard (Arber's *English Garner*), p. 270; cf. E. K. Wilson, *England's Eliza*, chap. 1.

she exploit the enthusiasm of revolution without succumbing to its philosophy and its extreme courses? Unlike her sister she was no *dévote*: she rejoiced in her own description of herself as 'mere English'.

In the early weeks of the reign, her watchword was caution. With France nominally at war — peace was not concluded until March-April 1559 — and the latent but by no means negligible threat to the throne represented by the Dauphin's wife, Mary Queen of Scots, there was reason to be prudent. To sober down the clash of creeds, Elizabeth issued a proclamation forbidding preaching and religious innovations; but she gave her Protestant followers a sign when on Christmas Day she instructed the bishop celebrating Mass before her not to elevate the Host — symbol of the Catholic doctrine of a real presence in the sacrament — and, on his refusal, left the service before this was done. There was no doubt which way she intended to go, but what would be her destination and how fast she would travel remained uncertain.

In this situation, and urged on by the popular demonstration at her Coronation procession on January 14th, Elizabeth met her first Parliament on January 25th. She had now to declare her hand. In many ways this was the crucial occasion of the reign. Certainly it set the pattern for the future; and we should never forget that the Queen, whose personal part in the story, though it must be largely inferred, was obviously vital, was a young woman of twenty-five. It is a lasting wonder that in so masculine a society, a woman, and one so young, managed to formulate policy and dominate those about her.

The House of Commons proved to be, like the citizens of London, overwhelmingly radical in its religious sympathies. Outside the House, remaining purposefully in London, were gathered the eminent divines, back from exile. Along with their friends in Parliament, they acted as a pressure group, whose programme was the instant overthrow of Catholicism and a wholesale conversion of the country to an extreme form of Protestantism.

The Queen, for her part, was beset by advice and pressure from all parties. There was no obligation on her to consult her Council: she may not even have asked for a formal lead, preferring to sound them individually and frame the policy herself. Her will was supreme. Amidst the babel of tongues about her, she seems to have been swayed by two lines of thought: profound respect for her father's statesmanship, and a desire to obtain as comprehensive and tolerant a settlement as possible. Even Protestants — those who were realists — stressed the perils, from abroad as well as at home. Move slowly seemed to be the most cogent advice in January 1559: it was certainly what Elizabeth's instinct prompted her to do.

When government policy declared itself, it was confined to an Act of Supremacy, with a clause conceding the cup as well as the bread to communicants. The Reformation — the Revolution as Protestant zealots thought of it — was in its initial stage to be a milk-and-water affair, confined to severance from Rome. The Catholic order of Church service was to continue until time and a second Parliament produced the propitious conditions for a Protestant Prayer Book. In this way Elizabeth hoped to stay any Catholic *démarche* from abroad, avoid trouble at home, and wean the more moderate leaders of the Marian Church from their Catholicism. If she could do the last, then she would be less dependent for staffing her Church on radical *émigrés*, and a conservative settlement might be feasible. She wanted revolution without tears.

The policy failed. First, the Marian bishops would not co-operate. Then, the Protestant divines and their agents in the House of Commons took the bit between their teeth. They altered the government bill and inserted the minimum programme they were inclined to accept. This involved the restoration of the second and more radical Prayer Book of Edward VI's reign. Elizabeth's reply was to get the House of Lords to strike out their amendments. She was still clinging tenaciously to her policy and her lone, strange Supremacy Bill; still clinging to these, when suddenly, within a few hours of dissolving the Parliament, she changed her mind and adjourned the assembly over Easter, instead of dissolving it. News had arrived that peace had been concluded with France, and with that news the last imperative reason for delaying a full Protestant settlement disappeared.

The true revolutionary character of the situation had asserted itself; and, with the Catholic leaders refusing to follow the moderate lead from the Government, it looked as if control of affairs would pass to the *émigrés*. They attempted to impose their own settlement: a more radical Protestant regime than that achieved by the end of Edward VI's reign. Elizabeth resisted them. The ultimate destination which she had set herself went no farther than the first, very conservative Prayer Book of 1549: one that the Catholic bishop, Stephen Gardiner, in those days had not found impossibly obnoxious. The final struggle between the revolutionary leaders and their Queen was obstinate: so obstinate that her officials contemplated the possibility of a deadlock. But Elizabeth was forced to compromise. So were the radicals; and our Prayer Book to this day retains the results. The decorous character of the Anglican Church is perhaps the most distinctive element in Elizabeth's personal, if limited, triumph.

The Queen had put the reins on revolution, and for nearly half a century she kept a firm grip on them. It was to her advantage – indeed, it was her triumph – to drive that restive steed. Throughout the rest of her days she had to cope with the effects of the disappointment that she inflicted in 1559. The revolutionary spirit did not die down: rather, it spread and intensified. Yet, to the zealots, she, whose firmness alone kept them in check, remained their Deborah and Judith. Her Accession Day – November 17th – became known, and was known in this land for nearly two centuries, as the Birthday of the Gospel. For this remarkable achievement her own consummate art as a ruler and leader of the nation was largely responsible; but it also rested on the stark fact that her votaries had no alternative person to worship. To be 'England's Eliza' she had also to be England's Virgin Queen.

THE ELIZABETHAN POLITICAL SCENE[1]

A STUDENT of Elizabethan history, delivering the Raleigh Lecture, might be expected to centre his attention on the great Elizabethan whose fame he commemorates. No doubt there are fresh things to be said about Raleigh's career, puzzling incidents to be set in better perspective. But man does not live in a vacuum, and on occasions it profits more to describe an environment than to write another biography. Though Raleigh's name finds only a casual place in my narrative, let us bear in mind that he was a figure, if a less conspicuous one, in the political scene that I have chosen as my theme.

The pattern of government in Elizabethan England looks relatively simple to the casual eye: Queen, Privy Council, Councils in the North and the Marches of Wales, Exchequer, Parliament, law courts, the organs of local government. It is all familiar enough in our constitutional histories. And if we wish to fill in the administrative framework, we may turn to a well-known table of 'Queen Elizabeth's annual expense, civil and military', which contains a list of all officials in the Queen's pay, with the amounts of their salaries and allowances.[2]

This traditional approach to the subject gives us the façade, but it is no sure guide to what lay behind. Consider the administrative framework. Our list of officials in the Queen's pay is precisely what it purports to be. Nevertheless, it is misleading — astonishingly so — about the income that officials received, and far from complete as a list of those in the administrative service.

[1] The British Academy Raleigh Lecture, 1948; published in the *Proceedings* of the Academy for that year.

[2] Peck, *Desiderata Curiosa*, i, 51 seqq.; *Ordinances for the Royal Household* (1790), pp. 241 seqq.

Official salaries had taken little account of the passage of time or monetary inflation, and in some instances were scarcely more than token payments. Obviously, there had to be compensation somewhere. It was found in payments by people using an official's services, whether as clients or suitors. Such payments were of two kinds: 'fees', which conformed to a tariff; and 'gratuities', which occasionally became fixed and figured as new fees, though normally they remained flexible and might, with unscrupulous givers and receivers, merge into what even that insensitive age termed bribery. No wonder that a correspondent, calculating the earnings of certain great officials at Court, made a triple estimate, according as the official wished for Heaven or Purgatory as his ultimate destination or was indifferent about his soul's welfare. The Lord Keeper of the Great Seal, for example, received from the Crown, in fees and annuities, £919 per annum, the Lord High Admiral £200, and the Principal Secretary £100.[1] Yet John Manningham noted in his diary in 1601 that the Lord Keeper's office was 'better worth than £3000 per annum', the Lord Admiral's 'more', and the Secretary's 'little less'.[2] He was certainly not taking a gloomy view of their after-life.

Similarly with the number of officials. In addition to those appearing in our list because they were on the Queen's pay-roll, there was a host of minor officials who received no salary from the Crown and are therefore not mentioned. These men were paid out of the fees and gratuities of suitors and litigants. Originally they had often been servants, aiding their masters in the labours of office; and a trace of private service still survived in their appointment, which was generally in the gift of the higher officials, not the Crown, and, incidentally, was a source of profit. The transition from servant to official was still proceeding, as new items appeared in the scale of fees confronting suitors. It was the way the civil service grew.

[1] Peck, op. cit. i, 51, 58, 61.
[2] *Manningham's Diary* (Camden Soc.), p. 19.

Clearly, the administration looks very different when approached in this way. Perhaps a similar emphasis on the realities of life at Court will throw fresh light on the nature of personal monarchy. If we can penetrate its secrets of power, reveal the stresses and strains to which it was subject, and uncover its inherent weaknesses, we may do more than write a chapter in Elizabethan history. We may revive past experience as a warning of the dangers to which a particular type of government is exposed.

We must begin by focusing attention on the two extremes of the picture; and first on the Queen, whose personal decisions controlled a wide range of governmental and administrative activity, and whose will or whim could both make and unmake careers and fortunes. A vast amount of patronage was at her disposal. There were hundreds of offices in her gift, and others which could be diverted to her use by the device of recommendatory letters or verbal orders, sometimes amiable in tone, sometimes hectoring, but at all times difficult, if not dangerous, to resist. There were also royal lands to be leased or sold, or to be granted as reward for services; a source of great wealth, and most eagerly solicited. Finally, there were all those grants by letters patent, whether charters, licences, monopolies, or whatever they were, which conferred some benefit on the recipient.

At the other extreme were the customers in this colossal business — the suitors, who thronged the Court (thus, incidentally, guaranteeing a large 'presence' by which the reputation of monarchy was sustained) or alternatively pursued their petitions more precariously from a distance. Competition was bound to be keen. It was intensified by the custom of primogeniture, which forced out the younger sons of the landed gentry to seek their own fortunes.

Between monarch and suitors were interposed members of the inner ring of the Court; broadly, those with access to the privy chamber, more specifically, those officials and courtiers — not excluding the ladies of the Court — whose place or friendship gave them the Queen's ear. Of necessity these were the intermediaries whom very many suitors had to employ to press on the sovereign their requests for office or favour, and pilot their suits through treacherous currents to the safe harbour of the royal signature. As Spenser feelingly wrote.[1]

> Full little knowest thou that hast not tried
> What Hell it is in suing long to bide;
> To lose good days that might be better spent;
> To waste long nights in pensive discontent;
> To speed today, to be put back tomorrow;
> To feed on hope, to pine with fear and sorrow;
> To have thy Prince's grace, yet want her Peer's;
> To have thy asking, yet wait many years;
> To fret thy soul with crosses and with cares;
> To eat thy heart through comfortless despairs;
> To fawn, to crouch, to wait, to ride, to run,
> To spend, to give, to want, to be undone.

Unalloyed friendship might occasionally procure a suitor the support he needed, but usually support was purchased. Bribery we should call it; and bribery it sometimes deserved to be called. However, it was not so immoral as we might think. Ministers and courtiers were compelled to sell their influence, for even if the Queen had jumped the centuries in her thoughts and seen the wisdom of paying servants adequately, her revenues would not have permitted it. Nor, indeed, was the practice strange in a society based on the principle that anyone seeking a service paid for it. It was analogous to our custom of 'tips', except that 'tips' were not restricted to menials. Everyone, from the Lord Treasurer or a countessdown, accepted them. 'I ever took it that a man may with honesty accept a gratuity given', said an official whose actions were under scrutiny in 1597.[2]

[1] *Mother Hubberd's Tale*, ll. 895 seqq. As *pièce justificatif*, cf. *Hatfield MSS*. vii, 393.
[2] *Hatfield MSS*. vii, 363.

In the nature of things, evidence about gratuities is fitful. But, whether pursued openly or surreptitiously, the practice was generally recognized. One of his mother's chaplains, making suit through Robert Cecil for a prebend at Windsor in 1594, declared: 'As I cannot promise rewards after the custom of the world, so I unfeignedly promise my poor prayers for your Honour and yours.'[1] As early as 1559 we find Lord North acting as intermediary for a man who sought Sir William Cecil's support for his device to reform the coinage. He 'will give you 500 marks for your pains', North wrote to Cecil, 'and offers me 500 marks to dispose at my pleasure. I am desirous to bestow unto yourself 200 marks, unto Mr Treasurer 200 marks, and to take the rest myself'.[2] The suit was unsuccessful. So far as one can judge, Burghley was not open to crude bribery, nor did he let his advice to the Queen be deflected by prospects of monetary gain. Herein lay one reason for Elizabeth's unique reliance on him. But do not let us imagine that he was a stranger to gratuities.[3] If we attempted to construct a budget of his income and expenditure, we should undoubtedly become aware of the gap that they filled;[4] and certainly in the Mastership of the Court of Wards he possessed a constant source of such income. He 'grew rich' by means of this office, 'and ofttimes gratified his friends and servants that depended and waited on him', wrote one of two panegyrists, members of his household; though it is fair to add that the second writer stressed his moderation.[5] In 1582 a second Lord North wrote to tell him of a wardship: 'Forgo not this occasion. I have known but few such fall in my time. Get her into your possession.'[6]

[1] Ibid. iv, 527.
[2] Ibid. i, 154-5.
[3] e.g. in 1587 the representative of the merchant adventurers with Drake was authorized 'to promise and assure to pay or deliver to your use ... the full sum of £1000', 'for the obtaining of our portions in those goods brought home' by Drake (ibid. iii, 281-2).
[4] Some idea of his expenditure can be obtained from Peck, op. cit. i, 22-3.
[5] B.M. Additional MS. 22925, fol. 28b; Peck, op. cit. i, 20-1.
[6] *Hatfield MSS.* xiii, 208.

Burghley may or may not have profited from this particular wardship; but after his death someone compiled what I think must be interpreted as a list of gratuities that he received between January 1596 and August 1598 for granting wardships. It is endorsed, 'This note to be burned.' There are eleven items, totalling £3103 6s. 8d. One is a gratuity of £1000 paid by Attorney-General Coke for Walter Aston, an exceedingly rich heir, aged thirteen, who afterwards became the poet Drayton's patron. And a very good bargain it was – for Coke and Burghley, though not for the Queen. Officially, the lands – which a century later were said to be worth £10,000 a year – were assessed at £256 6s. 8d. per annum, and the wardship of the body, which carried the right of marriage, at a capital sum of £300 – payments which went to the Crown and were distinct from the gratuity to Burghley. Aston later compounded for his marriage by paying Coke £4000.[1]

Our minds will now be attuned to a letter from that shameless if reverend place-seeker, Tobie Matthew, who rose to be Archbishop of York and once provoked a tart comment from the Queen by oft-repeated reference in a sermon to rewards for the deserving.[2] On his appointment to the bishopric of Durham he wrote to Burghley, acknowledging that he owed his promotion to him. Not having a suitable office to bestow, he sent him £100 in gold by the bearer. Of course, the gift may have been returned, but as the bishop a few weeks earlier had declared that he would express his thankfulness in deeds as well as words, we may reasonably doubt if it was.[3]

[1] S.P. Dom. Eliz. 268, no. 41; P.R.O. Wards Misc. 348; B. H. Newdigate, *Michael Drayton and his Circle*, pp. 146-8. I am indebted to my former pupil, Mr J. Hurstfield, for the manuscript information, and for much of my knowledge about wards.

[2] T. Birch, *Memoirs of Queen Elizabeth*, i, 48. 'Well, whosoever have missed their rewards, you have not lost your labour.'

[3] B.M. Lansdowne MSS. 78, fol. 40; 79, no. 40. In 1597 the new Bishop of Chester wrote to Robert Cecil: 'Having received so great a benefit by your means, I ... will further express my thankfulness by some special gratification' (*Hatfield MSS.* vii, 351).

Offices were bought and sold. Burghley once denounced the practice as insufferable, to which it was retorted that 'the the same fault ... is winked at, and the mart kept within the Court'.[1] Perhaps his denunciation was directed less against gratuities than against officials bargaining to surrender their patents of office to particular purchasers, who then set about securing their own appointment — a practice with obvious dangers. All the same, in the later part of the reign there was often little distinction between gratuities and plain sales. For example, there were several candidates in 1594 for the vacant Receivership of the Court of Wards — a royal appointment carrying a fee of 100 marks plus £70 diet and allowance. One aspirant offered Burghley and Robert Cecil £1000; another offered £1000 to Robert Cecil along with £100 for his wife 'to buy her four coach horses', and on learning from him that the Queen intended to let one of her ladies, Lady Edmunds, enjoy the patronage, promptly offered to pay her the £1000. Someone else got the post, and presumably Lady Edmunds netted at least £1000.[2] This same lady — who with the Countess of Warwick appears to have dabbled in many suits — when offered £100 to intervene with the Queen over a Chancery case, treated the offer as too small.[3] 'As a man is friended, so the law is ended' was a contemporary aphorism. Incidents in Judge Manwood's career show that it had point.[4]

The accident of evidence has centred our attention on the Cecils. Others were in the game, much more deeply in relation to their opportunities than Burghley, no doubt. When Sir

[1] *Cal. S.P. Dom. Add. 1566-79*, p. 46. Nevertheless, Burghley advised Heneage about buying an office for his brother (*Hist. MSS. Com.*, *Finch MSS.* p. 6).

[2] *Hatfield MSS.* iv, 497, 529, 531-2, 534, 537.

[3] Birch, op. cit. i, 354.

[4] Cf. *D.N.B.*; Lansdowne MS. 104, fols. 76-9; Harleian MS. 6995, fol. 49. John Wynn's lawyer wrote: 'Mr Wynn, I am wearied to see the tumbling and tossing of law and conscience, for both are ended, as the proverb is, as a man is friended.' Incidentally, he paid tribute to Sir Christopher Hatton's probity: 'The old Chancellor is gone that esteemed neither letters nor would be carried with means or rewards' (N.L.W., Wynn of Gwydir Papers, Panton group, 9051 E, no. 135).

John Carey, a relative of the Queen, heard that she was critical of his wife for selling petty places in the garrison at Berwick, he commented: 'If her Majesty would search into takers so narrowly ... she might find takers of another kind nearer hand, such as take more in one day than she – Lady Carey – hath done in all her life.... It is not the use in any place where she hath been, to do good turns *gratis*.'[1] Unfortunately, we know very little about this aspect of the Earl of Leicester's career, and it is not satisfactory to quote from so gross and malevolent a libel as *Leicester's Commonwealth*. All the same there is some interest, whatever degree of truth there may be, in the writer's accusation that 'no suit can prevail in Court (be it never so mean) except he be first made acquainted, and receive not only the thanks, but also be admitted unto a great part of the gain and commodity thereof'.[2] Sir Thomas Heneage was another statesman of baser metal than Burghley. In 1592 the Earl of Essex wrote to his friend and follower, Sir Henry Unton, reporting that he had spoken about some suit to Heneage, who 'gave me his word to do his best, and the more for my sake. But', he added, 'I think your best friend unto him will be your £1000'.[3] Once, as we know, Heneage was paid £60 to subscribe a bill for a minor duchy official.[4]

Statesmen and courtiers were not the only ones on whom the refreshing rain of gratuities descended. They, too, were remote, and as a rule had to be approached through intermediaries – very often their secretaries. Michael Hicks, one of Burghley's secretaries in his later years, in a letter to a friend, casually referred to certain minor appointments with which, as occasion offered, he could demonstrate his affection – 'as welcome and acceptable to you as twenty fair angels laid in

[1] *Cal. Border Papers*, ii, 787. Cf. Spenser's lines (*Mother Hubberd's Tale*, ll. 515-16):
For nothing there is done without a fee:
The Courtier needs must recompensed be.

[2] *Secret Memoirs of Robert Dudley*, ed. Drake (1706), p. 53. Cf. Collins, *Sydney Papers*, i, 297.

[3] *Hatfield MSS*. iv, 276.

[4] Ibid. xiv, 29.

the hands of us poor bribers here in Court'.[1] If a suit involved attendance on the patron — and we read of Burghley and Essex overwhelmed with suitors[2] — there were more menial servants to be tipped. A suggestive glimpse of the process is offered by the city of Exeter's bill for a suit before the Privy Council in Mary Tudor's reign. 'For remembering' their masters and 'preferring our suit', the secretaries or servants of the Lord Treasurer, the Earl of Pembroke, the Lord Chancellor, the Secretary, and the Lord Admiral were paid varying, not unappreciable, sums; the Lord Treasurer's porter was tipped 'for letting us in, and other his pains'; and the three clerks of the Council, in addition to their legitimate fee, were given two and a half times this sum as a gratuity.[3]

'The gentlemanly profession of serving men' was a common career for younger sons of the gentry, and the vast households of Court magnates offered attractive prospects. The pressure to enter some great man's service, or place a protégé, was constant. Burghley declared that 'it was his disease ... to have too many servants', but he could do little about it:[4] the Earl of Essex, youthful, exuberant, ill-disciplined, kept adding to his retinue. Such men could no more pay their servants adequately than the Queen could hers. Defending himself — on an odd, whimpering note — against the charge of being a councillor that abused his credit to his private gain, Burghley once declared that, unlike many others, he kept no servants 'to whom I pay not wages and give liveries'.[5] But if we were to infer from this that his servants did not depend on gratuities, we should be egregiously wrong. The most revealing evidence about the bribery of those days comes from the correspondence of his secretary, Michael Hicks; and long before the time

[1] Lansdowne MS. 107, fol. 162.
[2] Cf. T. Wright, *Queen Elizabeth and her Times*, ii, 427; Birch, op. cit. i, 168.
[3] *Hist. MSS. Com., Exeter MSS.* pp. 362-3.
[4] *Hatfield MSS.* v, 293.
[5] Lansdowne MS. 103, fol. 46 (printed Strype, *Annals*, III, ii, 379-83); Conyers Read, *Sir Francis Walsingham*, iii, 119.

of Hicks, John Wynn of Gwydir, who in 1572 had a letter for this statesman, told his father that it would be handed to one or other of Burghley's chamber, 'who will look for a reward, which should be measured in accordance with his speeding much or little or none at all'.[1]

Burghley's statement that some people did not pay wages to their servants happens to be confirmed by Sir Christopher Hatton's sententious secretary, Samuel Cox. 'I never charged you with any kind of wages, nor other gift or bounty of your own whatsoever', he wrote. Accused of selling his master's justice and favour, he unfolded his defence:

> There liveth not so grave nor so severe a judge in England, but he alloweth his poor clerk under him, even in the expedition of matters of greatest justice, to take any reasonable consideration that should be offered him by any man for his pains and travail. It is the poor man's whole maintenance, and without it he could not live.... If this be to sell justice and favour, sometimes to take a gratuity of 10s. for one letter among one hundred, sometimes more, sometimes less, according as the party was benefited, or as myself had deserved, I then confess ... I ignorantly erred, as all the rest of your servants have done.[2]

How many other servants served their masters, as Cox did his, for board, lodgings, and tips, we do not know.[3]

Gratuities were fundamental in Elizabethan Court life. All important officials and many minor ones depended upon them; and though it seems impossible to estimate the proportion of his income that any eminent statesman derived from this

[1] *Cal. Wynn Papers*, p. 7. Also cf. *Hist. MSS. Com.*, *Various Coll.*, vii, 260.

[2] Nicolas, *Memoirs of Hatton*, pp. 389-93. Cf. *Cal. S.P. Dom. 1595-7*, p. 254.

[3] On the death of Heneage, one of his servants, a duchy official, explained to Cecil that he had received £20 yearly, plus diet, lodgings, etc., from Heneage, and £20 from official sources. Further, he had his master's 'honourable speech and letters for himself and friends very readily' — i.e. a source of gratuities. All this he estimated as equal to £100 yearly, which leaves an ample gap for gratuities (*Hatfield MSS.* v, 525).

source, we can safely say that he could not otherwise have sustained his splendour. The household servants of such men were as dependent on these gifts as the staff of a modern hotel on tips.

The Queen, of course, knew what went on. In fact, from time to time we find her diverting a suit to some courtier or lady of the Court – as, for example, to Lady Edmunds in the instance already cited – obviously as a reward. Perhaps there was deliberate policy in her actions – an attempt to spread the benefits of patronage as widely as possible; though her closest advisers, and certain officials such as the Masters of Requests, were strategically too well placed to be victims of much levelling. The Queen's concern was not to stop gratuities but to prevent abuses; to see that her own discretion was not undermined by corrupt conspiracy between suitors and courtiers, and to ensure that bribery did not get the wrong person into office. Her habit was to seek assurance of a man's fitness from those not monetarily or otherwise interested in his appointment. Burghley she seems to have consulted almost invariably. The rivalries at Court also served her well. She took advantage of these to check the plausible arguments of patrons, so promoting efficiency while safeguarding her own independence. From this point of view Court factions were essential to the well-being of the governmental system: there could be no greater disaster than single-faction rule. If she suspected deceit, or perceived that the factions were in unholy alliance to secure some appointment of which she disapproved – as the Essexites and Cecilians united to procure the Solicitorship for Francis Bacon – a common device of hers was to fall back on delays. No one could be sure of obtaining her signature. In 1593, in a suit evidently sponsored by Robert Cecil and presumably carrying a gratuity with it, she refused to grant an office to father and son, saying that 'she would make no continuance of inheritance in any her offices'.[1] Though kept ignorant of many things, she was watchful

[1] Ibid. iv, 364.

and ready to express her wrath at abuses that came to her notice. In 1591 Judge Manwood incurred her displeasure for selling an office in his gift, perhaps at too high a price. He defended himself — very much as Sir John Carey defended his wife in similar circumstances — by citing the more heinous acts of other judges.[1] Corruption and inefficiency would have become rampant without such an alert will and discipline at the centre, reinforced by at least one leading statesman of integrity.

The effect of the system on the structure of politics was profound. In Elizabethan England there were no political parties as we know them. True, from time to time there were political differences among statesmen; but, since privy councillors played a merely advisory role in matters of policy, owed a personal and not corporate obligation to the Queen, and, being resident at Court, were constantly consulted in personal conversation, there was neither the mechanism nor the mentality to foster party politics. 'All these Lords', wrote Sir William Cecil to his friend Sir Thomas Smith in 1565, 'are bent towards Her Majesty's service, and do not so much vary amongst themselves as lewd men do report.... I have no affection to be of a party, but for the Queen's Majesty.'[2] The place of party was taken by faction, and the rivalry of the factions was centred on what mattered supremely to everyone: influence over the Queen, and, through that influence, control of patronage with its accompanying benefits.

The competition at Court was ceaseless. Success not only meant money: it meant power. On it depended the quality and size of a statesman's faction — his entourage of household servants, followers, and clients, thronging his chamber and constituting a minor court within the Court proper. The world saw his greatness reflected therein. Every magnate had his circle of friends and followers, some of whom might don his livery as occasion demanded or pay their respects when

[1] Harleian MS. 6995, fol. 49. [2] Wright, op. cit. i, 209.

they were in London or he in their locality. It was an association of self-interest, a mutual-benefit society. Members expected their patron to sponsor their interests at Court and cast his mantle over them whenever the prestige of his name or the cogency of his recommendatory letters might help. 'My desire is to be protected ... under the shadow of your wings, as I was by his Lordship', wrote a member of the noble Manners family to Robert Cecil, offering himself as his follower on Burghley's death.[1] If the association did not pay dividends, members might transfer their investment elsewhere, thus weakening the faction they deserted and strengthening a rival one. 'Who will be desirous to come under a roof that threateneth ruin?' asked the Earl of Essex when his prospects seemed gloomy; while on another occasion, when two of his friends were placed in high office and the Council, a follower wrote, 'Those which are lukewarm will trust more in him; and such as be assured unto him will be glad to see he hath power to do his friends good.'[2]

Within this circle, or among those he counted as his friends, a patron did not necessarily take monetary rewards for his services. 'Sir John Stanhope told me it was your practice not to take anything of charge from those you liked best of', wrote one of Robert Cecil's followers, whose gratuity had been declined.[3] But even here there is a qualification to make, for New Year's gifts were no negligible part of a patron's perquisites — nor, for that matter, of the Queen's.[4] Thomas Bilson, the divine, wrote of Burghley's manifold favours, which, as he put it, 'make me careful at this time, when all men acknowledge their patrons', to show some remembrance.[5] And that dauntless beggar, Julius Caesar, who in the opinion of the Dowager

[1] *Hatfield MSS.* viii, 310. [2] Birch, op. cit. ii, 176, 423.

[3] *Hatfield MSS.* ix, 8. Perhaps for the same reason Burghley refused 'a small piece of plate' from Lord Audley, who thereupon sent a horse (ibid. iii, 362-3).

[4] Cf. Collins, *Sydney Papers*, i, 382. In December 1595 there was a rumour that the Queen 'will make both councillors and officers of Household'. A courtier was sceptical; 'but,' said he, 'it will increase the Queen's New Year gifts'.

[5] Lansdowne MS. 77, fol. 44.

Lady Russell had by 1596 'enough already, if these days could acknowledge what is enough',[1] placed his New Year's gifts with nice calculation. In 1591, in addition to Burghley, he sent gifts to the Lord Chancellor, the Lord Admiral, the Earl of Essex, a master of requests, and my Lady Howard. 'It may be that I shall by the next year be enabled to yield a greater gift', he wrote to Burghley.[2] The innuendo was obvious. On the other hand, Burghley refused a cup of gold as a New Year's gift from Sir Thomas Shirley, a month or so before he was appointed Treasurer at War.[3] It overshot the mark, and the recipient had scruples. At his death, Burghley's plate was worth fourteen or fifteen thousand pounds – a fortune in itself, and yet, as a servant-biographer thought, modest in comparison with his opportunities.[4]

With the chief competitors for power it was a vital point of strategy to place their friends and followers in Court offices and the Privy Council, thus surrounding the Queen with persons who would echo the same advice, promote the same suits, and generally enhance the credit, and through that the wealth, of their faction: as one of Essex's followers put it, to 'bring in any of his friends to strengthen him (of which all the world thinks he hath need) or keep out his greatest enemies, who will seek by all possible means to overthrow him'.[5] *Leicester's Commonwealth* contains an acute analysis of the strategy of power, though otherwise one blushes to quote the passage.

> In the Privy Chamber, next to her Majesty's person, the most part are his [Leicester's] own creatures (as he calleth them) – that is, such as acknowledge their being in that place from him; and the rest he so over-ruleth,

[1] *Hatfield MSS.* vi, 215.
[2] Lansdowne MS. 47, fols. 8 seqq.
[3] *Hatfield MSS.* iii, 206.
[4] Peck, op. cit. i, 27.
[5] Birch, op. cit. ii, 185.

> either by flattery or fear, as none may dare but to serve his turn. His reign ... is so absolute in this place, and likewise in all other parts of the Court, as nothing can pass but by his admission, nothing can be said, done, or signified, whereof he is not particularly advertised; no bill, no supplication, no complaint, no suit, no speech can pass from any man to the Prince (except it be from one of the Council) but by his good liking.... Whereby he holdeth as it were a lock upon the ears of his Prince.[1]

Interesting, but fantastic! The writer maligned the Queen as well as Leicester. She allowed no monopoly, but played the factions one against the other; and there can be little doubt that she paid more heed to Burghley, whose advice was most disinterested and least corrupt. This supreme statesman was wont to tell his intimates 'that he had gotten more by his patience than ever he did by his wit'.[2]

Absence from Court was perilous to faction-leaders. It gave opponents the opportunity of poisoning the Queen's mind with malicious stories; it was their chance to fill vacant offices with their friends. 'I pray you to stand fast for your poor absent friends against calumniators', wrote Leicester to Walsingham, when he was away in the Netherlands,[3] and his absence was seized upon – by Burghley, said the French ambassador – to have Whitgift, Cobham, and Buckhurst, all opponents of his, made privy councillors.[4] The illustration *par excellence* of this strategy is the career of Essex. He failed hopelessly to place his nominees in Court office. 'Not that the Earl meant to stand alone like a substantive (for he was not so ill a grammarian in Court)', wrote Sir Henry Wotton, who once was a secretary

[1] *Secret Memoirs*, ed. Drake, p. 52. Cf. *Spanish Cal. Eliz.* iii, 267, and the reference to 'the wonderful power of this man' at Court, in *Cal. S.P. Dom. Add. 1580-1625*, p. 203.

[2] Add. MS. 22925, fol. 29b.

[3] *Foreign Cal. Eliz.* XXI, iii, 233.

[4] *Scottish Cal.* viii, 248.

of his; but the Cecilians frustrated him, 'as very well knowing that upon every little absence or disassiduity, he should be subject to take cold at his back'.[1] And on his last, fateful absence from Court, Essex himself wrote bitterly to the Council from Ireland: 'I provided for this service a breastplate and not a cuirass; that is, I am armed on the breast, but not on the back.'[2]

In its broad lines this analysis of the Elizabethan political scene might have proceeded, not inductively from the printed and manuscript sources of the period, but deductively — as an essay in the logic of human behaviour — from a system of personal monarchy, with immense patronage at the disposal of the Crown, and inadequate salaries in both royal and private households; though whether, in view of man's insatiable cupidity, inadequate salaries constitute an essential element in the argument, is perhaps open to doubt.

There are two weaknesses or dangers inherent in such a system of government. Corruption may get out of hand, or, to employ the Elizabethan distinction, gratuities degenerate into plain bribery; and rivalry at Court may become so intense as to threaten the stability of the state. Our Elizabethan story has light to throw on both.

If our evidence can be trusted, the standard of public morality was declining sharply during the last decade or so of the reign. True, this gloomy view owes much to a unique collection of letters[3] — the correspondence of Michael Hicks, secretary to Burghley and subsequently to Robert Cecil; and one cannot but wonder how the picture would look if the correspondence of earlier secretaries had survived. Nor can we close our minds to doubts, knowing that after Burghley's death Hicks went through his papers, and coming across many letters from Sir Robert Sidney offered them to him 'to burn'.[4] Was this a purge? Perhaps not; but if it was, how far did it go?

[1] *Reliquiae Wottonianae* (1654), p. 25.
[2] Birch, op. cit. ii, 420.
[3] In the Lansdowne MSS.
[4] *Hist. MSS. Com., Penshurst MSS.* ii, 403.

All the same, if we compare Burghley and his son, Robert Cecil, it is difficult to imagine the father – at any rate in his prime – figuring as Cecil does in many documents. 'You may boldly write for his favour in this matter', John Wynn of Gwydir was told by his London lawyer in 1592. 'You paid well for it.'[1] Two years later we find Cecil writing an obscure letter to Hicks – with instructions to burn it – the gist of which was to keep secret his part in the choice of someone for a post, since he did not wish the Queen to suspect that he thought of anything but her service, nor his enemies to realize what had occurred.[2] Hicks, as this letter indicates, was more than a servant; he was an intimate friend of Robert Cecil. When in 1596 he ended a letter with a 'prayer to give you your heart's desire either in promotion or profit', how much the servant revealed both of himself and his young master![3] In 1603 Cecil was offering him advice on a suit he was making to the Queen. Warning him of the need to secure the Lord Treasurer's support, he told him to go to Lady Glemham, the Lord Treasurer's daughter, and promise her £100 if she 'will win her father to you'. There were two postscripts to the letter, one a caution against being cozened by Lady Glemham, the other a promise to find him a ward to pay for the bribe, whether it cost £100 or £200.[4] Or consider the letter that he wrote Hicks about a wardship which the latter was seeking, and which was reckoned so exceptional a prize that the Court was 'absolutely full of importunity for it'. After putting him gently but firmly in his place for his effrontery in asking for so valuable a gift, in competition with his betters, Cecil – who was now Master of the Court of Wards – explained that he intended to 'draw some benefit' from this wardship for himself, but through a nominee

[1] N.L.W., Wynn of Gwydir Papers, 9051 E, no. 135.

[2] Lansdowne MS. 77, fol. 192. Cf. Cecil's letter to the Earl of Northumberland (*Hatfield MSS.* x, 347) where he adopts a high moral tone in contrast with his intimate letters to Hicks.

[3] *Hatfield MSS.* vi, 395.

[4] Lansdowne MS. 88, fol. 105, printed in Ellis, *Original Letters*, 3rd ser. iv, 150-1.

whom no one would suspect of being merely his 'figure'.[1] There is a lack of scruple about these incidents which one can hardly associate with Burghley. Nor can one imagine him advising a suitor, as Cecil did on another occasion, to pay Sir John Stanhope, Treasurer of the Chamber and a follower of his, £100 to speak to the Queen on his behalf.[2]

As for Cecil's merry friend Hicks, he became a wealthy man and played money-lender to courtiers, including Francis Bacon, Fulke Greville, and the Earl of Pembroke.[3] It would not be rash to guess that in the last decade of the reign he received more gratuities than any other servant in England. Many of his surviving letters are from correspondents sending or promising him tokens of their goodwill. One sends £20 and hopes for his favour.[4] Another, desirous to be a clerk of the signet, 'will deliver unto whom he [Burghley] will please to appoint £100, and to yourself 100 angels'.[5] Still another vows that if, through Hicks, Burghley is pleased to move the Queen for his suit, 'I shall ever after be bound to do him and his family honour and service, show myself thankful unto him' – euphemism for a gratuity – 'in sort as I acquainted you, and for your own travail therein assuredly perform what I have promised.'[6] 'A Welsh nag worth five pounds' is another bait.[7] Being so close to two successive masters of the Court of Wards, he was approached by persons seeking wardships;[8] and no doubt Robert Cecil saw that he had occasional bonuses from this source.

To judge the tone of the period, let us glance at a few of the gratuities offered to statesmen – though not necessarily accepted – in the years 1590 to 1603. A receiver-general of

[1] Lansdowne MS. 88, fol. 91.
[2] *Hatfield MSS.* x, 31.
[3] Cf. *D.N.B.*; Lansdowne MS. 88, fol. 23.
[4] Ibid. 72, no. 72.
[5] Ibid. 107, no. 71.
[6] Ibid. 78, fol. 62.
[7] Ibid. 83, no. 39. Cf. also ibid. 77, fols. 36, 164, 168; 87, fol. 214; 88, fol. 79; 107, fol. 46; 108, fol. 19; 109, fol. 119.
[8] Cf. ibid. 77, fols. 112, 180; 87, fol. 37; 108, fol. 41.

the Court of Wards, who had followed the all-too-prevalent practice of holding on to Crown revenue as long as possible, meanwhile employing the money to his own gain, died £25,824 in debt to the Queen — a scandalous episode. His son not only had the effrontery to ask for his father's office, but offered Robert Cecil £1000 to secure the Queen's consent to a certain device for handling the debt.[1] Nothing came of his proposals, but he retained Cecil's friendship. A man offered Cecil £100 a year to join with three other councillors in securing a patent, which was obviously contrary to public interest. Again, it is unlikely that anything came of the offer, though Cecil's relations with this promoter of suits look rather suspicious.[2] Then, in 1597 Sir Anthony Ashley wrote that he had the disposition of a lunatic, and if Robert Cecil would take the wardship for himself, it would bring him 'some thousand pounds per annum', or, alternatively, the lunatic's younger brother would pay him £2000 for it.[3] The same year a man offered him 2000 marks to procure a legal office in Judge Anderson's gift.[4] On this occasion Cecil probably did not even try, for Anderson was the judge who, as John Chamberlain tells us, on the death of a high official in the Court of Common Pleas 'had given the place and sworne an officer before eight a clock the next morning; and within an hour after, came the Queen's letters for another, which by that means were frustrate'.[5] The pursuit of office or wardship in these years grew so feverish that the mere prospect of a death set suitors busy.

[1] P.R.O., Wards Misc. 88, fols. 419b-21; *Hatfield MSS.* iv, 515. There are references to this affair in several volumes of the *Hatfield MSS.*

[2] Ibid. iv, 608, and index to vols. iv and v *sub* Margitts, George. Cf. Margitts' letter to Cecil, October 8th, 1593 (ibid. 384-5): 'I will not leave, with God's help, before your Honour be someways furnished with one good suit or other.' Pressing one particular project, he writes: 'You shall have good assurance for the payment of £5000 in five years, and 500 marks yearly afterwards', and only Burghley and the writer will know 'that you have any dealing in the same'.

[3] Ibid. vii, 4-5. For other references to wardships, cf. ibid. iv, 353, 522-3, 554-5, 597; v, 128; vi, 363, 425 (£1000 offered to Burghley's secretary, Maynard); vii, 115; ix, 378; x, 107.

[4] Ibid. vii, 210.

[5] N. E. McClure, *Letters of John Chamberlain*, i, 75.

In 1593 no less a person than Sir John Fortescue, Chancellor of the Exchequer and privy councillor, wrote to Lord Keeper Puckering — apparently a corrupt person, whose death few deplored[1] — offering 100 angels for the office of *custos rotulorum* in his county. He explained that he wanted it more 'for credit than commodity', though as he stipulated for nomination of the Clerk of the Peace, he could presumably have made commodity out of it: at any rate, in Devon the clerkship was bought for £300.[2] In 1591 John Wynn of Gwydir, actuated by a feud, tried to rig the choice of sheriff for his county. His agent employed the Countess of Warwick, who 'promised sure to stop' Wynn's enemy, William Williams, and get in his nominee; but she happened to be unwell when the Queen pricked the sheriffs, and as the agent wrote, 'William Williams is sheriff by the means of my Lord of Buckhurst. It is reported he paid dear for it.' However, in the neighbouring shire of Merioneth, Wynn's intervention succeeded. His brother acted as agent in this instance, was more fortunate in his choice of patron, and 'laid out money' as instructed.[3]

This downward trend in public morality was noted by one of Burghley's panegyrists. 'I will forbear', he wrote, 'to mention the great and unusual fees exacted lately by reason of buying and selling offices, both judicial and ministerial, as also the privileges granted unto private persons to the great prejudice and grievance of the common people.'[4] Of course, the bribers were to blame as well as the bribed; and no doubt economic causes were also at work along with social. The growing wealth of the nation, in contrast with that of the state; monetary

[1] Birch, op. cit. i, 481, and cf. p. 354.

[2] Harleian MS. 286, fol. 219; *Hatfield MSS.* iv, 517. For other payments offered for local office, cf. *Hist. MSS. Com., Gawdy MSS.* p. 75; N.L.W., Wynn of Gwydir Papers, Add. MS. 464 E, no. 111 (£10 offered to the Earl of Leicester's servant to make Owen Wynn and Thomas Vaughan J.P.s).

[3] N.L.W., Wynn of Gwydir Papers, Panton group, 9051 E, no. 129. For other gratuities, cf. *Hatfield MSS.* iv, 253, 362, 499; vi, 139, 146, 259, 545; vii, 106, 258, 288-9, 332, 349; *Cal. S.P. Dom. 1591-4*, p. 424; *Cal. S.P. Dom. 1601-3*, p. 41; *Cal. Border Papers*, ii, 439.

[4] Additional MS. 22925, fol. 23.

inflation; industrial expansion, coupled with the scandal of monopolies; perhaps, also, an undue concentration of money on the domestic market owing to war conditions: all these probably help to explain soaring bribes and the feverish competition for place and favour. It has the appearance of an inflationary movement: too many suitors pursuing too few privileges. Nor must we forget that the Queen was ageing, and her discipline – dependent in any case upon the loyalty and probity of those about her – losing its old resilience. The balance of factions was also weakening, and there was the threatening spectre of single-faction rule. Even Burghley, in the last eight years of his life, when his son so frequently acted as his deputy, seems to have been affected by the new moral climate.

In leaving this tale of growing corruption, we may reflect that pressure tends to concentrate on the weak features of any social system, thus undermining it; and that a new generation does not respond so readily to the restraints of a moral code which it inherits and does not create. The generation coming into power in the 1590s was out of tune with the old Queen and her ways. It fawned, but it deceived. Elizabeth herself voiced this feeling to her faithful antiquary, William Lambarde, in 1601: 'Now the wit of the fox is everywhere on foot, so as hardly a faithful or virtuous man may be found.'[1]

In the first decade of Elizabeth's reign there were occasions when faction seemed to be getting out of hand. But there was then a fundamental harmony in age and outlook between sovereign and statesmen. Leicester was not an Essex, and the loyalty, authority, and uprightness of such men as William Cecil, Nicholas Bacon, and the Earl of Bedford, to mention no others, were sufficient steadying force. Sir Robert Naunton, in his *Fragmenta Regalia*,[2] has an astute comment on the Queen's method of government. 'The principal note of her reign will

[1] Nichols, *Progresses of Queen Elizabeth* (1788), vol. ii.
[2] In the essay, 'The Queen'.

be, that she ruled much by faction and parties, which herself both made, upheld, and weakened, as her own great judgment advised.' As Sir Henry Wotton wrote, it 'was not the least ground of much of her quiet and success'.[1]

The 1590s, however, were a political climacteric. The great statesmen and faction-leaders of the reign were passing in rapid succession to the grave; and power had to be transferred to the new generation at a pace dangerous to the digestive capacity of the system. The 'quiet and success' which Elizabeth had derived from the rivalry of the factions were shattered, principally by the nature of the young Earl of Essex, but also by the survival of Burghley, whose unrivalled experience, authority, and subtlety were all concentrated on securing the succession to his very able son, Robert Cecil.

> O grief of griefs, O gall of all good hearts
> To see that virtue should despised be
> Of him, that first was raised for virtuous parts,
> And now broad spreading like an aged tree,
> Lets none shoot up, that nigh him planted be.

So wrote Spenser,[2] and though he was not an impartial spectator, there was perhaps an element of truth in his words. For the followers of Essex, there was certainly a semblance of truth. 'Old *Saturnus* is a melancholy and wayward planet, but yet predominant here', wrote Sir Robert Sidney's man in 1591, warning his master that the way to favour was through Burghley, not Essex.[3] And in 1596, Anthony Bacon, the Earl's right-hand man, described the Cecils as 'the omnipotent couple'.[4] '*Regnum Cecilianum*' or 'Cecil's Commonwealth' was a phrase which had been frequently used.[5]

[1] *Reliquiae Wottonianae* (1654), p. 44.
[2] *The Ruins of Time*, ll. 449 seqq.
[3] Collins, *Sydney Papers*, i, 331.
[4] Birch, op. cit. i, 481.
[5] Strype, *Annals*, III, ii, 380; Add. MS. 22925, fols. 29-30.

But if there was a *regnum Cecilianum* in these later years, it was the creation of the Earl of Essex. This impetuous young man was the architect of his own ruin. He could not live and let live, but wanted everything. He would tolerate no divided loyalties. He virtually reduced the factions to two; and would have reduced them to one – his own. There was no subtlety in his tactics. He recklessly engaged his reputation in the suits he supported, so that failure brought humiliation. Even over an Irish office worth £300, for which in 1593 there was great competition and round sums offered 'in the Chamber and elsewhere', while Burghley planned to suppress it in the interests of economy, we are told that he backed his man with such assurance and publicity that all the Court knew of it.[1] Inevitably he embarrassed the Queen; and as his megalomania developed, feeding on the idolatry of the people for a romantic war-leader, he left her in no doubt that she must resist or be enslaved. He believed that he could carry her mind by storm – his policy of 'hot waters', against which Francis Bacon shrewdly advised him. He would get his way by constant iteration: '*saepe cadendo*', as he termed it.[2] On one occasion Elizabeth bade him go to bed, if he could talk of nothing else. It was impossible for her to follow her old policy of balancing the factions. Instead, she was driven to backing one faction – the Cecilians. At the time of Essex's fall Robert Cecil was Secretary, Chancellor of the Duchy of Lancaster, and Master of the Court of Wards – a unique combination of offices; and if we reflect on the power and patronage they conferred – particularly the rich patronage of the Court of Wards and the Duchy – we can appreciate how near to creating a rival monopoly Elizabeth was forced to go. After the Earl's death she took the Chancellorship of the Duchy away from Cecil.

Never was the danger for a faction-leader of absence from Court more clearly demonstrated. While present, Essex could

[1] Birch, op. cit. i, 130.
[2] Cf. *Unton Correspondence*, ed. J. Stevenson, p. 317.

often by his tantrums prevent the Queen from making unwelcome appointments; but when away, he was too weak to resist his enemies. All Robert Cecil's offices were conferred while his rival was absent on one expedition or another; and news of Cecil's appointment to the Mastership of the Court of Wards, which Essex had strenuously solicited for himself, was one of the gravest blows he suffered during his Irish campaign.

How passionately Essex fought for his friends, Sir Robert Sidney and Francis Bacon! In 1596, when Lord Hunsdon was dying, he promised to put forward Sidney for the great office of Lord Chamberlain — an insensate proposal.[1] Instead, Lord Cobham, his enemy and Burghley's friend, was appointed. Next year, on Cobham's death, he waged implacable battle over the Lord Wardenship of the Cinque Ports, to keep out Cobham's son and put in Sidney. For some months his outrageous behaviour kept the post vacant; but then Cobham got it.[2] He next pressed for the Vice-Chamberlain's office, vacant since the death of Heneage in 1595. Raleigh had ambitions that way; but Essex told him that he would be an enemy to all who sought the office.[3] He so terrified other candidates that the Queen left the office vacant until his death opened the way for a Cecilian. He also promised Sidney a peerage.[4] He got him nothing. The violence with which he pressed his suits for Francis Bacon, first for the office of Attorney-General and then of Solicitor-General, is well known. He tried to make him Master of the Rolls.[5] He failed in all. He could get anything for himself, said a supporter, but nothing for his friends; and Essex's own view in 1599, in the darkening weeks before his departure for Ireland, was that he could 'procure nothing for himself nor any of his friends'.[6]

[1] *Cal. S.P. Dom. 1595-7*, p. 181.
[2] Collins, *Sydney Papers*, ii, *passim*.
[3] Ibid. p. 80.
[4] Ibid. *passim*; *Hatfield MSS.* viii, 29.
[5] Birch, op. cit. i, 488.
[6] *Hatfield MSS.* ix, 10.

As our analysis of the Elizabethan political scene will have suggested, there was another side to this story. Court rivalry was not merely concerned with power and prestige. A leader's own solvency and the livelihood of his servants were at stake. Like a financier in our modern world, he was poised upon a great credit structure. Blow upon it: the result might be ruin. This was Essex's position.[1] Early in his career, in 1589, he confessed to Sir Thomas Heneage that his debts were at least twenty-two or twenty-three thousand pounds, and his revenue no greater than when he came of age. Life seemed to him then, and was, a game with fortune.[2] He obtained the lease of the sweet wines which Leicester had held, and with it the means of raising substantial loans from the wine merchants. In 1597, when it lapsed, statements of his debts were compiled to show that he would be bankrupt if it were not renewed, and his credit with these merchants prolonged.[3] Meanwhile, with the inordinate growth of his household and his splendour, the stakes in the game mounted. He began with two secretaries. In 1595-6 the number was increased to four and then to five — much to the chagrin of the oldest, who, though he gave other reasons for discontent, feared a drastic diminution in gratuities.[4]

Apart from his natural incapacity to accept reverses with equanimity, Essex must have been concerned about the financial effects of continual rebuffs in his major suits to the Queen; and so too must the members of his household, many of whom were ambitious, able men, and some reckless. How long would the indispensable gratuities continue to flow? From this point of view his Irish campaign was a gambler's last throw; and with our knowledge of the great monetary gains which the Master and his friends and servants made out of the Court of Wards, we can appreciate how bitter was the news, which came in the midst of his Irish misfortunes, that

[1] For Leicester's position at his death, cf. Ellis, *Original Letters*, 3rd ser. iv, 75-9.
[2] *Hatfield MSS.* iii, 459.
[3] Ibid. vii, 283, 375-6.
[4] Birch, op. cit. ii, 105 seqq.

Cecil had been appointed to this office. The Earl's mad, unauthorized return to Court was followed by a prolonged disgrace. It brought him face to face with ruin. His licence for sweet wines, as valuable 'in credit as in profit', lapsed: it was not renewed. An incomplete catalogue of his debts at this time showed over £16,000 owing; and his creditors, distrustful as they had cause to be, were pressing for payment and lying in wait to arrest those servants of his who had stood pledge for him.[1] The credit structure was collapsing. His household must have been in worse case. For sixteen months – the duration of his disgrace – there can have been no gratuities. No wonder that the prime villain of the piece, his secretary Cuffe, and others were reckless. The rebellion was an act of financial desperation.

In these last years of Elizabeth's reign, with the inherent flaws of a political system apparent, we are moving into a new age. The accession of James I, a weak sovereign who had neither the character nor the political skill to maintain the discipline of the past, gave rein to the forces of corruption. The episode of Essex was also repeated, though in a different way and with a different ending. This time it was the sovereign himself who encouraged single-faction rule. If Queen Elizabeth had really been infatuated with Essex as tradition pictured her, or as James I with the Duke of Buckingham, then Sir Henry Wotton's *Parallel* between the two favourites would indeed have deserved its name. But Elizabeth strove to maintain the old, balanced order. Under James I it broke down, and the scandal and discontent caused by a putrefying political system helped to provoke the Civil War.

[1] *Hatfield MSS.* x, 110, 128, 312, 348.

THE SAYINGS OF QUEEN ELIZABETH[1]

THE occasion of this article is the publication under the same title of a book by Mr Frederick Chamberlin.[2] Four years ago he achieved considerable popular success by a work on *The Private Character of Queen Elizabeth*, which ran into four printings. Neither book has been reviewed in any serious historical journal, and since Mr Chamberlin's literary programme is by no means complete, it may be useful, before making any excursion of my own into the entertaining field chosen by him, to say something of his more recent work and to assess the scholarship of one whose pretensions are, to put it mildly, a little extravagant.

Mr Chamberlin prefaces his collection of the sayings of Queen Elizabeth with an exuberant introduction, in which he presents himself as the champion of Elizabeth and Leicester against the misrepresentations of former historians. The Queen, he tells us, once said, 'The truth will at last be made manifest', and 'If I had not come along now,' he adds later, 'how many years would have passed before the truth would "at last be made manifest"?' Such passages it is needless to comment upon, as it is needless to rebut his charges against John Bruce, the editor of the *Leycester Correspondence* published by the Camden Society, and against professional historians in general. They are best left to the sober judgment of his readers. But his criticism of Froude is more than mere *obiter dicta*. It pretends to be an elaborate examination of his historical method; and in consequence I must devote a little space to it.

Mr Chamberlin quarrels with Froude because he was

[1] Published in *History* (October 1925), x, 212-33.
[2] John Lane, 1923.

critical of Elizabeth, seeing behind her the figure of Burghley, digesting and docketing documents with an amazing capacity for work, drawing up the arguments for and against some policy in that characteristic Italian hand of his, and displaying a solid common sense, which, if seemingly timid and unimaginative, yet gave the turn to the rudder that saved the ship of state from wreck. Mr Chamberlin does not see the Elizabethan age as Froude saw it. Burghley is to shrink under the blast of his criticism, Leicester to take his place as the master-mind of the reign, and the Queen, her name cleansed from scandal, is to stand out peerless. Consequently he attempts to dethrone Froude by submitting his technique to a detailed study.

Faulty as the study is, it shows conclusively that Froude was no respecter of inverted commas; and this is a legitimate and a useful line of criticism. In these days we hold by an exacting historical method, but it would be lamentable if that robbed us of a sense of values. Froude was a great literary artist. He felt the rhythmic possibilities of sixteenth-century prose and made occasional alterations in his quotations that lent an incomparable melody to them. He abridged documents, often without warning. He translated in a free, because an artistic, manner. He felt that history could not be literature were it to consist of documents strung upon a commentary; that both must pass into the crucible of an artistic mind and be fused into one. And yet his sin was not that he amended his documents, which was sound literary instinct, but that he sanctified his own handiwork by inverted commas. It was, however, the fault of another age of historians than our own, and cannot be judged fairly by recent standards. Nor is it serious, once we recognize that Froude is not to be trusted to quote his documents *verbatim*. In fact, it is a venial sin. But if in using his documents the historian inverts or deflects their sense, that cannot be excused. Unfortunately Froude did, and if only Mr Chamberlin had been less concerned with trivial inaccuracies and had enabled us to judge how extensive was

Froude's serious offence, he would have performed a valuable service.

The critic must pay the penalty of submitting his own work to be judged by the standards which he himself sets up. Mr Chamberlin attempts to demonstrate the worthlessness of Froude's quotations by printing alongside of them what he says is the true text. One of his columns he heads, 'What Froude says Elizabeth wrote'; another, 'What Elizabeth actually wrote'.[1] It is perhaps a quibble to remark that Elizabeth neither wrote nor composed the document in question; but be that as it may, when Mr Chamberlin quotes his second column from the *Calendar of State Papers, Scottish Series*, and describes it as 'a correct reproduction of the entire document', he betrays, first that he has not looked at the original document, and secondly that he has not yet realized that generally a Calendar does not reproduce a document *verbatim*.

His idea of what constitutes historical proof is also a measure of his scholarship. 'I am giving to the public', he says on p. vi, 'one of the most epochal facts in all the life of Elizabeth.' It purports to be Elizabeth's own statement of her reason for favouring Leicester, and comes from a letter of Hubert Languet, in which he is retailing the gossip at Antwerp, at a city where, as Guicciardini puts it, one always knew everything that was going on in every other country in the universe.[2] In other words, Mr Chamberlin's evidence is as unreliable as a news-letter. Nor does he improve matters by citing Gregorio Leti in confirmation of it. I can hardly enter here into proof of my estimate of Leti as a historian; but his *Historia ... di Elizabetta* is utterly worthless, and is adorned with letters of his own fabrication.[3] Written between 1680 and 1693, it is obviously not an original authority for Elizabeth's reign.

[1] *Sayings of Queen Elizabeth*, p. xxiv.

[2] *Description de Touts les Pays-Bas* ... (1598), quoted by Tawney and Power, *Tudor Economic Documents*, iii, 157.

[3] Mary Wood in her *Letters of Royal Ladies*, and F. A. Mumby in his *Girlhood of Queen Elizabeth*, have both reprinted apocryphal letters from Leti.

The body of Mr Chamberlin's book consists of 'sayings' of Elizabeth. Many are quoted without any reference to their source, and there are few people who would not be tempted to invoke the shade of Macaulay's schoolboy when told that the authority is 'obvious or readily found from its context'. Nor is Mr Chamberlin quite fair to Miss Strickland. Something like half of his 'sayings' are taken from her *Life of Elizabeth*. In most instances he makes no acknowledgment to her, and often he borrows her reference, also without acknowledgment. Here is an example. Miss Strickland's reference is, 'Autograph letter in the imperial collection at St Petersburgh ... '; Mr Chamberlin's, 'Translation from the French original, preserved in the Imperial Autograph Collection at Petrograd. I cannot now vouch for the existence of this MS., but it was at Petrograd before the Great War.'[1] Whatever may be Mr Chamberlin's explanation of his own gloss upon the original reference, the fact remains that the translation which he uses is Miss Strickland's; and since she quotes her documents with much the same freedom as Froude, we have the curious result that she imposes upon Mr Chamberlin throughout his book just those very faults which he criticizes so drastically in his introduction.

Much might be said about the sayings which flow through other channels into Mr Chamberlin's book. He resurrects Sir Nicholas Bacon (d. 1579) to deliver one of the opening speeches in parliament in 1601, and attributes the speech, with what authority I do not know, to the Queen's composition.[2] Some sayings appear more than once in different guises, an example being the famous 'Aye or No' speech of 1593, which again he wrongly attributes to Elizabeth, and the best version of which[3] he does not know. Two sayings are from Carlyle – a 'very reliable' authority, says Mr Chamberlin,[4] who clearly cannot have heard of the Squire papers.

[1] Strickland, *Lives of the Queens of England* (1851), iv, 641 n.; Chamberlin, op. cit. p. 193 n. For another example see ibid. p. 47 n. (Strickland, iv, 644 n.).
[2] Chamberlain, pp. 148-9.
[3] See *Eng. Hist. Rev.* xxxi (1916), 128.
[4] Op. cit. p. 28 n.

And so I might go on; but it is enough to add that as grapes are not gathered of thorns, so sound history does not come from an unsound critical equipment.

One merit Mr Chamberlin's book possesses: it sets us wondering whether the sayings attributed to Elizabeth were really hers. Needless to say, he offers no help to the answer. Whether true or false they went into his collection; and so far as I know there has hitherto been no attempt to set up a canon and apocrypha of stories. The reason is simple. It would involve elaborate criticism of a hundred and one books, and even then we could say no more than 'probable' or 'improbable' about most of the stories. Such criticism I do not pretend for a moment to have undertaken; but in the remaining pages of this article I hope to make a preliminary essay towards a differentiation between the true and the false in regard to a few of the reputed sayings and stories.

It goes almost without saying that some are apocryphal. Wit was in fashion at the Court of Elizabeth, as it is in a community like Oxford, and we hardly need reminding that the men of established reputation in such circles are often strangers to their own fosterlings. At the peace conference of 1919, where there was a company of experts adept at word-play and a few statesmen at the centre of things distinguished politically and not incapable of a *bon mot*, we are told that the epigrams which were invented were fathered with astonishing regularity upon the same few, and especially upon M. Clémenceau. It would be difficult to say what mordant epigrams Clémenceau was responsible for, and what not; and equally difficult is it, and for the same reasons, to tell what sayings were really Elizabeth's. Her wit was equal to them all. She was a woman of ready and vigorous mind and considerable culture, and the figurative style of her writing and speaking gave her excellent practice in turning phrases. She loved metaphor and simile, antithesis and epigram, and sometimes got herself so involved in her conceits that her listeners and correspondents must have been as perplexed about her meaning as her statesmen were. 'No man can knowe the inward entencyon of her harte ... but God and her selfe', said her councillors when consulted about the Anjou marriage negotiations;[1] and Walsingham, when advising the Queen on the same project, wisely wrote, 'If you mean it ... If you mean it not ... '[2]

But even when most involved, her style rarely lacked vigour and distinction, and when passion kept her love of finery in check, she could rise to magnificent heights. Here is a passage from a letter to James VI where vigour and affectation struggle for mastery:

> And since it so lykes you to demande my counsaile, I finde so many ways your state so unjoynted, that it needs a skilfuller bonesetter than I to joyne each part in his right place. But to fulfill your will, take, in shorte, theise few words: ... Who to peril a king were inventores or actors, they should crake a halter if I were king. Such is my charitie. Who under pretence of bettering your estate, endangers the king, or needs wil be his schoolemasters, if I might appoint their universitie they should be assigned to learne first to obay; so should they better teach you next....[3]

Whilst here, in a brief passage taken from a speech to the Commons, which, though a report only, is a full, and, I believe, a faithful one, and well worth reading in its entirety, her language is simple and forceful:

> As for myne owne part I care not for death, for all men are mortall, and though I be a woman I have as good a courage, aunswerable to my place, as ever my father had. I am your anoynted Queene. I will never be by violence constrained to do any thing. I thanke God I am endued with such qualities that if I weare turned out of the

[1] *Hatfield MSS.* ii, 239.
[2] Ibid. p. 427.
[3] *Letters of Elizabeth and James VI* (Camden Soc. 1849), pp. 76-7.

Realme in my peticote I wear able to live in any place in christome [Christendom].[1]

Elizabeth was merely the centre of a Court in which the wit and culture of her age were mirrored, and there were men about her like that imp of a godson, Sir John Harington, who shocked her – so she pretended – by his broad humour, yet amused her and won her love as much by his ready tongue and pen as by his claims as a godson. Inevitably good stories must have been fathered upon her, whether she knew it or not. If she knew, she smiled, no doubt, and let them float down to posterity on the strong support of her fame. Being a very human being, she loved praise, and being a sovereign – and a Tudor sovereign at that – got more of it than was good for her; for if adulation be the common lot of an attractive woman and a prince, only a Diogenes could have resisted a combination of both. 'My heart was never broken till this day', wrote Raleigh to Sir Robert Cecil in an outburst which in its extravagance parodies the eulogies of the Court:

> My heart was never broken till this day that I hear the Queen goes away so far off, whom I have followed so many years with so great love and desire in so many journeys, and am now left behind her in a dark prison all alone. While she was yet near at hand, that I might hear of her once in two or three days, my sorrows were the less, but yeven now my heart is cast into the depth of all misery. I that was wont to behold her riding like Alexander, hunting like Diana, walking like Venus, the gentle winde blowing her fair hair about her pure cheeks like a nymph, sometime sitting in the shade like a goddess, sometime singing like an angel, sometime playing like Orpheus – behold, the sorrow of this world once amiss hath bereaved me of all. Oh! love that only shineth in misfortune, what is become of thy assurance! All wounds

[1] *Eng. Hist. Rev.* xxxvi (1921), 516.

have scars but that of phantasy: all affections their relenting but that of woman kind.[1]

The Court cried her praises, and the City, when it was in the humour, was Echo's voice which Elizabeth kept well tuned by bewitching it. 'Now, if ever any persone had eyther the gift or the stile to winne the hearts of people, it was this Queene', wrote Sir John Hayward, who had little to thank Elizabeth for save imprisonment and a lucky escape from worse:

> and if ever shee did expresse the same, it was at that present, in coupling mildnesse with majesty as shee did, and in stately stouping to the meanest sort. All her facultyes were in motione, and every motione seemed a well guided actione; her eye was set upon one, her eare listened to another, her judgement ranne uppon a third, to a fourth shee addressed her speech; her spirit seemed to be every-where, and yet so intyre in her selfe, as it seemed to bee noe where else. Some shee pityed, some shee commended, some shee thanked, at others shee pleasantly and wittily jeasted, contemning noe person, neglecting noe office; and distributing her smiles, lookes, and graces soe artificially, that thereupon the people again redoubled the testimonyes of their joyes; and afterwards, raising every thing to the highest straine, filled the eares of all men with immoderate extolling their Prince.[2]

That Elizabeth had an irresistible way with her the documents of the time prove amply enough. Let me illustrate it by a letter from Sir William Brown to Sir Robert Sidney, who had sent him over from the Netherlands with letters to the Queen in 1601. Like so many of her servants abroad, Brown had become a disgruntled creature. This Elizabeth knew, and she set herself to charm him.

[1] *Hatfield MSS.* iv, 220. The date is July 1592.
[2] *Annals of Elizabeth* (Camden Soc. 1840), pp. 6-7.

> I had no sooner kyssed her sacred hands, butt that she presently made me stand upp, and spoke somwhat lowd, and sayd, Com hether Browne; and pronounced, that she held me for an old faithful servant of hers, and said, I must give content to Browne, or som such speeches: And then the Trayne following her, she sayd, Stand, stand back, will you not let us speake but you wilbe hearers? And then walked a turne or twoo, protesting her most gracious opinion of my self: And before God, Brown, sayd shee, they do me wrong that will make so honest a servant be jealous that I should mistrust him.... Having walked a turne or twoo, she called for a stoole, which was sett under a tree, and I begann to kneele, butt she wold not suffer mee; in so much as that after twoo or three denyalls which I made to kneele, still she was pleased to say, that shee wold not speake with me unles I stood upp.

Brown began to explain the position of affairs in the Netherlands: 'Tush, Brown,' said she, 'I know more than thow doest', and thereupon she poured forth her own comment and prophecy. She turned to talk of the French king, and, Brown venturing a remark, 'Tush, Browne,' said she, 'do not I know?'—and so the conversation went on. With a final pat on the back poor Brown was sent away, so deliriously happy that it was only in a postscript to his letter that he remembered he had been sent to England by Sidney on business.[1]

Many other examples could be given of the Queen's genius in winning affection. There was little Byzantine aloofness about her sovereignty. Majesty spoke with the captivating modulations of a woman's voice, employed a woman's every art, and felt with her sensitiveness. She breathed her spirit even into the formal documents of the time, and expressions of loving affection are often found in strange harness with the conventional diplomatic formulae of proclamations and official

[1] Collins, *Letters and Memorials of State* (Sydney Papers), ii, 229-30.

letters. In 1589 Lord Willoughby received a letter under the signet, beginning in the usual form, thanking his troops in France for their services:

> Wee have ... thought good to take knowledge thereof to your comforte, and to let you knowe ... how much we hould ourself bownd to thanck allmighty God for blessing us with subjects of that worthines and valure as you have shewed to be.... And further we will you to make knowen to all the colonels, captaines and souldiars our subjectes ... our princely and grateful acceptance of this their worthy service ... and to assure all and every of them that they shall fynde us myndefull of yt to their comfortes.[1]

And as though she found the formulae of such letters too cold, instead of the simple superscription of her name, she wrote, 'Your most lovinge soveraine, Elizabeth.' To another, extremely formal, signet letter sent to Willoughby she added in her own hand, 'Good peregrin suppose not that your travail and labours ar not gratiusly accepted and shalbe ever kept in good memorye.'[2] And when Cecil drafted a letter of thanks to Lord Hunsdon after his victory over Leonard Dacre in 1570, she set the more restrained language of her secretary to shame by a glowing postscript of her own:

> I doubt much, my Harry, whether that the victory were given me more joyed me, or that you were by God appointed the instrument of my glory; and I assure you that for my country's good, the first might suffice, but for my heart's contentation, the second more pleased me ... ; and that you may not think that you have done nothing for your profit, though you have done much for honour, I intend to make this journey somewhat to increase your livelihood, that you may not say to yourself, *perditur quod factum est ingrato*. Your loving kinswoman. Elizabeth, R.[3]

[1] *Hist. MSS. Com., Ancaster MSS.* p. 295.
[2] Ibid., p. 198.
[3] *Cal. S.P. Dom. Add. 1566-79*, p. 246.

Nor did she hesitate to flatter by seeming to deceive her ministers. There is a letter, fortunately preserved by Sir Henry Sidney, which was written to him in 1565. 'Harry,' it begins – and goes on in Elizabeth's most euphuistic style, ending, 'Let this memoriall be only committed to Vulcanes base keping, without any longer abode than the leasure of the reding therof, yea, and with no mention made therof to any other wight. I charge you, as I may comande you. Seme not to have had but Secretaries letters from me. Your lovinge maistris, Elizabeth R.'[1]

Now how can historical science, or, to use Lord Bryce's less pretentious phrase, refined common sense, hope to separate the false from the true in the traditional stories about such a woman as this? *Omnis fabula fundatur in historia*, it has been said. Perhaps; but we must examine the foundations, none the less; and it is only by a critical review of our sources that our problem will be solved, if at all. Let me illustrate the point by examining one of the best known of Elizabethan stories. In 1566 Sir James Melville was sent to England by Mary Queen of Scots to announce the birth of her child. Melville tells us in his *Memoirs* that Cecil first whispered the news to Elizabeth in the course of a dance. Thereupon 'all her mirth was laid aside for that night', and sitting down she put her hand under her cheek and burst out with the moan 'that the Queen of Scots was Mother of a fair son, while she was but a barren stock'.[2]

'When men's memories do arise', said Fuller, who was himself a delightfully garrulous offender, 'it is time for History to haste to bed.'[3] Melville's *Memoirs* were the child of his old age, and though he had some of his papers by him on which to rely, fickle memory played its tricks, and his narrative is by no means reliable. If not conclusive proof that this particular story is false, it is at least sufficient to make us pause in believing it, that the Spanish ambassador, Silva, who was not

[1] Collins, op. cit. i, 7-8.
[2] *Memoirs* (1683), p. 70. The best edition is the Bannatyne Club's (1827).
[3] Fuller's *Worthies* (1811), i, 349.

at all one to miss the chance of retailing such a story, and who saw Melville the day after his audience, merely tells Philip that 'the Queen seemed very glad of the birth of the infant': nor had he a different tale to tell, though he was an assiduous collector of Court gossip, when he wrote again four days later.[1] Other stories go back to Melville for their parentage, the best known of which is probably the amusing debate which he says took place between Elizabeth and himself in 1564 on the relative accomplishments and qualities of his mistress and herself.[2] We cannot say that its pedigree is above suspicion and we cannot test it, although I confess a sneaking desire to keep the tale.

Few of the Queen's sayings are so choice, though their charm depends upon their setting rather than any intrinsic brilliance, as are those connected with her progresses. The supreme moments of her genius were these, and if with their masques and verses her progresses belong to the history of the drama, they are no less part of the unwritten story of government propaganda. Old age failed to cloy her appetite for them, and we find her in her sixty-seventh year resolutely determined to go on her long progress to Tottenham, and with fine spirit replying to the lords who were grumbling at the prospect of the fatigue, by bidding 'the old stay behind, and the young and able to goe with her'.[3] The accounts we have of these progresses are strictly contemporary, written generally immediately after the events, by eye-witnesses.[4] Some are printed tracts, and their sale surely fostered that popular interest in Elizabeth which made her the symbol of a quickening national consciousness. Their evidence is not beyond cavil. Narrators could not have heard all they report. Some of the Queen's sayings must have come from the story of the visit which immediately gained currency in the neighbourhood; and perhaps the writers, no

[1] *Spanish Cal. Eliz.* i, 562, 563.
[2] Op. cit. pp. 49-51.
[3] Collins, op. cit. ii, 210.
[4] They are printed in Nichols, *Progresses of Queen Elizabeth* (1823).

less than the simple folk who constructed the epic in their taverns, did not leave the tale unadorned.

There is a delightful tract describing Elizabeth's passage through London the day before her Coronation,[1] which was in print nine days afterwards. Never was princely play so perfect as on that occasion. It was this which called forth the eulogy from Sir John Hayward that I have already quoted. 'I warrant you it is for gladness,' said the Queen when a gentleman called attention to an alderman who was weeping; and when she was seen to smile and was asked the reason — it was, she said, 'for that she had heard one say, Remember old king Henry theyght'. At Warwick in 1572 she made a perfect speech to the Recorder after his public welcome of her. 'Come hither, little Recorder,' she said: 'it was told me that youe wold be afraid to look upon me, or to speak boldly; but you were not so afraid of me as I was of youe, and I nowe thank you for putting me in mynd of my duty, and that shuld be in me.' And at the same place she sent for a poor man and his wife, whose house had been burnt down by a firework display, comforted them and saw them compensated.[2] At Sandwich she flattered her citizen hostesses at a banquet by taking their food without the usual preliminary tasting, and then had some of the dishes reserved for her and sent to her lodging, a compliment as supreme as it was womanly.[3] There was a similarly incomparable touch at Norwich in 1578. The schoolmaster was very ill at ease at having to make a speech. 'Be not afrayde,' said Elizabeth, and afterwards she purchased a loyal heart at the cost of a small lie, for she told him that it was the best speech ever she had heard. Nor did she stop there. After the Court party had moved on she sent deliberately back to know the schoolmaster's name, capping her conventional courtesies in a way of which she alone was mistress.[4]

[1] Ibid. i, 38 seqq.
[2] Ibid. i, 315, 320.
[3] Ibid. i, 338-9.
[4] Ibid. ii, 155, 159.

I give free rein to scepticism when we come to our next two sources. They are Bacon's *Apophthegms*, and Fuller's *Worthies*. In both, wit or love of a good story prompted most of the tales, and Clio must needs cover her face and hide her blushes, for the inveterate raconteur is without scruple. Everything was fish that came into Fuller's net. His 'bare skeleton of time, place, and person, must', he confessed, 'be fleshed with some pleasant passages'; and consequently he 'purposely interlaced ... many delightful stories, that so the Reader, if he do not arise ... *religiosior* or *doctior* ..., at least he may depart *jucundior*'.[1] He is not a contemporary authority (he was born in 1608), and even supposing we could believe that his traditional stories had contemporary origins, their parentage would still be doubtful. The *onus probandi* is on the narrator when merry tales are in doubt.

From Fuller come two stories about Sir Walter Raleigh at which one cannot but strain. The first is the famous story of the new plush cloak which he spread in the mud to keep the Queen's feet from being soiled, by his gallantry winning her attention and favour, and gaining, as it has been punningly said, many good suits by the spoiling of a cloak. Where Fuller got the story from I do not know. Naunton, a younger contemporary of Raleigh's, does not tell the tale, apt though it would have been in his *Fragmenta Regalia*, and I am inclined to think that it was the invention of a later generation wishing to explain so rapid a rise to favour. As an explanation it has the misfortune to be needless. Raleigh may have been introduced at Court by Katherine Ashley, a relative of his, or by the Earl of Leicester, and being a man of good parts, mentally and physically, a ready talker and a wit, an introduction was sufficient to make him a free of a company loving pride of life, 'the cowrtes vanitie, ambition's puff ball',[2] for, as Fuller puts it, the Queen well knew *Gratior est pulchro veniens e corpore*

[1] *Worthies* (1811), i, 2.
[2] Harington, *Nugae Antiquae* (1804), i, 170.

virtus.[1] The other story belongs to his early days at Court and tells that he wrote on a glass window, 'Fain would I climb, yet fear to fall.' Upon seeing it, the Queen completed the distich by subscribing, 'If thy heart fails thee, climb not at all.'[2] It is impossible, and naturally so, to show that a tale of this sort is apocryphal; but if we set out to credit all that we cannot disprove, we shall write strange history, and I am content to state my argument as frank scepticism. Other sayings of the Queen rest upon the uncertain authority of Fuller, amongst which is her reply to Burghley's servant when he bade her stoop as she entered the door at Burghley House to visit the sick minister: 'For your Master's sake I will stoop,' she is made to say; 'but not for the King of Spain's.'[3] This also I would put in our apocrypha.

Bacon's *Apophthegms* contain quite a number of Elizabethan stories, amongst which are some of the Queen's sayings. Most of the apophthegms were dictated from memory by Bacon in 1624. Others appeared only after his death, and though it is probable that they were copied from his papers, one cannot be quite certain of it.[4] Supposing, however, that we accept Bacon's authority for these stories, we must still remember that in collecting them he was not concerned with their historical accuracy, but with their wit or moral, and accordingly neither his scholarly sense nor his position in Elizabethan society can be held to establish the stories as genuine. Only when he was himself an ear-witness need we receive them into our established canon. For example, Bacon tells how Seckford, a master of requests, who had been many times disappointed in his attempts to secure an audience, came at last into the Queen's presence, wearing a pair of new boots. 'Fie, sloven,' said Elizabeth, who disliked the smell of new leather, 'thy new boots stink.' 'Madam,'

[1] *Worthies,* i, 496.
[2] Ibid. p. 287.
[3] Ibid. ii, 14.
[4] Cf. editor's preface to the Apophthegms in *Works,* ed. Spedding and Ellis, vii, 113 seqq.

answered Seckford, 'it is not my new boots that stink, but it is the stale bills that I have kept so long.'[1] Now Sir Nicholas L'Estrange, who flourished in the first half of the seventeenth century and collected a large number of stories, tells the same tale in a slightly different form, but tells it of Sir Roger Williams, not Seckford;[2] and it is perhaps one of many stories current even in Elizabeth's lifetime — whether genuine or not, who can say? On the other hand, when Bacon tells of an interview of his with the Queen concerning Hayward's *Life of Henry IV*, the jest in which is not Elizabeth's but his own, we may probably accept the tale as true.[3]

Between Bacon and Sir John Harington there may seem to be little to choose in the way of reliability, and that little in Bacon's favour: I draw a distinction, resting not upon the qualities of the men but upon the character of those writings of theirs in which sayings of the Queen are found. Unsatisfying as the editing of Harington's papers is in *Nugae Antiquae*, they still are his private papers, consisting of letters and diary entries as well as of more definitely literary pieces; and Harington was well placed both to hear himself and to learn of others when the Queen shone in repartee. His parents had earned the gratitude of Elizabeth by their service to her in the perilous days of Mary, a service which brought them into prison; and when their son John was born in 1561 the Queen repaid their loyalty by standing as godmother to him. As the boy grew he became welcome at Court, not alone as the Queen's godson, but as a wit of no small repute. Consequently his tales, when no appreciable time intervenes before their telling, carry a certain weight; but he was too much the established wit to look closely at a good story, and the value of his evidence diminishes considerably when he is engaged upon a literary composition like his *Briefe View of the State of the Church*.

[1] Cf. *Works*, vii, 137-8.
[2] Thom's *Anecdotes and Traditions* (Camden Soc. 1839), p. 47.
[3] *Works*, vii, 133.

It is in this work of his, which was written in the latter part of 1607, that the well-known story is told of Elizabeth's insulting remark to Archbishop Parker's wife. The Queen often visited Parker. Once, after she had 'greatlie feasted' at his house, she took her leave, thanking her hostess in the following brutal words: 'And you, *Madam* I may not call you, and *Mistris* I am ashamed to call you, so I know not what to call you, but yet I do thanke you.'[1] The saying, it is true, may not have been quite so pungent in the sixteenth century, when 'mistress' had a wider content and moved more frequently in respectable than in other circles; but if that blunts the point it does not remove it, and Harington's meaning was obviously ours. What, then, can be said for and against the genuineness of the story? There can be no doubt that Elizabeth was strongly, nay bitterly, opposed to marriage of the clergy: she had a curious obsession on the subject of marriage, and she horrified Parker by a tirade against it in 1561, driving the distracted man to murmur to Cecil, 'oportet Deo obedire magis quam hominbus'.[2] Also she could show a coarse and venomous tongue on occasions. Yet even so I find it difficult to believe in this deliberate insult following upon the enjoyment of Parker's hospitality; though I confess that if there is one thing too wonderful for us, it is the way of a woman's mind, and that the mind of Elizabeth, who, as Sir Robert Cecil said, 'was more than a man, and (in troth) sometymes less than a woman'.[3] The late date and studied art of the *Briefe View* make me sceptical of the stories which are deliberately introduced into it; and there is this also to be urged against the truth of the story, that Harington is not a first-hand witness, for he could not have been above nine years old, and may not have been born, at the time of the Queen's visit to Parker. I let the reader decide which way the balance leans. Unfortunately we must

[1] Harington, op. cit. ii, 16.
[2] *Correspondence of Archbishop Parker* (Parker Soc.), pp. 156 seqq.
[3] Harington, op. cit. i, 345.

take our leave of Harington, with but a single story examined. His papers give many glimpses of a Court where men experienced the elations and depressions of a passionate love. When the Queen smiled, he tells us, 'it was a pure sun-shine, that every one did chuse to baske in, if they could, but anon came a storm from a sudden gathering of clouds, and the thunder fell in wondrous manner on all alike'.[1]

I turn from a criticism of various sources which are rich either in the quality or the quantity of their Elizabethan sayings, to discuss a well-known verse with which the Queen's name is always associated. It is the following, and is deservedly famous:

Christ was the Word that spake it;
He took the Bread and brake it:
And what the Word did make it,
That I believe, and take it.[2]

The problem of its authorship started a discussion in the second series of *Notes and Queries* which dragged its inordinate length over four series of that journal, only to end with no verdict. So far as I know, the verse was first attributed to Elizabeth in Baker's *Chronicle*, where it is said that she gave this answer in Mary's reign when someone tried to catch her in a net by asking what she thought of the words, 'This is My Body.' The chronicle was published in 1643. It contains a list of its authorities, but in none of these does the quatrain appear, and it is highly significant that Speed, who published a chronicle in 1611, does not quote it. Baker, however, was not the first to print it, for it was included in the second edition (1635) of Donne's poems, although modern editors, believing it to be Elizabeth's, have discarded it as spurious. Some light was thrown on the subject by the discussion in *Notes and Queries*. The quatrain apparently was found painted in black letters

[1] Harington, op. cit. i, 362.
[2] Baker's *Chronicle* (1679), p. 320.

on a pillar of the village church at Walton.[1] Also it is to be found, with slight differences of reading, written at the end of a New Testament belonging to Bishop Cosin's library at Durham;[2] and a substantially different version, 'in an Elizabethan hand', occurs on the fly-leaf of a book of Hours at Lambeth.[3] None of these examples is described precisely enough to date it; but the Lambeth version is less pithy and probably more primitive than the version with which we are familiar, and I would therefore suggest that in one form or another the quatrain was current as an anonymous verse for a considerable time before it was given its permanent form. Perhaps it was Donne who rounded it off, and Baker, a friend of his, knowing this version, quoted it from memory. Its connection with Elizabeth is easily explained. Her fame was a magnetic centre for any unattached story that could possibly be fitted into her history, and it was absorbed into her legend probably in the second or third decade of the seventeenth century. Certainly Baker is too late an authority to guarantee his story, and Elizabeth was too hard put to avoid the dangers of Mary's reign to have uttered so equivocal a reply when her loyalty was being tested through her faith: equivocation heightens and does not allay suspicion, and suspicion she wisely was anxious to avoid.

After so much destructive criticism of the Elizabethan legend, it is refreshing to try and rehabilitate one of the Queen's sayings, and that among the most notable. It is the prose version of her speech at Tilbury camp at the time of the Armada in 1588.

[1] 6th ser. x, 248. [2] 2nd ser. v, 438.
[3] 5th ser. vii, 111-12. The version reads:

As christe willed it and spacke it
And thankeffullie blessid it and brake it
And as the Sacreid woord dothe make it
So I beleve and take it
My Lyffe to geve
Therefor in Earthe to leve
No More.

My loving People, we have been perswaded by some that are careful of our safety, to take heed how we commit our self to armed multitudes, for fear of treachery; but I assure you, I do not desire to live to distrust my faithful and loving people. Let tyrants fear. I have always so behaved my self, that under God, I have placed my chiefest strength and safeguard in the loyal hearts and good will of my subjects, and therefore I am come amongst you, as you see, at this time, not for my recreation and disport, but being resolved, in the midst and heat of the battle, to live or die amongst you all, to lay down for my God, and for my Kingdom, and for my People, my honor, and my blood, even in the dust. I know I have the body but of a week and feeble woman, but I have the heart and stomach of a King, and of a King of England too, and think foul scorn that Parma or Spain, or any Prince of Europe should dare to invade the borders of my Realm; to which, rather than any dishonor shall grow by me, I my self will take up arms, I my self will be your general, judge, and rewarder of every one of your vertues in the field. I know, already for your forwardness, you have deserved rewards and crowns; and we do assure you, in the word of a Prince, they shall be duly paid you.[1]

In a recent number of the *English Historical Review*,[2] Mr Miller Christy, when examining the various accounts of the Queen's visit to Tilbury, cast a doubt upon this version of the speech. He was unable to trace its source, and its language seemed to him more like that of a report drawn up afterwards by some skilled literary hand. In fact, the speech first appeared in print in the *Cabala*, an anonymous collection of the letters of illustrious persons, the first edition of which was in 1651; and it is part of a letter from Dr Leonel Sharp to the Duke of Buckingham. Sharp was a divine whom we know to have been

[1] *Cabala* (1691), p. 343. [2] xxxiv (1919), 55.

chaplain to the Earl of Essex, to Queen Elizabeth, and to Prince Henry.[1] In 1614-15 he was in disgrace and was imprisoned in the Tower; and this letter, written probably after Buckingham's marriage expedition to Spain in 1623, like others, was meant to ingratiate the writer with the Duke. In it Sharp discusses England's policy towards Spain, and draws upon his memory of events in Elizabeth's reign, giving in that connection an account of the Queen's visit to Tilbury. 'The Queen', he writes, '... made an excellent oration to her army, which, the next day after her departure, I was commanded to redeliver to all the army together, to keep a publick Fast.... This I thought would delight your Grace, and no man hath it but my self, and such as I have given it to....'[2]

I see no serious reason for rejecting the speech. The letter itself is probably genuine, despite the fact that we know only too little about the collection in which it appears; Sharp's statement that he was at Tilbury, waiting upon the Earl of Leicester – presumably as chaplain – may be accepted; and his story of the way in which he came by the speech is circumstantial and natural enough. That James Aske's account of the delivery of the speech, in his *Elizabetha Triumphans*,[3] seems not to square with Sharp's, is no strong argument against the latter's story, which, at any rate, will fit in with Deloney's verse narrative.[4] Then, so far from agreeing with Mr Christy's stylistic argument, I think that some of the phrases have every appearance of being the Queen's, and the whole tone of the speech is surely very much in keeping even with the few Elizabethan quotations that I have had room for in this article. Since the Queen, like Mr Micawber, revelled in her own words, it is very probable, if Sharp's tale be true, that it was she herself who ordered the speech to be re-delivered to the troops, in which event she would certainly not have entrusted

[1] Cf. *Dict. Nat. Biog.*
[2] *Cabala*, pp. 343-4.
[3] Printed in Nichols, *Progresses*, ii, 545 seqq.
[4] *Works*, ed. F. O. Mann, pp. 474 seqq.

her phrases to another's memory; and so I have little doubt that Sharp's version is a copy, at two or three removes, of a speech actually written by Elizabeth herself.

Legend clouds over us as we turn from the incidents of the Queen's life to those of her death, for there is a dramatic sense in popular story which demands of its famous people that they shall die fittingly, so acquitting themselves on their death-beds as to point a moral or adorn a tale. The biographer of Elizabeth may, like Mr Chamberlin, choose as the Queen's last words a highly moral reflection – 'My lord, the crown which I have borne so long has given enough of vanity in my time'; or he may finish his portrait of a frivolous woman with the cry, 'A million of money for a moment of time': only, if he does, he will be the dupe, in the latter instance of someone, I know not whom, and in the former of the egregious Leti. Mr Chamberlin devotes four pages of his book to the sayings of what he calls 'the inevitable hour'. I might dispose of most of them by an individual examination of their sources, but such a method of attack would be involved and wasteful, and it will be more useful and equally effective if I review the various accounts of Elizabeth's death, separating the reliable from the unreliable.

One counsel of safety there is in such a review, and one only – to start from strictly contemporary narratives, that is, from letters written actually during the illness. Much the most informative are the dispatches of the French ambassador, Beaumont,[1] who evidently drew his bulletins from the Court, despite the fact that Cecil and the Council, nourished on an inherited fear of what might befall at the Queen's death, were at first doing their best to prevent news leaking out and alarming the country. It is an ordinary death-bed tale that the dispatches tell, unadorned by terrible visions and with few random flashes of Elizabethan temper. Unable to sleep, parched in throat and body, and plunged in a deep melancholy;

[1] Included in Baschet's transcripts at the Public Record Office.

refusing for days to enter what she instinctively felt would be her death-bed, spurning medicine, and having little taste for food, the Queen gradually sank, plagued by the solicitations of doctors and councillors, until she passed into a stupor and the end came. Chamberlain, writing to Carleton on March 30th – the Queen died in the early hours of March 24th – says nothing more; and the moment we venture beyond some such general outline to fill in any details, especially of words which Elizabeth may have spoken, we are in a whirl of uncertainty, for gossip got to work immediately. 'Even here', says Chamberlain, writing six days after her death, 'the papists do tell strange stories as utterly voyde of truth, as of all civill honestie or humanitie.'[1]

One problem with which I must deal, before examining the set narratives of Elizabeth's death, is whether she did or did not name a successor. There is no hint that she did in any letter written during her illness. Beaumont appears to have been in touch with the Earl of Northumberland, and was told by him in all secrecy that the councillors had determined to proclaim James the moment Elizabeth was dead;[2] but as late as the day following her death he states definitely that she had named no successor.[3] Eleven days later his news was different. Nottingham and Cecil had seen him and had told him that a few days before her death Elizabeth had said to them in confidence that she recognized no other successor but James, and did not want her kingdom to fall into the hands of rascals. When they later asked her to confirm this before other councillors, being speechless she made a sign by putting her hand to her head.[4] The story may be true. Cecil certainly did announce that Elizabeth had named James as her successor;[5] and perhaps we should believe him. But one contemporary at least looked a

[1] S.P. Dom. Jas. I, i, no. 6.
[2] Beaumont to Villeroy, March 18th/28th.
[3] *Venetian Cal.* vol. x, 1603-7, pp. 15-16.
[4] To Villeroy, April 4th/14th.
[5] Baildon, *Les Reportes del Cases in Camera Stellata*, pp. 164, 227.

little askance at the tale,[1] and it may be that it was an invention given currency after Elizabeth's death to justify the action of the Council. It has found its way into the narratives of her death, sometimes with elaborations.

Of these narratives the most sober and the best known is Sir Robert Carey's.[2] Carey was about the Court during Elizabeth's illness, waiting for the moment when he was to set forth on his famous ride to Edinburgh, harbinger of a flock of time-servers hastening north to worship the newly-risen sun. He saw the Queen twice during her last days, and, apart from his own knowledge, had a sister in waiting on Elizabeth and a brother at Court, from whom to draw further information. His narrative, I have said, is sober. It contains one remark of the Queen's only. Its sobriety makes it an admirable check on other accounts; for considering what his sources of information were, and considering also that he did not write his *Memoirs* until about 1627, by which time the legend of Elizabeth's death was practically complete, his deliberate rejection of the details which we find in other narratives — 'false lies', he termed them — is strong argument against their authenticity.

There are four of these narratives which I must notice. All but one may be dismissed without much discussion, for they were not written by eye-witnesses. The first is an account found in the State Papers[3] — a fact which goes for nothing in the way of reliability — in the Cotton manuscripts,[4] and elsewhere. Written during the year 1603, its distinguishing feature is that it elaborates the story about the naming of a successor. We may certainly reject the additional remarks of the Queen

[1] Ellis, *Original Letters*, 2nd ser. iii, 195.

[2] In his *Memoirs*, best edition, 1808. The narrative is reprinted in Firth, *Stuart Tracts*.

[3] S.P. Dom. Jas. I, lxxxvi, no. 150.

[4] Titus, C. VII, fol. 57, printed in Nichols, *Progresses*, iii, 607-9. There is also a copy in the Petyt MSS. at the Inner Temple, which Isaac Disraeli printed in his *Curiosities of Literature*. As Camden used the Cotton copy, Disraeli's argument is invalid.

which it gives. The second account[1] apparently was written in November 1603 by one formerly in the service of Lord Burghley. It contains a sober enough description of Elizabeth's illness, adding one or two ordinary remarks of hers in which I neither believe nor disbelieve, since persons having 'good means to understand the truth of things', from whom the remarks profess to come, are often licensed deceivers, striving to live up to their reputation, and disarming one's critical faculties. But even this writer quotes from the apocrypha. 'It is credibly reported', he says, 'that not long before her death she had a great apprehension of her own age and declination by seeing her face (then lean and full of wrinkles) truly represented to her in a glass, which she a good while very earnestly beheld: perceiving thereby how often she had been abused by flatterers.' For its point the tale needs the explanation which is found in another narrative,[2] to the effect that for twenty years she had only seen herself in a false mirror, made to deceive her sight. This legend furnished a piquant story to Ben Jonson, who told Drummond that the Queen's ladies 'painted her, and sometymes would vermilion her nose'.[3] Our third narrator is Camden. It is easy to recognize that in his account of Elizabeth's death, in addition to the tradition of the time, he used the first narrative referred to above and the fourth narrative, which we must next examine; and it is enough to add that the less this writer is regarded as an original authority, and the more as a historian whose sources can and ought to be discovered, the safer a student will be.[4]

With the fourth narrative I come to the real problem of our sources. It is an account, existing in manuscript at Stonyhurst College and endorsed in the hand of Robert Persons — or Parsons — the Jesuit, 'The relation of the lady Southwell ...

[1] B.M. Sloane MS. 718, part only printed in Ellis, op. cit. pp. 189 seqq.
[2] The Southwell narrative, dealt with later.
[3] *Conversations*, ed. R. F. Patterson (1923), p. 30.
[4] Cf. in this connection Camden's account of the trial of Mary Queen of Scots, and my remarks thereon in *Eng. Hist. Rev.* xxxviii, 446.

primo Aprilis, 1607.'[1] Lingard, who was the first of modern historians to use it, did not know that part of it had actually been printed, but in fact Persons first referred to it in a tract of his, *The Judgment of a Catholic English-man*, published in 1608,[2] and when challenged by Bishop Barlow to leave his innuendoes and produce his evidence,[3] printed more than half of the narrative, omitting all names, in his *Discussion of An Answer*, a pamphlet that appeared in 1612.[4] It is the most vivid of all the accounts of Elizabeth's death, revelling in witchcraft and nightmare, decking itself out in sayings of the Queen, and working to a climax of horror, so that the sceptic might be inclined to dismiss it as worthless without more ado. But 'improbable' and 'impossible' are not synonyms, and however sceptical he may be, the historian must attempt to justify his scorn by a process of reasoning.

We may accept Persons' statement that the narrative is the relations of a lady named Southwell. She was Elizabeth, daughter of Sir Robert Southwell, goddaughter to Elizabeth, and granddaughter of Lady Nottingham, a young woman of surpassing beauty, romantic in temperament and career, and, at the time of the Queen's death, one of her maids of honour. In 1605 she set the Court of James in a flutter by eloping to the continent, disguised as a page, with Sir Robert Dudley, who left his wife behind. Abroad the two lived together irregularly until the Pope granted Dudley a dispensation, and they were married. Elizabeth Southwell is said to have eloped on the pretext of religion: at any rate, both she and Dudley became Catholics.[5] Consequently our narrative is that of an eye-witness, written, however, four years after Elizabeth's death by a romantic young woman who had turned Catholic. The first question

[1] Printed, apparently in full, by Tierney in his edition of Dod's *Church History*, iii, 70 seqq. Lingard, Miss Strickland, and Beesly print it in part.

[2] pp. 31-2.

[3] *An Answer to A Catholike English-man* (1609), p. 86.

[4] pp. 217-20.

[5] *D.N.B.*, under Dudley, Sir Robert; J. T. Leader, *Life of Sir Robert Dudley* (Florence, 1895).

one naturally asks is whether it was tendentious. The reply may be found in the words of Persons: 'It will remayne to posterity', he said, 'as a dreadfull patterne of a miserable end, after a lyfe of so much joylitie.'[1] Obviously, to him it was a sermon. But I would not make too much of the point, for if this was her aim Mistress Southwell did not make the best of her opportunity. None the less, neither its author nor the circumstances under which it was written encourage trust in the narrative.

But we may use stronger arguments in criticizing it. In the first place, Sir Robert Carey probably had read the account in Persons' *Discussion*. What Elizabeth Southwell knew — and more — Carey's sister, Lady Scrope, must have known; and yet Carey repeats none of the stories. Implicitly they are part of the 'false lies' which he denounces. Especially is this true of one story, for it was to Lady Scrope, according to the narrative, that Elizabeth said, 'she saw one night her own body, exceedingly lean and fearful, in a light of fire'. The argument from Carey may be strengthened by an argument from other sources. The Southwell narrative closes with a gruesome tale. Elizabeth, it relates, gave instructions that her body should not be embalmed, but despite her wishes it was opened by her surgeons at Cecil's secret command. The account continues:

> Now, the queen's body being cered up, was brought by water to Whitehall, where, being watched every night by six several ladies, myself that night watching as one of them, and being all in our places about the corpse, which was fast nailed in a board coffin, with leaves of lead covered with velvet, her body burst with such a crack, that it splitted the wood, lead, and cere-cloth; whereupon, the next day she was fain to be newtrimmed up.

The French ambassador,[2] the Venetian ambassador,[3] and

[1] *The Judgment of a Catholic English-man*, p. 32.
[2] Beaumont to the King, March 29th/April 8th.
[3] *Venetian Cal.* x, 2-3.

Chamberlain,[1] all refer in their letters to the body lying at Whitehall, all three state definitely that it was not opened, as was customary, and, needless to add, they do not mention the gruesome story of it bursting. If in consequence it be reasonably certain that part of the Southwell narrative is false, then my point is made, for it becomes impossible to distinguish between the false and the true in the greater part of the account except by the test of probability, and it is just that test which it will not stand. And so I would reject all the set narratives of Elizabeth's death except Carey's, either as adding nothing new of which we can be certain or as most likely false, and with them reject most of the sayings in Mr Chamberlin's four pages.

Here my essay must end. It has touched only the fringe of the subject. There is the whole range of ambassadors' dispatches, there are Foxe and Naunton and a traveller's tale in Hentzner, none of which I have criticized. And beyond contemporary authorities lies a less reputable but extensive collection of sayings which has grown continuously, aided by the prolific Leti and by wits of all centuries and many localities.[2] To take the formidable weapon of historical criticism to some of these might seem like taking a sledge-hammer to a pea-nut; whilst so far as the more securely-based stories that I have overlooked are concerned, they may be criticized along the lines that I have already indicated. Neither space nor the purpose of this essay allows of it being exhaustive.

[1] S.P. Dom. Jas. I, i, no. 6.
[2] Cf. *Notes and Queries*, 5th ser. iv, 139.

THE VIA MEDIA IN POLITICS

A HISTORICAL PARALLEL[1]

We are living in an age of ideological conflict and are troubled by the strains it imposes on society. The totalitarian state spreads alarm; we fear doctrinaires with their subversive organizations; we suspect fellow-travellers; we endure the Cold War; we think of quislings and the fifth column as instruments of foreign conquest. The fanatic's way of life we know to be dynamic; and though we say 'It shall not happen here,' we are not inclined, after our experience of the last twenty years, to boast that it cannot happen here. We are at odds about the policy we should pursue. Passion breeds passion; and unless we feel deeply about our own ideals, inevitably we are at a disadvantage against the enemies of society. Moderation, which is a liberal virtue, takes on a watery appearance. It seems uninspired and inglorious, prone to defeat.

In such a dilemma it may be useful to turn to history, which is the treasury of recorded experience. History never repeats itself, but it offers analogies. Just as the historian, consciously or unconsciously, uses the present to understand the past, so there is a reverse process. It is the most weighty of the justifications for the writing and study of history; and a nation which is historically minded is more likely to be fortunate in its affairs than one which is not.

For an analogy with our own times we cannot do better than turn to the Elizabethan period in English history. Such terms as fifth column, fellow-traveller, cold war, and the totalitarian state may be of recent origin, but the ideas for which they stand were as familiar to the Elizabethans as they

[1] Published under the title 'Elizabeth I and her Cold War' in the *Saturday Review* (New York), October 1st, 1955.

are to us, and their ordeal was as long drawn out as ours. In their case, moreover, we know the outcome and can judge more or less dispassionately. By common consent it is one of the great success stories of history.

Few historians nowadays would hesitate about ascribing the chief credit for this success to the Queen herself. In her own day her prime enemy, Pope Sixtus V, acclaimed her as great. Her Protestant subjects had no doubt about it. They believed that they were living at the summit of their country's glory; and their temper and achievements proclaimed the dynamic character of the age. Nevertheless, the Queen's policy, which she pursued with impressive tenacity, was that of the *via media*: one we do not normally associate with exuberance and glory. To examine the situation which confronted her, explain her policy, account for its success, and, above all, discover why the spirit of the nation, so far from being deflated, was never more buoyant: this surely cannot be an exercise remote from our present-day interests.

When Elizabeth I came to the throne in November 1558 she found her country, and the western European world in which it was set, divided by the great conflict of the Reformation. In due course and after much suffering, men learnt to separate religion from the State, at least to the extent of tolerating divergent creeds. But for the sixteenth century, inheriting the medieval conception of the Christian Commonwealth, that solution of the problem was beyond comprehension and therefore outside practical politics. Church and State, for the time being, were indissolubly joined, and the Reformation imposed the choice of Catholic or Protestant. In other words, the State was ideological in an age of conflicting ideologies. Its problems were similar to ours; and since the Catholic Church, like Communism today, was universal in its claims and international in its organization, the parallel with our predicament was very close.

Elizabeth may be described as Protestant by destiny and

upbringing. Educated by able Renaissance scholars of liberal outlook, experience during the short reigns of her brother and sister deepened her distrust of fanaticism. She was only twenty-five when she came to the throne, but for five years she had watched Mary Tudor govern the country as a Catholic devotee, and had learnt much from her own personal danger. If ever there was a lesson that passion and politics do not mix well, it was that reign. Instead of making England united and Catholic, as was fondly hoped, Mary had intensified faction, alienated moderate and patriotic men, and cast a gloom over the nation by the clerical character of her government, the excessive use of the stake against dissidents, and the subordination of English to foreign interests.

Several hundred of the most active Protestant divines and laymen fled abroad to escape her persecution. There, developing the single-mindedness of the revolutionary, they lived for the day when they would return, destroy Catholicism, and build their new Jerusalem in its place. Their hopes were centred on Elizabeth, their Deborah; and they looked to her to justify the blood of the martyrs by setting up a more extreme Protestant regime than the country had yet known. A counter-revolution was what they wanted; and the mood of London citizens, as Elizabeth's Coronation procession and other events demonstrated, was similar. When the first parliament of the new reign met in January 1559, the House of Commons proved to be like-minded.

Elizabeth understood what was expected of her and rose to her destiny to the extent of deciding on an immediate break with the Papacy, in this proving more courageous than some of her advisers. But beyond, caution ruled. With her eye on danger from abroad and disunity at home, she proposed to defer doctrinal changes; and, indeed, so far was she from sharing the crusading ideals of her triumphant supporters, that for her ultimate settlement she wanted a Church as conservative, comprehensive, and tolerant as possible. She even hoped to carry the more moderate of Mary's bishops with her: which would have rendered her less dependent on the radicals. In the event, the bishops refused to co-operate and so the Elizabethan Religious Settlement — the famous *via media* of our history books — emerged from a stubborn struggle between the Queen and a pressure-group of Marian exiles, directing the agitation of the House of Commons. Elizabeth was forced to make concessions — they can be seen in the Anglican Prayer Book of today — but she denied the radicals their thorough reform. It was in this opportunist way that the Anglican Church, which time has made so venerable, came into being.

Thus at the outset fanaticism was checked. The advantages of the policy were quickly apparent. During the early, critical years of the reign, while Elizabeth was consolidating her authority, Catholic forces abroad were not provoked into attempting her overthrow, Catholics at home remained quiescent, national instead of factional sentiment was fostered, and domestic peace was preserved. England escaped the religious wars of western Europe. That was one of the signal achievements of the reign: a miracle profoundly appreciated, though few grasped its secret. True, the radicals proved troublesome. They persisted in regarding the Settlement as a temporary measure, dictated by expediency. They practised nonconformity in defiance of the law, and they maintained their agitation. The Queen, however, knew that she could rely on their loyalty; and had time and circumstance permitted, they might have ceased to be a serious political problem.

The opportunity of unfolding its merits in peaceful isolation was unfortunately denied to the religious *via media*. England was drawn into the great storm of the Catholic Counter-Reformation and subjected to strains quite as severe as those we ourselves have endured. The Religious Wars broke out in France, continuing intermittently for a generation. The Netherlands revolted against Catholic Spain; and that struggle lasted even longer. Protestant zealots in England became convinced that at the Council of Trent and subsequently at a Franco-Spanish conference a universal Catholic conspiracy had been planned, its object to root out Protestantism by every means, in every country.

Then, in 1568, occurred the event which was to end all hope of insularity: the flight of Mary Queen of Scots to England. Mary was a Catholic. Through her mother she was a daughter of the House of Guise, leaders of militant Catholicism in France. It could be argued that she was the rightful Queen of England: certainly, on ground of mere descent, she had the best title to be Elizabeth's successor. And Mary as Queen of England foretold a return to Catholicism, the nightmare of all good Protestants. She instantly became a focus for discontents, political as well as religious. Her mere presence revived Catholic hopes and attracted conspirators, both foreign and English. The relative tranquillity of the first decade of the reign was ended. English statesmen foresaw the peril, but the alternative of allowing this dangerous woman to leave the country was even more perilous. 'Our good Queen', wrote one of them, 'has the wolf by the ears.' The Queen of Scots was kept in honourable captivity, and remained a captive till her execution in 1587.

In little more than a year trouble matured with the Northern Rebellion, a coalescence round Mary of political and religious discontent. More serious than that, the Papacy seized the opportunity to issue a Bull deposing Elizabeth, thus openly ranging international Catholicism against Protestant England. It was the beginning of a period of cold war and aggressive devices, similar to those we ourselves have experienced in our time. English Catholics fled to the continent, where they were trained for the English mission field and sent back secretly to convert their countrymen. Throughout the 1580s the Papacy and the Guise party in France were busy planning the invasion of England by an international Catholic army, to be aided by a revolt of English Catholics: the Enterprise of England, as it was called. The ever-increasing band of missionaries, however innocent their intentions, were, from the standpoint of the Enterprise, a stratagem of war. They were recruiting a fifth column, to be called into action at the Pope's command when the invaders landed.

Against this general background there occurred plot after plot, beginning with the Ridolfi Plot of 1572. Plans were made and remade for the assassination of Queen Elizabeth and ultimately – as the English government discovered – received the official blessing of the Holy See, through the Papal Secretary. Add the Massacre of St Bartholomew in France in 1572, and the assassination of William the Silent by a Catholic fanatic in 1584, and we have a picture of the times as seen by Elizabethans: ideological warfare without scruple or limit, the sort of nightmare experienced by many of our contemporaries.

The reaction of the nation and the policy of the Queen are both of interest to us today. They are best seen in Parliament, where, as each phase of the danger developed, new legislation was required for the defence of the Queen's person and the country. One notes the constant extension of the law of treason; and it is worth reflecting that in the ideological State treasons inevitably multiply.

The general scene is of an angry, fanatically-tempered House of Commons, supported in some of their most extreme proposals by the more sober-minded House of Lords and Privy Councillors. It is not surprising. Nothing stood between Protestant England and the threat, bordering on certainty, of Mary Queen of Scots obtaining the throne, with the backing of international Catholicism – nothing, except the life of Queen Elizabeth. And that life was subject to the hazards of epidemic illness and assassination. The religion, the careers, the fortunes, possibly the lives of these men were at stake. They wanted to root out Catholicism in England by any and every means, stop the missionaries by merciless laws, answer terror by terror. Many spoke and acted as if the only good Catholic was a dead one.

Standing against Parliament and her Councillors, often in stark isolation, was the Queen. She proved herself a *politique*: which is not to say that she was indifferent about her faith. Her own experience in her sister's reign, reinforced by temperament, had taught her the principles by which to rule. They might be comprehended in the phrase, civil obedience. The State was Protestant; the law demanded attendance at church; the people must conform. But she would be content with outward obedience. She was opposed to forcing conscience, 'Her Majesty', as Francis Bacon expressed it, 'not liking to make windows into men's hearts and secret thoughts.' She had assured her people of this in 1570, at the time of the Northern Rebellion; and when, in the Parliament of 1571, both Houses, with the cordial support of bishops and Councillors, passed a bill to compel attendance at the Communion service – in order, as one Puritan zealot declared, that 'not only the external and outward show' but 'the very secrets of the heart' should come to a reckoning – the Queen vetoed the bill. The relevance of such an incident to our own days needs no stressing.

The Queen continued to restrain her Parliaments. In 1581, when the first Jesuit mission and other events had invested the Catholic threat with a new intensity, Lords and Commons joined to frame a bill imposing orthodoxy on the country with the ruthlessness of a modern totalitarian regime. Missionaries and their converts, without qualification, were to be guilty of treason; and for other Catholics there were Draconic provisions. Elizabeth intervened to reduce the penalties, and so qualified the treasonable offence that it was made dependent, not on the simple act of conversion but on treasonable intention. Here she applied her second principle of policy, namely – as Bacon defined it – that matters of conscience cease to be such when they exceed their bounds and become matters of faction, involving overt threats to the established government. It was a principle that she extended to the Puritans as well.

Needless to say, these Parliaments of Elizabeth would have

destroyed the focus of all troubles, Mary Queen of Scots, long before 1587 if they had been allowed. The Queen's reaction to their fearful anger makes one of the most astonishing stories of the reign. In 1572, after the Ridolfi Plot, Privy Council, Lords and Commons united in a passionate determination to attaint and execute Mary. When Elizabeth demurred, they repeated their demand with all the vehemence and argument they could devise; and it was only after a second, emphatic denial that they turned, in disgust and tears, to the milder alternative of excluding her from the succession to the throne. At the end of the session, Elizabeth confounded them all by vetoing their second bill. Next, in 1585, following further plots and the assassination of William the Silent, Council and Parliament wanted to fight the cold war, now degenerating into murder, with its own weapon. They proposed to legalize lynch-law against Mary. Elizabeth intervened to amend the bill in the interests of decency. Even after the Babington Plot, when the nation could no longer be denied its vengeance, the Queen did her utmost to avoid the inevitable. No historical legend could be more ironic than the one, still cherished by Scotsmen, which saddles Elizabeth with unalloyed responsibility for the execution of this unfortunate woman.

In such an atmosphere it is not surprising that the Religious Settlement of 1559 was threatened by radicalism. We in our day have witnessed the expansion of Communist sympathy during the struggle with Nazism and Fascism. The Marian exiles had won the support of the House of Commons in the revolutionary mood at the opening of the reign. That mood, renewed by the cold war, restored the alliance of Puritan clergy with Members of Parliament. After all, a distinguishing feature of Puritanism was hatred of every vestige of Popery; and, on the political side, that was the flamboyant symbol of patriotism. The men who pressed most relentlessly for the execution of Mary Queen of Scots and urged ruthless legislation against Catholics were also earnest Puritans. In this curious world of conflicting ideologies, Queen Elizabeth found herself — like American statesmen in recent years — fighting a triangular duel and suffering from the shots of the other two duellists, Catholics and Puritans. The latter, though the most ardent of her supporters, gave her almost as much trouble as the common enemy.

In the 1570s the Puritan party among the clergy developed a younger left wing of extremists, who became Calvinist and wanted to change the polity of the Anglican Church, substituting Presbyterianism for the episcopal and hierarchical system inherited from Rome: a change so far-reaching in its political and social consequences that revolution is the only adequate term for it. Their programme suited the times. Its claim to be the apostolic form of the Christian Church caught the prevalent mood of truth-seeing, just as the doctrinaire character of Communism has attracted visionaries in our generation. Similarly with its sombre and severe discipline: this was the spiritual complement to the totalitarian regime desired by the fanatics in Parliament. Moreover, in the city of Geneva these Puritans had a contemporary working model of the new Jerusalem, as infectious in its influence as Russia in our time.

The parallel carries further. One of the conspicuous features of Communism is its party organization and discipline. The same is true of Elizabethan Presbyterianism. Both might be described as singularly well adapted to subversive, minority movements. Both have made remarkable use of propaganda. Though primarily a clerical concern, the Elizabethan movement won wide support from the gentry, and even included Privy Councillors among its patrons and sympathizers. Many laymen were convinced adherents; still more were fellow-travellers.

To Queen Elizabeth, Puritanism was an abomination. She hated and scorned its doctrinaire character, disliked its radicalism, and detested its inquisitorial discipline. Long before its conspiratorial nature and secret organization were revealed, and while some of her bishops and statesmen, beguiled by its lively virtues, were playing the role of fellow-travellers, she sensed the danger. Puritan divines briefed their supporters in the House of Commons and maintained a constant agitation there; but Elizabeth was adamant in resisting every parliamentary effort to interfere in Church affairs. The struggle reached its climax in the Parliament of 1587 when the Puritan extremists, who had set up their secret presbyteries and were undermining the Church from within, attempted to impose their revolution on the country by legislation. The Queen imprisoned the group of M.P.s responsible, and set her best orators to expose the true character of their bill, thus shocking fellow-travellers into some awareness of the company they had been keeping. A few years later, having uncovered the secrets of the Puritan clergy's organization, she was able to strike at its leaders and destroy a very dangerous conspiracy.

It remains for us to assess the merits of the Queen's policy. The history of the reign — in particular the parliamentary history — leaves no doubt that but for Elizabeth's firm rule the period would have been much more cruel and bloody. Her statesmen — including the moderate Lord Burghley — were always bemoaning her merciful nature, perilous to herself and the country. We have observed in the totalitarian states of our own time that ideological regimes tend to evoke the worst instincts in men and bring brutes to the fore. The administration of the Elizabethan penal laws, in any case, was not free from tyranny: nor, be it added, from astonishing lenity. The career of that notorious hunter of Catholics, Richard Topcliffe — a cultured gentleman, but a fanatic and sadist — shows that the Gestapo and the OGPU, with their abhorrent methods, are not so much the product of particular countries or a particular era as of a political system. But there would have been many more Topcliffes in Elizabethan England if Parliament had had its way and a different sovereign been on the throne. If life had been made intolerable for ordinary Catholics, their patriotism would have been submerged under fear, hopelessness and passion. They knew, however, that their Queen was no fanatic, and though they suffered from recusancy fines and other troubles, they continued to be Englishmen first. Only the exiles and a few extremists of their faith welcomed the Spanish Armada.

Even more important: the damping down of ideological passion enabled the nation, when dangers eased, to recover balance. Fanaticism is not an enduring feature of civilized society. A new generation rarely experiences the same exaltation of spirit as the old: unless, indeed, the same causes persist; and perhaps, even then, only reluctantly, since it is not of their own creation. How foolish the first Stuart kings were, who provoked a new Catholic scare and so revived old passions. As Elizabeth's reign moved into its fourth decade, the execution of Mary Queen of Scots, the successful – nay, glorious – weathering of the international storm at the time of the Armada, and the gradual passing of the generation that had known persecution under Mary Tudor and endured the long nightmare of the cold war under Elizabeth, all made for a relaxation of tension. A new mood is perceptible, strikingly perceptible, where the fanaticism of the high Elizabethan period was most apparent – in Parliament. The Parliament of 1593 saw two government bills introduced against Catholics. They emerged as a bill against Protestant sectaries and only one against Catholics – the last anti-Catholic bill of the reign, with its penalties reduced by a Parliament, now closer in sentiment to the Queen and more tolerant than her Privy Councillors.

If Parliament had had its way in the 1570s and 1580s and fastened on the community a merciless totalitarian system, with the consequent inflammation of passions and the inevitable momentum or inertia, as also the vested interests, that any regime acquires, who can say when the country would have recovered? Certainly, a very different, a spiritually impoverished England would have emerged. To inject poison into the body politic is to take grave risks.

One question remains: How was it that a Queen, so antipathetic to Puritanism, managed to preserve and nurture in her people an exuberance of spirit derived largely from the emotions she opposed? Accident enters into the answer. She was all these zealots had. There was no obvious successor to look to. They cherished her as parents do an only child. As an explanation of Elizabethan England, this, however, is utterly inadequate. Positive qualities were there, lots of them: personality, ability, complete absorption in her country and task. Her people were left in no doubt that she was, as she claimed to be, 'mere English'. Moderation can be a gutless policy. We have biblical authority for disliking people who blow neither hot nor cold: and an occasional hot-gospeller did not hesitate to quote the passage to Queen Elizabeth. But her moderation was the reverse of gutless. As she knew and was repeatedly told, it increased the risk to her own life immeasurably: thus, incidentally, inspiring more passionate love. In fact, her policy was a calculated and courageous gamble – trusting, for example, to outlive Mary Queen of Scots, rather than destroy her; trusting that the threatened storm would not come or could be weathered, rather than consent to courses detestable to her. Had her gamble failed, the name of Queen Elizabeth – as Peter Wentworth was bold enough to tell her – would have been infamous.

This woman was as vital as Winston Churchill, and, like him, made romantic leadership an art of government. The name 'Gloriana' and the phrase '*via media*' seem odd companions. But the liberal way of life is richest and fullest, and it was well for England that when men's passions led them from it, Queen Elizabeth preserved the tradition. Her Puritan fanatics had no more obstinate opponent: she, in turn, had no more devoted worshippers. It is the strangest paradox of her reign and the supreme tribute to her greatness.

THE DIPLOMATIC ENVOY[1]

AMBASSADORS became a necessity among men when Pandora's box was opened and the evils escaped into the world. So say sixteenth-century authors of manuals for ambassadors, claiming an antiquity for the art of diplomacy as remote as society itself and the distinction of *meum* and *tuum*. They might have added that it was the reopening of Pandora's box, when princes were consolidating the nation-state, that made resident ambassadors a necessity in Europe and gave the art its modern significance.

The nursery of European diplomacy was Italy. Not only did the Papacy develop a ceremonial attaching to the dispatch and reception of envoys so elaborate as to become an intolerable nuisance to officials in Rome, but among secular states Venice won a prestige for its service by careful regulation and sustained tradition that was unique. By common consent it had no need of the manuals that the development of diplomacy inspired: it was itself the mirror for ambassadors. The orders governing the conduct of Venetian envoys date back to the thirteenth century and were revised and expanded from time to time. But until the middle of the fifteenth century the embassies to which they referred, as the embassies of other secular states, were what later would have been called missions or special embassies. It was in 1479 that Venice sent an ambassador to reside at the court of France. At the Duke of Burgundy's court she had a resident ambassador rather earlier, but extended the practice to England only in 1496. Princes followed the example—slowly, however, and with suspicion. For long an ambassador's

[1] A lecture, one of a course on historical sources to students in the Honour School of History, delivered in the University of London (at King's College), on May 14th, 1928; published in *History* (Oct. 1928), vol. xiii, no. 51, pp. 204-18.

principal business was to supply his government with information, and the contemporaries of Philippe de Commynes were prone to think that ambassador might be more simply spelt spy. This coming and going of embassies, Commynes remarked,[1] is by no means safe:

> It is unavoidable, but, if my advice be sought, here are the precautions that I would take. If they come from true friends of whom there can be no suspicion, treat them with good cheer and grant them frequent audience, but dismiss them soon, for friendship among princes does not endure for ever. If from hostile courts, send honourably to meet them, lodge them well, set safe and wise men about them to watch who visits them and keep malcontents away, give them audience at once and be rid of them. Even in time of war one must receive envoys, but see that a keen eye is kept on them, and for every one sent to you, do you in return send two, and take every opportunity of sending, for you can have no better spies, and it will be hard to keep a strict watch over two or three.

This represents an attitude of mind that hindered the development of permanent diplomatic relations; but if Ferdinand of Aragon and Henry VII of England shared Commynes' distrust, the intricate diplomacy of the new century and the interminable disputes of commerce drove their successors to follow where Venice had led.

The establishment of resident ambassadors at the various European courts brought into existence a class of documents of bulk, interest and importance such as to vie with that other great class of documents created by the new monarchy, the domestic state paper. My purpose here is to give you some idea of the content and worth of these documents, and perhaps you will forgive me if I do not pretend to knowledge of them in more than a very limited period of history — the Elizabethan.

[1] *Mémoires*, III, viii.

Their bulk may be indicated by the fact that though Elizabeth had fewer resident ambassadors abroad than France, Spain and several less important states — this because of her religion — yet the foreign state papers of the reign fill some 300 volumes at the Public Record Office, and much besides exists in the way of semi-official correspondence between ambassadors and leading statesmen. We must recollect that similar great collections once existed in the more important states of Europe, and smaller ones in the archives of minor states; and though acts of God and of man have made sad havoc of documents, the volume of material still in existence is enough to startle the most intrepid of researchers. Glance at the footnotes to Lucien Romier's two large volumes on *Les origines politiques des guerres de religion* and you will obtain some notion of the wealth of diplomatic correspondence in Italian archives bearing on a very short period of French history.

Bulk we may accept; but what of the information these documents contain? It is still the business of an ambassador to keep his government informed of events and opinion in the country where he serves, and a Walter Page, in his admirable comments on English society, may emulate the great Venetian ambassadors of the sixteenth century. This duty has, however, lost its ancient importance, for nowadays the various movements of national thought find their expression in print and can generally be interpreted by foreign governments without an ambassador's help. The raison d'être of an ambassador today is the preservation of peace, not the supplying of news; and it is in the reversal of the order of these duties that he is chiefly distinguished from his sixteenth-century predecessors. The dispatches of ambassadors in those days were virtually the sole regular source of foreign news that had much value, and since the diplomacy of Elizabeth and her fellow-sovereigns had to be framed upon this news, the success or failure of their representatives depended upon the constancy and accuracy of their reports. What little leisure a zealous ambassador had may be judged from the fact that one, a Venetian, who was resident at Rome, wrote 394 dispatches in 365 days! All were not as model as he. But in addition to writing his official dispatches, it was often essential for an ambassador to keep up a regular correspondence with one or more of the influential councillors at home. For example, our ambassadors addressed an occasional letter to the Queen herself, and frequent ones to the secretary charged with foreign affairs — for a long time, Walsingham. This was his official correspondence. Burghley, however, was a power at Court and needed information, not merely to frame his policy but to maintain his dominance in the Council, which was founded on his knowledge of affairs. An ambassador dare not ignore his wishes, and when that ambassador was Sir Edward Stafford, who belonged to Burghley's party at Court and was disliked by Walsingham, the correspondence with Burghley became almost as voluminous as the official dispatches to Walsingham, and certainly more intimate.

In his role of foreign correspondent to his sovereign an ambassador had to see to the organizing of his news service. Hotman, in his sixteenth-century manual *The Ambassador*,[1] advises him to set about this at once on his arrival at the foreign court. He ought to see that he is kept posted with the news from other countries; but this was of negligible importance beside the necessity of penetrating by every means in his power into the secrets of the country where he was serving. He must intrude his agents wherever information was to be had. He must entertain at table, which, says Hotman, obligeth many people, and especially those who to have a free recourse thereunto, or to draw from the ambassador some dozen of crowns, smell out all the news and report them unto him. He must suborn both high and low: money maketh the closest cabinets of princes to fly open. In fine, he must establish a secret service of his own.

Let me give one or two illustrations. De Spes, the Spanish ambassador in England, writes in 1570 of a friend, whom he

[1] English translation, London, 1603.

has always found to be true, who has undertaken to make for him a note of all that passes in the Council, keeping himself as free as possible from other things in order the better to remember. Perhaps it was that secretary of the Council to whom he had alluded before.[1] Mendoza had an agent employed in Walsingham's office whose death was a great loss to him, for in addition to his knowledge of Walsingham's affairs (which, says Mendoza, was absolutely trustworthy), he heard many things that went on in the Queen's chamber through a lady with whom it was almost impossible for Mendoza to communicate after his death. In consequence, the ambassador continues, 'I have to lose much time in finding out what goes on, and have, so to speak, to go about begging for intelligence.'[2] Perhaps the most remarkable example of spying that I have noted — if it is to be taken at its face value — is an instance of one Spanish agent spying on another in 1572. The one agent wrote to Alva on December 22nd detailing a conversation which he had had with Burghley. 'This conversation', he writes, 'took place in his [Burghley's] room on the 19th instant, only he and I being present.' On the same day the other — and rival — agent also wrote to Alva telling him that this conversation had taken place on the 19th. 'What passed between them,' he adds, 'and the answer given to him I leave for Guaras to tell, as no doubt he will write to your Excellency about it; although I have heard the whole of the conversation from a person who overheard it.'[3]

It was also the custom for sixteenth-century sovereigns to dispense pensions through their ambassadors to certain councillors and others at foreign courts. As one might guess, it was not a practice that Elizabeth liked to follow, her scruples, however, being financial, not moral. And even with Philip II there was many a slip and much delay between promise and performance. But by this means both Spanish and French ambassadors obtained claims on a number of courtiers. That

[1] *Spanish Cal. Eliz.* ii, 248; cf. ibid. 93, 96, 227.
[2] Ibid. 663, 653. [3] Ibid. 452, 454.

they secured Court gossip and news in consequence is no doubt true, but that their pensioners betrayed state secrets I think it well not to believe except when there is conclusive proof. Dr Conyers Read, following Martin Hume, has argued that our ambassador in France, Sir Edward Stafford, sold important state secrets to the Spanish ambassador there for a bribe. If true it is peculiarly infamous, but for my own part I have not been able to bring my credulity to this leap and do not believe that the facts are quite as Dr Read thinks. It was, however, not pensioners amongst the nobility who told ambassadors most, but malcontents. The religious and political dissensions of the time gave Elizabeth, Philip II and Catherine de Medici their chance of weakening one another by encouraging the discontented in each other's realms, the result being that an ambassador's residence was apt to become a resort or a centre of intrigue for rebellious nobility. De Spes and Mendoza, Spanish ambassadors in England, flagrantly abused their positions by their intrigues, and so did the English ambassador, Sir Nicholas Throckmorton, in France.

If it was the business of an ambassador to penetrate the secrets of a rival Court, it was the concern of that Court to bamboozle the ambassador and in its turn to discover any intrigues in which he might be engaged. An ambassador might even have his correspondence waylaid. Spy was set against spy, and bluff against bluff. The age of Machiavelli knew that there is nothing on occasions so sure to deceive as the plain truth. Or, alternatively, that to misinform one's ambassador lent to his report of a lie all the semblance of truth. If princes wish to deceive their adversaries, said Guicciardini, let them begin by deceiving their own ambassadors: their words will seem more free and be more calculated to inspire confidence.[1] The authors of those early manuals for ambassadors loved to enumerate the qualities demanded of an ambassador by his office. They would have him to be a divine, astrologer,

[1] Quoted by Janet, *Histoire de la science politique* (5th edition), i, 544.

logician, an excellent orator, as learned as Aristotle, and as wise as Solomon; and to these requirements the practice of the age added the subtlety of the serpent. No wonder that Hotman remarks, 'The perfect image of an Ambassador ... was never amongst men.'

However, I must not leave a jaundiced impression of an ambassador's activities in your minds. Spies and intrigue were more or less important according as the relations between two courts were strained or friendly. My remarks may or may not amount to a caricature of any particular embassy. Let me add that they really do not misrepresent such embassies as those of De Spes and Mendoza in England or Throckmorton in France. Their point, however, lies not in their sufficiency or insufficiency as a portrait of a sixteenth-century ambassador, but in the caution they must engender when we are assessing the value of his dispatches as historical evidence.

I turn to make that assessment. And it is not with the obvious — the value of diplomatic correspondence for diplomatic history — that I shall deal, but with the less obvious, for it has become increasingly less important in later times — its value for domestic history. I have already said that an ambassador had to report — generally at intervals of a few days — whatever news he could ferret out: Court gossip, meetings of the Council, the trend of policy, events and rumours of importance in the country; and if he was a wise man, and was writing to Elizabeth or Catherine de Medici, he would flavour his letters with lengthy descriptions of Court ceremonies, personalia and lighter gossip. His dispatches constituted a fairly elaborate Court diary and a less elaborate diary of national events.

It is this fact which gives diplomatic correspondence its peculiar value for sixteenth-century history. We should suffer gravely without it in England, for in those days we were very much behind the continent — at any rate behind Italy and France — with our historical literature. It is astonishing, if explicable, that we have no memoirs at all to set beside the great wealth of France. Brantôme, Marguerite de Valois, Monluc, are three amongst scores of French memoir-writers of the sixteenth century. Memoirs are, of course, notoriously untrustworthy. These were written late in life, and generally to the greater glory of the writer or to set his career in a more agreeable light. The Italian wars produced quite a number of would-be Caesars dictating their Commentaries in the enforced idleness of old age, imprisonment or unemployment. And in all the memoirs facts have been distorted by the tricks of memory and the passing of time. With all their faults, however, they give us a picture of Court life in France and a survey of events for which in England we are dependent on the dispatches of foreign ambassadors. Not indeed that French historians can ignore similar dispatches. Anything in the nature of a diary has very obvious advantages over a memoir, and however strong may be one's cautions against too easy a faith in an ambassador's facts, they were recorded at the time and avoid the snares that beset facts in memoirs.

England boasts no memoirs for the sixteenth century, but she can boast great wealth in domestic state papers and private correspondence. This is due to Providence. We have had no social revolution and have preserved our county families singularly well. Only moth and rust — unless we add the death duties of the last few years — have entered in and destroyed. But neither from domestic state papers nor private correspondence could one reconstruct a connected story of events at Court, and over discussions of important state affairs hangs an almost impenetrable cloud. No records were kept of them. We have a very occasional memorandum of Council discussions made by Burghley, but matters of state were *arcana imperii*, and those sharing the secrets divulged them and forswore themselves at their peril. On the other hand, it was the business of an ambassador to discover what had been said and done in Council, and however uncertain his reports may be, they present, I think, a more connected story than we could piece together from other sources. Similarly with the intrigues of conspirators. It was the height of folly for them to commit their thoughts or plans to paper, but the confidences which they whispered into the ears of ambassadors were immediately transmitted by the latter to their sovereigns. To take a single instance: the Duke of Norfolk, at the time of the Ridolfi Plot, would have cut a still sorrier figure if only Elizabeth had had before her the dispatches of the Spanish ambassador. Norfolk ultimately bolted out a good deal of the truth after repeated examinations before his trial, but his confessions can be checked and supplemented from the Spanish and French ambassadors' dispatches.

I have said enough to suggest the peculiar position which diplomatic correspondence holds among the historical sources for the sixteenth century. This, however, implies no estimate of its reliability; and let me say at once that, indispensable as such correspondence is, I nourish the deepest distrust of it. In the first place, ambassadors in England were almost always in a country whose language they could not understand. The manuals of the time give lists of languages which the perfect ambassador ought to know. Latin, Italian, French, Spanish, German are included, and one Italian writer even includes Turkish. None thought to include English, and even as late as 1716 a manual could omit our language from the tongues of diplomacy.

Now an ambassador, unable to understand the language of the country, was half blind and dependent on others to lead him — a fruitful source of half-truths and misconceptions. How difficult communication was may be illustrated by the following examples. The first is from the *Spanish Calendar* and refers to an interview between De Spes on the one hand and the Admiral and Cecil, the Secretary, on the other. 'The Admiral', says De Spes, 'spoke first, and briefly said in French that he and the Secretary had been sent by the Queen, but that as he did not speak much Latin the Secretary would communicate her Majesty's message in that tongue, which he [the

Admiral] understood, although he had little practice in speaking it.'[1] It is easy to imagine what flounderings there would have been had Cecil not borne the brunt of the conversation, and easy to imagine, not only how useful Cecil's linguistic knowledge was to him in the competition to control affairs, but how useful the Queen's was to her. Elizabeth spoke Latin, French and Italian and understood Spanish. Her accomplishments have more than the interest of cultural frills, though her love of showing them off and her courtiers' love of indulging her whim might prevent one from realizing it. They are indeed as much the explanation of her control of policy as her masterly temper. As a woman in the age of John Knox she would have been hard put to it to direct policy had she not been as able as the best of her councillors, and more able than most of them, to conduct the interviews with foreign ambassadors. My impression is that she kept a closer monopoly of these interviews than other sovereigns of her age, who were apt to refer ambassadors to their councillors – closer even than Catherine de Medici. But I must return to my examples of an ambassador's linguistic difficulties. I take my second from the same year, but from the French ambassador, La Mothe-Fénélon's correspondence. Fénélon had the Duke of Norfolk, the Earls of Arundel and Leicester, Lord Howard of Effingham, Cecil, and other lords of the Council to dine with him. He notes that Cecil translated his speech into English for the benefit of the Councillors and that after they had conferred together, Norfolk said a few words in English and then told Lord Howard of Effingham to explain them to Fénélon in French.[2]

The information that an ambassador collected was a rather indiscriminate mass of rumour and gossip, truth and falsehood, sometimes with a good leavening of official bluff. For example, while the Ridolfi Plot was brewing Sir John Hawkins, with the full cognizance of Burghley, was offering to go over with his

[1] *Spanish Cal. Eliz.* ii, 117.
[2] La Mothe-Fénélon, *Correspondance diplomatique*, ii, 132.

ships to the Spanish side and betray his country; this in order to penetrate the plot. He easily tricked the credulous Spanish ambassador and even convinced the more cautious Philip. 'I have written to your Majesty', says De Spes, 'of the great desire which Hawkins expresses to serve you ... and I can discover nothing suspicious about it. He has gone to Plymouth, taking artillery and munitions from London, leaving a person here in case I should wish to call him back.... He may render great service by manning his ships with a very few men and filling them up with others chosen by your Majesty.'[1]

Similarly, in the negotiations which Burghley had with a Spanish agent in October and November 1572, when events in the Netherlands made our strained relations with Spain seem dangerous, I am sure that he was often mildly pulling the agent's leg; and I have frequently suspected, in reading the diplomatic correspondence of the time, that the seemingly disloyal overtures of a councillor like Leicester to some ambassador were moves in a game of bluff. Doubly a foreigner by his ignorance of the language, it was difficult for an ambassador to sift the true from the false, and if his relations with the Court were unfriendly his sympathies tended to go out to malcontents, and the eddies of faction ever threatened to destroy his discretion. The effect of keeping such company upon a particularly intemperate mind may be illustrated by the following quotation from a dispatch written by De Spes:

> The principal person in the Council at present is William Cecil, now Lord Burghley. He is a man of mean sort, but very astute, false, lying, and full of artifice. He is a great heretic, and such a clownish Englishman as to believe that all the Christian princes joined together are not able to injure the sovereign of his country, and he therefore treats their ministers with great arrogance.
>
> This man manages the bulk of the business, and by

[1] *Spanish Cal. Eliz.* ii, 329; cf. 346, 351.

means of his vigilance and craftiness, together with his utter unscrupulousness of word and deed, thinks to outwit the ministers of other princes. This to a certain extent he has hitherto succeeded in doing. Next after him, the man who has most to do with affairs is Robert Dudley, Earl of Leicester, not that he is fit for such work, but because of the great favour with which the Queen regards him. He is a light and greedy man who maintains the robbers and lives by their plunder. He is ungrateful for the favours your Majesty has granted to him, and is greatly inclined to the French party, from whom he receives an allowance. The other man who has his hand in the government is the Lord Keeper of the Great Seal. He is an obstinate and most malignant heretic, and, being Cecil's brother-in-law, always agrees with him. The Admiral does not interfere very much in arranging matters, but he is a very shameless thief without any religion at all, which latter also may be said of the Earl of Sussex.... The Earl of Bedford also belongs to the Council. In person and manners he is a monstrosity and a great heretic. There are others of less authority than these men, lawyers, creatures of Cecil who only repeat what he says.[1]

Once more, perhaps, I have overdrawn my picture, or rather, put in the shadows and omitted the rest. All is not gloom, but he who would sail in uncharted seas must keep a sharp look-out for rocks, and I have known quite eminent historians founder.

It remains for me to give you a rather fuller conception of the information contained in diplomatic sources. I turn first, as every sixteenth-century diplomat would have done, to the *Relazioni* or Relations of the Venetian ambassadors. In origin they are the reports on their missions which ambassadors had to make on their return home, and there is a decree of the

[1] *Spanish Cal. Eliz.* ii, 364.

Venetian Grand Council as early as 1268 concerning them. Had they continued to be mere reports on the details of a diplomatic mission, they would not have become the famous and unique documents that they are. In fact, they might have been confined, as was more or less so in other states, to ambassadors returning from special missions, since resident ambassadors gave full reports of their negotiations in their dispatches and it was generally needless — and indeed impracticable when the residence had been of long duration — to review their work on their return. Consequently, it was a happy accident that led the Venetians to add to their reports a geographical, social and political description of the country from which they had returned. The pattern became established custom, and I imagine that it was with the introduction of resident ambassadors that what had been a mere frill became the very substance of a 'Relation'. The document was read before a solemn gathering of the Doge and Senate within a fortnight of the ambassador's return, and was listened to with critical interest. Tradition and the fame which these reports won throughout Europe in the sixteenth century established very high standards, and one can see the effects of emulation in the formidable length to which some of them grew in the second half of the century. Though formally they were confidential documents, manuscript copies got abroad. They were sold in Rome at 15 pauls per hundred sheets, and contemporary transcripts are to be found in the great libraries of England and other countries. A group of *Relazioni* was actually published at Cologne in 1589.[1]

No doubt it was largely the commercial character of the Venetian state and the high level of its culture, but it was also the traditions of a great service which made its ambassadors the ablest and most detached of observers. Their Relations have these advantages over travellers' descriptions: first, that there are very many more of them — for a country like France they recur at intervals of a few years; and secondly, that their

[1] Cf. Introduction to *Venetian Cal.* vol. i.

authors were generally shrewder observers, lived longer in the country they are describing, and had peculiar advantages in noting and collecting their information. It is true that a foreigner is almost sure to go wrong in some measure in commenting on institutions, which are too elusive to understand readily. But against native writers must be set a freshness of view that notes points which are so familiar to an inhabitant that they cannot become objective.

Let me sample one or two of these Relations for you. The earliest known, written about 1500, concerns England and opens in the following matter-of-fact way:

> Magnificent and most illustrious Lord!
>
> The Kingdom of England is situated in the island named Britain, which ... is in the Ocean, between the north and the west. Her form is triangular, like that of Sicily, and she lies, though at a considerable distance, over against Germany, France and Spain....

On Englishmen its comment is as follows:

> The English are, for the most part, both men and women of all ages, handsome and well-proportioned; though not quite so much so, in my opinion, as it had been asserted to me ... ; and I have understood from persons acquainted with these countries, that the Scotch are much handsomer; and that the English are great lovers of themselves, and of everything belonging to them; they think that there are no other men than themselves, and no other world but England; and whenever they see a handsome foreigner, they say that 'he looks like an Englishman', and that 'it is a great pity that he should not be an Englishman'; and when they partake of any delicacy with a foreigner they ask him, 'whether such a thing is made in *their* country?' ... [1]

[1] *Italian Relation of England*, edited by C. A. Sneyd (Camden Soc. 1847), pp. 7, 20.

From a Relation of the year 1551, which is admirable in its description of our institutions, I take the following account of the mode of holding parliament:

> When they are assembled in the place appointed for this purpose, which is very vast and extremely handsome, after celebration of the mass the King makes the Lord Chancellor state the causes which have rendered it necessary to assemble the Parliament. In the next place, the King desires the inferior order, that of the burgesses, to elect as usual an able and eloquent member to announce their suits and grievances. This mover is styled Speaker of the Parliament, because as president of that order he prescribes the mode and place for speaking. These orders being separated one from the other, they commence regulating matters, as aforesaid; and first of all they inscribe in a bill[1] whatever has to be treated, after which they read the bill three times in three days, one day always intervening between each reading, for the purpose of giving time to the House in question to consult. The bill having been read, any member who pleases is at liberty to speak, but in turn, one after the other, nor is it allowable to interrupt anyone speaking. The arguments on both sides having been heard they proceed to vote, and all those who assent to a motion exclaim 'Aye, aye,' those who reject it exlaiming 'No, no.' If the number of one side is doubtful the Speaker counts it one by one, and thus the majority conquers the minority, and the deliberation being noted in a bill, is sent by three or four members selected from that House to the Upper House, wherein the whole affair is discussed in like manner. If the bill is disapproved they immediately tear it; if approved, it is kept until the last day of Parliament, when in presence of the King all bills of the sort are read; and if the King assents to them they all

[1] I have substituted 'bill' for the translator's 'book'.

become so many lasting and immutable laws; but if any of the bills do not please the King, they then say that the King will consider, and the matter is referred to another time.[1]

I might go on indefinitely quoting from these descriptions of England. Certainly I must not omit the fine portraits of Mary and her sister Elizabeth, drawn by the Venetian ambassador in 1557.

Queen Mary ... is of short stature, well made, thin and delicate, and moderately pretty; her eyes are so lively that she inspires reverence and respect, and even fear, wherever she turns them; nevertheless she is very short-sighted. Her voice is deep, almost like that of a man. She understands five languages, English, Latin, French, Spanish and Italian, in which last, however, she does not venture to converse. She is also much skilled in ladies' work, such as producing all sorts of embroidery with the needle. She has a knowledge of music, chiefly on the lute, on which she plays exceedingly well. As to the qualities of her mind, it may be said of her that she is rash, disdainful and parsimonious rather than liberal. She is endowed with great humility and patience, but withal high-spirited, courageous and resolute, having during the whole course of her adversity been guiltless of any the least approach to meanness of comportment; she is, moreover, devout and staunch in the defence of her religion ... The cabal she has been exposed to, the evil disposition of the people towards her, the present poverty and the debt of the Crown, and her passion for King Philip, from whom she is doomed to live separate, are so many other causes of the grief by which she is overwhelmed. She is, moreover, a prey to the hatred she bears my Lady Elizabeth, and which has its source in the recollection of the wrongs she experienced on account of her mother, and in the fact that all eyes and hearts are

[1] *Venetian Cal.* v, 342-3.

turned towards my Lady Elizabeth as successor to the Throne.

My Lady Elizabeth ... is a lady of great elegance both of body and mind, although her face may rather be called pleasing than beautiful; she is tall and well made; her complexion fine, though rather sallow; her eyes, but above all her hands, which she takes care not to conceal, are of superior beauty. In her knowledge of the Greek and Italian languages she surpasses the Queen. Her spirits and understanding are admirable, as she has proved by her conduct in the midst of suspicion and danger, when she concealed her religion and comported herself like a good catholic. She is proud and dignified in her manners; for though her mother's condition is well known to her, she is also aware that this mother of hers was united to the King in wedlock, with the sanction of the holy church and the concurrence of the primate of the realm.[1]

France — the France of the religious wars — offered a fine field of observation for the Venetians, and had I not been addressing an English audience it would have been from the French Relations that I would have drawn my main illustrations. The comments on persons are often notable. Catherine de Medici, says one ambassador, writing in 1561, in her role of mother keeps the king under her control. She allows no one but herself to sleep in his chamber; she never leaves his side. And her difficulties as regent are well analysed by another ambassador. 'It is sufficient to say', he writes, 'that she is a woman, a foreigner, and a Florentine to boot, born of a simple house altogether beneath the dignity of the kingdom of France.' Good also is this comment on Antony, King of Navarre: He is said to be intelligent and to talk well, but he is vain, imprudent and inconstant in his actions, readily enters upon great schemes, yet lacks the capacity to see them through. My final excerpt

[1] Ellis, *Original Letters,* 2nd ser. ii, 236-7; cf. *Venetian Cal.* VI, ii, 1043 seqq.

seems to me to be singularly penetrating. It is one of those simple but fresh comments which are the very essence of imagination. It was written in 1569 in the course of one of the religious wars. 'I believe', says the ambassador,

> I believe that in these troubles the Pope has gained more than he has lost; for before the religious dissensions there was so much licence of manners and so little respect for the Roman court that his holiness was regarded rather as a great Italian political power than as the head of the Church and universal pastor. But as soon as the Huguenots appeared, the catholics began to have a new respect for the pontiff and to recognize him as the true vicar of Christ, and the more the Huguenot party scoffed at him the more their faith increased.[1]

The Venetian ambassadors alone wrote these descriptive reports of the countries where they had resided. I know of only one exception, and that is a Relation of the State of France, written by Sir George Carew upon his return from his embassy there in 1609, and addressed to James I. It was avowedly an imitation of the Venetian Relations, but owed its existence to the ambassador's initiative and to that alone. It did not inspire an English series of Relations; nor indeed could there very well have been such a series without that form of audience for a returning ambassador which was peculiar to Venice. We may deplore the solitary character of the Venetian tradition, but it is more just to count our blessings than cry our losses; and, in fact, in their passing comments upon persons and affairs, the ordinary dispatches of an ambassador supply part at least of the picture that a Venetian deliberately drew. In Sir Edward Stafford's dispatches from France there are many touches which put together give us a portrait of Henry III – an unstable king, at one moment coercing even his mother, at

[1] *Relations des ambassadeurs vénitiens*, ed. M. M. Tommasio (Collection de documents inédits), i, 425, 549, 431; ii, 163.

another letting politics go hang while he mortified the flesh in religious processions. 'He is so strange a man of disposition', writes Stafford on one occasion, 'and so unknown in his proceedings, that no man can settle any judgment upon his actions. He is become, since Monsieur's death (whom he stood in fear of) to care for nobody, and so keepeth every one about him in awe that mother, counsellors, mignons and all quail when he speaketh.' He 'beginneth to reform marvellously the orders of his house', is the report a few weeks later; 'maketh three chambers afore they come to his inner bedchamber; in the first, to be gentlemen, modestly apparelled; in the next, men of greater quality; in the last, the princes and knights of the order of the Saint Esprit.... Into his private bed-chamber nobody to be allowed but who is called in, but only Epernon and Joyeuse, the Marshal Retz and Villequier ... ; all others being quite cut off, not to come in but when they are called for'.[1]

As we might expect, the most entertaining of all passages in the dispatches of ambassadors resident in England are those which describe their audiences with the Queen. Upon her progresses among her own people every faculty Elizabeth possessed was set in motion, and so it was at these audiences. At her accession to the throne she knew how to check the arrogance of the Spanish ambassador and remind him that her power depended upon the affection of her people and not upon the goodwill of his master; she could parry offers of marriage with maidenly yearnings for a cloistered life, and then pout because Philip II could not wait a month for her answer: 'Your Lordship', writes the ambassador, 'will see what a pretty business it is to have to treat with this woman, who I think must have a hundred thousand devils in her body, notwithstanding that she is for ever telling me that she yearns to be a nun and to pass her time in a cell praying.'[2] She knew how to

[1] *Foreign Cal. Eliz.* xix, 126, 184, 302.
[2] *Spanish Cal. Eliz.* i, 119.

receive the French ambassador after the Massacre of St Bartholomew, surrounded by her Court in profound silence, with a solemn and severe air, and yet without hostility, for she did not dare to break openly with France. She knew too how to trounce an insolent Polish ambassador, summoning her wrath and her Latin and rising lion-like from her chair. Infinite were her wiles. 'She caressed me more than I can describe', writes Mendoza, on one occasion; and on another he tells how at his last audience with her she gave the Portuguese ambassador a ring from her own finger, 'no doubt as a keepsake, for she is very clever at such little witcheries as these, when she thinks she can gain a point by them and disarm those with whom she is dealing. I fancy', he adds, 'she has fully succeeded in this with the ambassador.'[1]

These and many other such passages are to be found in the diplomatic correspondence of the time. I would counsel you, when next you read any well-documented history of the period, to note how many of the facts of domestic history are dependent on this type of source. It is not that the facts are best expressed in any ambassador's words. Too often it is that he provides our only evidence, and though I advise you to look the gift horse in the mouth, I would have you retain your gratitude.

And so I would end, but for a duty that I owe to our sixteenth-century ambassador. His was not a happy lot. His profit and loss account was a statement in two terms of which one was never operative. His equipment had to be costly, else he lost respect; his table had to be free and bountiful and his news service efficient, else he failed in his principal duty. He had to follow the Court in its perambulations and incur loss, fatigue and danger. One Venetian tells a vivid story of the alarms through which he passed when the Huguenots attempted to seize the king at Meaux. In Paris he kept his servants armed, water ready in the street lest his house was fired over his head, sentinels posted and himself ready at every sound to spring from

[1] *Spanish Cal. Eliz.* ii, 691, 663.

his bed and escape. Another tells of the inordinate price of victuals, of unhealthy lodgings, of dangers from soldiers and brigands.[1] Their pay was often irregular and never adequate, and they were lucky if their private estates were not hopelessly mortgaged at the end of an embassy. In 1511 an ambassador from the Low Countries in Spain had to slip out of the country and desert his post for lack of money. The consolation for the ambassador was that his reward came in some future appointment or grant from the state. The consolation for us is that what is generally assumed, so far as our ambassadors are concerned, to have had a peculiar source in Elizabeth's parsimony, was really the common practice of the time. We are an insular folk in our historical judgments.

[1] Tommasio, op. cit. ii, 199; i, 359.

THE FAME OF SIR EDWARD STAFFORD[1]

WHEN editing the last volume of the Elizabethan *Spanish Calendar* in 1899 Martin Hume identified with Sir Edward Stafford, our ambassador in France from 1583 to 1590, a certain Julio (or Julius), or the new friend, or the new confidant – all three, according to him, different names for the same person – who on the face of the documents he calendared seems to have been selling information to Mendoza, the Spanish ambassador in that country. The relationship began in January 1587, and Hume was so convinced of the identification that he indexed references to the three names under Stafford's name. To say the least, so grave a charge as that of treason, which Hume made, called for more argument than his footnotes supplied, and when reviewing the volume in this journal[2] – a review which should be read by anyone who has occasion to use the *Spanish Calendar* – Professor Pollard pointed out the striking discordances involved in Hume's identification. The argument which Hume omitted was supplied by Dr Conyers Read in an article written in 1915,[3] and his statement of the case against Stafford, reinforced – though less confidently – in his recent work on Sir Francis Walsingham, has not been refuted. Mrs Lomas, the editor of the *Foreign Calendar*, held strongly that Stafford was no traitor, and she promised to deal with the problem in the latest volume of her calendar. Unfortunately, ill health has made the fulfilment of her promise impossible, and in consequence I have ventured to convert

[1] Published in the *English Historical Review* (April 1929), xliv, 203-19.

[2] *Eng. Hist. Rev.* xvi, 572 seqq.

[3] *American Hist. Rev.* xx, 292 seqq.; and see his reply to my article, ibid. xxxv, 560-6. I still believe in Stafford's innocence.

my review of the volume[1] into an examination of the charges against Stafford.

There are two elements in the problem. The one is the identity of Stafford with one or more of the names mentioned above: that is, did Stafford receive money from Mendoza and supply him with information? The other is whether, if this be so, Stafford was acting treasonably. Dr Read wisely keeps the two questions apart, though he answers each affirmatively.

I will not say much about the first question, because it seems a waste of time to build a detailed argument on Hume's calendaring of the original documents, packed as it is with personal pronouns which he identifies with a certainty that others cannot share. In spite of this distrust, however, I accept Dr Read's contention that the evidence at places is so strong that one must, at any rate sometimes, identify Julio, the new friend, and the new confidant, with Stafford.[2] I thus accept the contention that Stafford received an initial sum of 2000 crowns from Mendoza, and further payments. However, it would be rash to write 'Stafford' or 'Julio' every time the new friend or the new confidant is mentioned. After the death of Charles Arundel, who acted as intermediary between Stafford and Mendoza, a new intermediary was found, and I think that he may sometimes be referred to under one of the pseudonyms.[3]

Conceding to Martin Hume and Dr Read the substance of their case on the first question, there still remains the crucial problem of Stafford's evil or good intentions. It is well to note first what is involved in proving the case against him. Assuming that he was the conscious source of Mendoza's information in each instance cited by Dr Read — an assumption we may make

[1] *Calendar of State Papers, Foreign Series, of the Reign of Elizabeth*, vol. XXI, i, June 1586-June 1588. Edited by Sophie Crawford Lomas (London: Stationery Office, 1927).

[2] *Am. Hist. Rev.* xx, 302 seqq.; *Spanish Cal. Eliz.* iv, 121, compared with ibid. pp. 87, 110, leaves no doubt of the identity of 'the new friend'. The references to Julio as though he were in London are easily explained if we assume that the object was to give the date of Stafford's letters from London.

[3] Cf. *Spanish Cal. Eliz.* iv, 430.

for the sake of argument – then everything turns on being able to prove that the information was accurate, that it was of a confidential character, that the divulgence of it was damaging to English interests, and if possible that Stafford really possessed it. I have tried to apply these tests and find it extraordinarily difficult to discover occasions when the proof can be made satisfactorily. The precision of facts and dates evaporates as one examines them attentively, and the gaps in the foreign state papers are so serious that when the *Spanish Calendar* offers a seemingly crucial occasion for the tests, the state papers fail us: sometimes the reverse happens. Hume's escape from this difficulty was an easy one. He simply assumed – or so it seems – that the statements in the *Spanish Calendar* were accurate, and by begging the question completely, arrived at his conclusion. Dr Read, for his part, refers to particular pieces of information, the giving of which to Mendoza he stigmatizes as 'the rankest sort of treason'; but generally his only evidence is a page reference, in a footnote, to the *Spanish Calendar*. Let us postpone judgment until we have examined some of the passages to which he refers.[1]

The first batch are concerned, in time if not always in subject, with Drake's Cadiz expedition, and the first reference is to news given by Stafford to Charles Arundel expressly for Mendoza. It contains the statement that Elizabeth had agreed to pay Don Antonio, the Portuguese pretender, three years of his pension, plus 18,000 crowns, and provide him with a fleet to operate against Spain. Dr Read offers no evidence that there was such a scheme afoot at the time, and on the other side there is this to be said: that Sir Julian Corbett had no suspicion of it when he was working over these years, nor is it reconcilable with the treatment of Don Antonio referred to a few pages later in the *Spanish Calendar*.[2] The second reference reveals Stafford as saying that Burghley had just written

[1] *Am. Hist. Rev.* xx, 310-11 and footnotes.

[2] *Spanish Cal. Eliz.* iv, 8, 17; Corbett, *Drake and the Tudor Navy*, ii, 65.

to tell him that the execution of Mary Stuart had been carried out against his will.[1] The statement is quite incredible. It seems easier to assume that on this as on the previous occasion Stafford was bamboozling Mendoza. With the next example we find Stafford saying that no living soul but the Queen and Burghley knew what Drake's plans were to be, and Elizabeth would not even have the Lord Admiral informed. On the face of it this is absurd, and it is hard to see how it can be reconciled with our evidence; though reconciliation is perhaps unnecessary since the new friend himself contradicts it in another of his revelations a month later.[2] Nevertheless, the passage in question refers to Cadiz as Drake's probable objective, and here at any rate it might seem that we have an instance of treason. Hasty conclusions are, however, generally false conclusions. We cannot, it is true, prove that Stafford was ignorant of Drake's intention to attack Cadiz, nor for that matter can Dr Read prove that he knew of it; but what seems to have escaped the notice of Stafford's critics is that Cadiz was an incident in Drake's plans, not the main objective, and had Stafford known of these plans he must have considered Cape St Vincent or Lisbon more important than Cadiz.[3] Couple this with the fact that Drake sailed on April 2nd and Mendoza only sent Stafford's news from Paris on April 9th/19th, and it looks as though treason is not here in question. I pass to another of Dr Read's references, where the passage evidently is supposed to give the gist of a letter from Walsingham to Stafford — a letter that is extant.[4] To a point it does — and the news is harmless — but the Indian flotilla of Spain, to which it refers, did sail that year and the text of Drake's counter-instructions suggests that the English authorities expected it;[5] so that in telling Mendoza

[1] *Spanish Cal. Eliz.* iv, 27.
[2] Ibid. iv, 69, 87; *Papers relating to ... the Spanish War, 1585-1587*, ed. Corbett (Navy Records Soc.), pp. 97 seqq.
[3] *Papers relating to ... the Spanish War*, pp. xxv seqq.
[4] *Spanish Cal. Eliz.* iv, 87; *Foreign Cal. Eliz.* XXI, i, 279.
[5] *Papers relating to ... the Spanish War*, pp. 101-2.

the opposite Stafford was probably lying, and lying with a purpose.

In another of his references,[1] this time to a letter of Mendoza's on June 16th/26th, 1588, on the eve of the Armada, Dr Read says that Stafford – that is, Julio – gave 'precise news' of the movements of Howard's and Drake's fleets. It is well to examine the precision. Julio says that the two fleets numbered 160 sail and not more than 8000 men: Sir Julian Corbett's estimate is 100 sail and 10,000 men. Julio further says that they sailed on May 30th/June 9th, their orders being not to sail into Spanish waters: actually they did sail on May 30th, but their intention was to sail to Spain and this their orders allowed; only the winds frustrated it. It is true that the plan was temporarily changed by the Queen on June 9th, but as Stafford does not mention the return of the fleet on June 6th, the information that he gave was in any event not up to date. Whether he knew or not of subsequent happenings, he clearly refers to the voyage of May 30th and he has clearly falsified its objective; while as information regarding this voyage, the news was scarcely prompt.[2] Dr Read is still more insecure when he argues that Stafford, in the spring of 1588, apparently tried to convince the English government that Philip had abandoned his intention of sending the Armada.[3] We do not possess the text of the letter to Howard in which Stafford told him that Philip had dissolved his forces, but I think there can be little doubt that he was merely passing on an advertisement that he had received. Seeing that he was telling Burghley at this very time that he did not believe in the possibility of peace with Spain,[4] while in March, April,

[1] I may also refer to Dr Read's sentence to which is attached footnote no. 65, which makes Stafford give Mendoza news on or before March 5th/15th of instructions only issued to Drake on March 15th. Cf. Dr Read's own reference to Corbett.

[2] *Spanish Cal. Eliz.* iv, 319; Corbett, *Drake and the Tudor Navy*, ii, 150, 156 seqq.; *State Papers relating to the Defeat of the Spanish Armada*, ed. J. K. Laughton (Navy Records Soc.), i, 192 seqq.

[3] *Am. Hist. Rev.* xx, 311, n. 67.

[4] *Foreign Cal. Eliz.* XXI, i, 481, 482; cf. Stafford's comment here (p. 481) – 'I see her [Elizabeth] out with Spain, and I think no intent in him ever to agree

and May he passed on the latest rumoured dates for the sailing of the Armada,[1] it is manifestly unreasonable to insinuate that Stafford was trying to deceive his own government.

There is some hyperbole in Dr Read's statement that Stafford 'betrayed to Mendoza every particular of the efforts of Elizabeth to form an alliance with Henry III of France against Spain in the spring of 1588',[2] and it is hardly convincing to base this statement on references to the *Spanish Calendar* alone. Even if one cannot prove the news items to be false, there still remains the duty of proving them to be true.

Let us take the first reference that Dr Read appends to his statement. Here 'the new friend' asserts that Elizabeth had written to Stafford on April 29th, 1587. I take this to be new style. Now on April 21st (old style) Walsingham wrote to Stafford, and as luck would have it I think we can infer from the postscript that Elizabeth had not written on April 19th (old style). But supposing that my inference is not altogether convincing, or that Mendoza is using old style — which I think very unlikely — the fact remains that Dr Read cannot prove that Elizabeth wrote the letter. And there is this argument also — though it is dependent on one's sense of the likeliness of things — that other revelations of the new friend on this occasion seem to be specially made for Mendoza's consumption: I do not, for example, believe the story about Philip's right to the English crown; much less do I believe that Elizabeth promised Stafford the viceroyalty of Ireland, or — as on another occasion Mendoza reports — a place in the Privy Council.[3]

It is, I think, needless to pursue the criticism much farther. Had Stafford really been betraying the course of Anglo-French

[1] *Foreign Cal. Eliz.* XXI, i, 532-3, 624; Harleian MS. 288, fol. 190b, Stafford to Walsingham, April 29th, 1588.

[2] *Am. Hist. Rev.* xx, 311.

[3] *Spanish Cal. Eliz.* iv, 86-7, 110; *Foreign Cal. Eliz.* XXI, i, 279-80.

with her' — with Mendoza's statement a few weeks later that he understood Julio was doing his best to induce Elizabeth to seek Philip and not draw closer to the French (*Spanish Cal. Eliz.* iv, 258).

relations at this time, one would have expected him in all haste to tell Mendoza of the most important private interview which he had with Henry III on March 29th, 1588, and of the subsequent interview with Secretary Pinart. In fact, it was a ludicrously inadequate and misleading account that Mendoza sent to Philip on April 4th/14th. Unfortunately, it is not quite clear that he received his information from the new confidant, although it seems likely; but, however this may be, one can at least say with certainty that Stafford had not divulged his secret by April 4th, and, but for the possibility of there being a gap in Mendoza's dispatches immediately after this date, one might be able to say that he did not divulge it at all.[1]

Dr Read then cannot be said to have proved his case against Stafford. But it is not sufficient merely to show this. We must attempt to supply a reasonable explanation of Stafford's actions, and it is only fair to Dr Read to point out that it is much easier to do this now that the foreign state papers for the period are calendared. If Stafford did not play the traitor — the thesis that I wish to maintain — and yet pretended to be a paid informant of Mendoza's, there was some reason for his conduct. Either it was for the money — not a great sum — or it was a phase of his secret diplomacy. I do not doubt that it was the latter. Stafford was in debt, but Dr Read makes altogether too much of the fact. It was not exceptional for an Elizabethan ambassador to get into financial straits, nor indeed was it for ambassadors of other countries in the sixteenth century. One ambassador had to desert his post for lack of money in 1511, and generally ambassadors had to face making inroads into their private estates.[2] Their allowance was fixed, but the expense of their establishment was not, and economy might easily mean inefficiency. Though the cost of the secret service of news that they had to organize and maintain might in a general way

[1] *Hatfield MSS.* iii, 314 seqq.; *Spanish Cal. Eliz.* iv, 266.

[2] Maulde-La-Clavière, M. de, *La Diplomatie au temps de Machiavel* (1892), ii, 7 seq.

be met, there were many outlays they could not recover. In 1586 Stafford advanced 6400 crowns to the Comte de Soissons in anticipation of a grant that he hoped Elizabeth would make, only to hear from Walsingham that Elizabeth's mood had changed and it did not look as though she would make the grant.[1] I have no doubt that Stafford recovered his loan, but I have equally no doubt that he made many advances which he did not recover; and in any event, it is difficult to believe that, after risking his own fortune through his enthusiasm for the cause, he should a year later start selling information to Mendoza. An ambassador's financial salvation was that he remained in a post for a brief time. Stafford was ambassador for an exceptional number of years and in exceptional times: 'Yf yow dyd knowe', he wrote to Walsingham in July 1588,

> whatt unseasonable tymes and unresonable I have had to passe an ordinarye bowndes of expense and especially the Queen of Scotts tyme above all other, and this last both for myne owne conservation and the preservation of thinges in good state for her majesties service heere, I thinke yow will nott wonder att the expense.[2]

It is true that Stafford added to his debts by gaming with Alençon and his companions in the first year of his embassy, but I think we may also accept his own statement that thereafter he abstained.[3] Unfortunately, this early frivolity gave his critics at home a weapon against him, and consequently we hear about it from the English side. The stress laid upon his debts in the *Spanish Calendar* is quite unconvincing, since if we assume that Stafford was fooling Mendoza, we must allow that by dinning into his ears the complaint that he was overwhelmed by debt he provided a natural setting for his relations with him. Unduly oppressed by Stafford's debts, Dr Read

[1] *Foreign Cal. Eliz.* XX, 554-5.
[2] Harleian MS. 288, fol. 216.
[3] *Foreign Cal. Eliz.* XXI, i, 128-9.

comes to the astonishing conclusion that he misappropriated public funds; this because he kept in his hands and used as a loan a sum of money that was to have been paid to the Comte de Soissons, but for legitimate reasons was not. Yet on Dr Read's own showing both Elizabeth and Walsingham knew that he had the money. Burghley also knew. The fact is that Elizabeth sometimes helped her servants by allowing them to be in her debt. It was not a peaceful position to be in, but Stafford's innocence is surely doubly clear when we learn that he asked Walsingham to show the Queen a letter in which this very charge over this very sum of money was made against him.[1]

If the suggestion that Stafford's conduct was the result merely of a desire for money does not carry conviction, then we must turn to explore the alternative explanation, namely that it was a move in his secret diplomacy. As an ambassador, it was his duty to supply his government with news of all projects and happenings that he could ferret out. He had to be, as it were, foreign correspondent for Europe generally as well as for France in particular, since we had no other resident ambassador abroad; and at the same time to be the centre of a spy service in France. The latter was abnormally elaborate because it was a question of probing the secrets of the English Catholic refugees, Mary Stuart's partisans, and the Guise party, as well as the usual business of securing informants at Court and suborning people in the households of prominent state officials; and in addition, the Spanish embassy became all-important since we had no ambassador in Spain, and our open intervention in the Netherlands led to Spain's preparations for invasion.

At the very beginning of his embassy Stafford asked his predecessor how he was to get information out of the Spanish ambassador's house, the Bishop of Glasgow's – Mary Stuart's agent – and the house of Guise.[2] There was nothing novel in this. Novelty, if it existed, was in the methods he devised

[1] *Am. Hist. Rev.* xx, 309; *Foreign Cal. Eliz.* XXI, i, 378, 483.
[2] *Foreign Cal. 1583-4*, p. 166.

to secure his ends. He was persistently inventing ways of obtaining intelligence and deceiving England's enemies, and — a point the importance of which we shall see later — asking leave from home to adopt them. Often Elizabeth refused permission and even chided him; but there is no need to assume with Stafford that Walsingham's malignant influence always inspired these refusals, nor to think that they reflected any suspicion at home of Stafford's good faith, as when he was commanded to have nothing to do with the more conspicuous English refugees like Charles Arundel and the Pagets. Elizabeth thought of the public character of Stafford; Stafford of a fine chance of securing intelligence.

Let us examine some of his schemes. On December 1st, 1583, he wrote to the Queen telling her of a Jesuit who had come to him pretending to be ready to play the spy and also warning him that his wife, Lady Stafford, was thought to be a Catholic at heart. Stafford explained to Elizabeth that he had taken care to encourage the Jesuit's suspicions of Lady Stafford; in fact that the rumour was one which he had himself devised. Four of the great ladies of the Court, who knew all state secrets through their intimacy with the leading statesmen, were fond of his wife's company, and religious sympathy, he thought, would lead them to speak more frankly to her.[1] Elizabeth would not let him go on with his plan — naturally enough, I think — but Stafford sorrowfully remarked that 500 marks would not suffice to make good the loss of news.[2]

In the following year Stafford was 'sought upon by the Duke of Guise's means'. We do not possess any details of the scheme. Perhaps it was an attempt to bribe him; perhaps not. At any rate, he was offered 'private conference', and his own comment

[1] B.M. Cotton MS. Galba E. VI, fols. 183 seqq. The letter is a copy in Stafford's hand, evidently sent to Burghley like the other copies in this volume. It is worth noting that Stafford did not mention his scheme in his letter to Walsingham of the same date (ibid. fols. 187 seqq.), and that Elizabeth did not betray Lady Stafford's name in telling Walsingham to write and scotch the plan (cf. *Foreign Cal. 1583-4*, p. 271).

[2] Cotton MS. Galba E. VI, fols. 194 seqq.

was that 'the only way to know those things that may hurt anybody is to haunt them that are their enemies'. He wrote to Burghley to know Elizabeth's will, and once more was rebuked. In a letter written to Burghley in the following year he attributed his rebuff to Walsingham's jealously: 'First she liked', he wrote, 'then the next day disliked it, which I thought came by her communicating it to those who will never like courses ... wherein I may do her Majesty service worth the thanks.'[1] We shall consider Walsingham's relations with Stafford later: for the moment it is enough to remark that he had become a bee in Stafford's bonnet. I think a quite adequate explanation of Elizabeth's objection is that Stafford himself was to visit Guise, which though done in secret could hardly remain unknown, and being known might have crossed Elizabeth's diplomacy unpleasantly. If this was the basis of the objection, then it would not hold against employing an intermediary, and after Stafford secured the services of Charles Arundel there were relations with Guise: in fact Stafford ostensibly sold information to Guise through Arundel as he later did to Mendoza, and Dr Read believes that he played his country false in this instance as in the other.[2]

In a similar vein to the foregoing is Stafford's device for penetrating the plans of Mary Stuart's supporters in France. In 1583 he seems to have been haunting the Bishop of Glasgow's house, unknown to the bishop. Walsingham advised him against it.[3] In 1585 he was approached by the Marian party and pretended friendship with them in order to help to keep watch on their actions. Once more he asked for the Queen's approval and once more was refused it. Again, I think, there is the same principle behind the refusal. Again, too, Stafford deplored the lost opportunity: he told Walsingham a year later that he would have been drawn in pieces by wild horses

[1] *Foreign Cal. 1583-4*, p. 475; ibid. vol. XIX, p. 654; Cotton MS. Galba E. VI, fol. 234b, Stafford to Burghley, May 7th, 1584.
[2] *Am. Hist. Rev.* xx, 300 seqq.
[3] *Foreign Cal. 1583-4*, p. 222.

if the Queen and he had not had in their hands both the recent Babington plot and anything yet to come, as plain as the conspirators themselves knew it. He added that he would one day tell the Queen and Walsingham the manner of it, which was not fit to be committed to writing; a comment which, with similar comments on other occasions, warns us that we must not look for details of all Stafford's devices in his letters.[1]

Now the mind which invented these tricks was quite likely to pretend to play its own government false in order to penetrate and disconcert the plans of its enemies. 'For my part', wrote Stafford to Walsingham once, 'I am of a mind to use the devil himself well, if he could come to me in the likeness of a man to serve the Queen withal.'[2] But not only can we place the main plan in its temperamental setting, the very incidents fit Stafford's genius. Somehow he had to impart a flavour of importance and genuineness to information generally harmless or false. I think he was often helped with Mendoza by being asked to confirm news the latter had received from agents in England. But the charge against him in connection with the Duke of Guise is that he showed his letters of intelligence out of England;[3] and Mendoza also notes from time to time that he had seen or had had read to him Stafford's dispatches.[4]

It is this apparently grave offence which we can reduce to the level of trickery. Twice in 1583 Stafford asked Elizabeth to write him dispatches occasionally, which he might show and so deceive other parties.[5] Once he acknowledged the receipt of such a dispatch from Walsingham, which he proposed to leave lying about so that a spy who was suspected to be in his house might see it; and to deceive this man further he added a knot to his signature when he wrote letters to Walsingham which he had allowed the spy to copy, and which therefore

[1] *Foreign Cal. Eliz.* XXI, i, 94, 127. Probably ibid. XIX, 653, refers to the same occasion.
[2] Ibid. *1583-4*, p. 173.
[3] Ibid. XXI, i, 34.
[4] e.g. *Spanish Cal. Eliz.* iv, 71, 194.
[5] *Foreign Cal. 1583-4*, p. 184; Cotton MS. Galba E. VI, fol. 186, Stafford to Elizabeth, December 1st, 1583.

were to be ignored at home.[1] Similarly he arranged a mark with Elizabeth which was to indicate that the particular passage in his letter was 'wrytten for a pourpose and nott for a truthe'.[2] In 1585 he told the Queen how he showed counterfeit letters from home in order to confirm confidential talks which he had with people who were sure to carry all they learned to Catherine de Medici.[3] And the year before, we find him telling how, after an interview with the French king, he wrote a fake dispatch home which was to be shown to the Spanish ambassador in Paris. It carried, he says, 'both matters which the Spanishe Imbassador knew to be trewe, and also introductions owte of cypher to helpe to discover partlye that which was in cypher'.[4]

Let me tell of a trick which he played on Secretary Pinart, and I think that we shall then have a repertory of devices quite rich enough to account for his practice with Guise and Mendoza. In March 1588 Stafford received an important letter from Elizabeth, the contents of which he made known to Henry III in a private interview. Afterwards the king sent his Secretary Pinart to Stafford, but warned the latter not to tell the Secretary of a certain point in the letter. Stafford carried out his instructions by showing Pinart the original letter in Elizabeth's hand, and then translating it into French as though he were reading it word for word; but he turned the beginning and omitted the passage mentioned.[5] The success of the trick depended on Pinart's ignorance of English, which was not a language that a foreign official was expected to know. Mendoza knew no English, and I think we may be sure that Guise also knew none.

If a case of treason cannot be proved from the information

[1] *Foreign Cal. 1583-4*, p. 184.

[2] Cotton MS. Galba E. VI, fol. 171b, Stafford to Elizabeth, November 7th, 1583.

[3] *Foreign Cal. Eliz.* XX, 252.

[4] Murdin, *Burghley State Papers*, p. 396.

[5] *Foreign Cal. Eliz.* XXI, i, 580 seqq.; cf. *Hatfield MSS.* iii, 314 seqq. It is very probable that Stafford played this same trick on Mendoza on the occasion referred to in *Spanish Cal. Eliz.* iv, 194.

given to Mendoza by Stafford, and if the latter's devices for deceiving his opponents suggest that his relations with Guise and Mendoza are instances of such deception – and thus far the argument has progressed – then we must see whether any evidence other than Mendoza's suggests a doubt about Stafford's innocence. That evidence is contained in the reports of two of Walsingham's spies. The first spy was Thomas Rogers, who was in France in the autumn of 1585 and returned to England, probably in the spring of 1586. We have a report of his on Stafford written apparently in June 1586 after his return. It accuses him of showing Guise his dispatches in return for 6000 crowns, and makes minor but grave charges against him in connection with Charles Arundel.[1] Probably it was another of Rogers' reports which Burghley told Stafford of in December 1585, but unfortunately we only possess Stafford's reply and this leaves the nature of the charges obscure. Evidently Stafford's relations with Arundel were condemned, and Arundel's with Guise. 'It is a thing', wrote Stafford,

> that carrieth no sense.... My dallying with Charles Arundel is not unknown to Mr Secretary, as I can show by the answers of his letters to me with his own hand in cipher; but which way I deal, it is not reason anybody should know it but them that I may trust well, which truly is not he. And in my opinion men should not in this place look with whom he that is in it dealeth, but look to the effect of his doings and let him answer it.[2]

It is not easy to determine whether Rogers was told to pry into Stafford's affairs or not; more probably one secret service happened to stumble across another, just as Stafford in 1588 stumbled across one of Walsingham's spies and did not know what to make of him, except that he was a dissolute and profane creature.[3] Nor is it easy to say what impression Rogers'

[1] *Foreign Cal. Eliz.* XXI, i, 34 seqq. [2] Ibid. XX, 221-2.
[3] Harleian MS. 288, fol. 218, Stafford to Walsingham, July 10th, 1588.

reports made on Walsingham, although it is well to remember that there is a vast difference between Walsingham seizing on certain points to criticize Stafford or undermine his credit, and his believing in the charge of treason. If a message of Walsingham's, to which Stafford replied on April 24th, 1586, referred to Rogers' accusations – and I think this very probable – then it would seem that Walsingham dealt honourably with Stafford and told him of them. 'I marvel what bad disposed people', wrote Stafford in reply,

> can have talked of me with such untruths as I find by your speeches with Tupper, and as I heard from others.... I have committed the truth to this bearer, and beseech you to give credit to him reporting it, and to me who send it, and crave your word in my absence to assure that which I send to you to be true.

Perhaps Stafford had Rogers in mind when he said that he suspected the author to be 'one that is gone naughtily and secretly from hence; ... as very a knave and as very a fool withal as any is in England or France'.[1] Walsingham's reply was reassuring. Probably it contained the promise referred to by Stafford when the second spy's report fell into Walsingham's hands; namely, to believe nothing of Stafford but when he had first, by making him acquainted with it, tried the truth, and to remain Stafford's friend.[2]

Unfortunately, the argument will not remain simple, for it is difficult to reconcile this friendly acquittal with the instructions given to Rogers – apparently by Thomas Mills, Walsingham's servant, and apparently in June 1586[3] – to restate his charges against Stafford. However, it is enough for our purpose, I think, to know that Stafford at this time repudiated such

[1] *Foreign Cal. Eliz.* XX, 574.
[2] Ibid. XX, 606; ibid. XXI, i, 662-3.
[3] Both the name of the addressee and the date of Rogers' letter are conjectural; but so is my interpretation of Stafford's letter of April 24th. I think it wisest to leave the difficulty merely stated.

charges against him as he heard of, and was able to explain the circumstances which gave rise to them. It may even be more significant to learn that he knew, before ever he entered upon his relations with Mendoza, that tales about his actions were likely to be told at home.

The second spy was the notorious Gilbert Gifford, Walsingham's tool in the Babington plot. When in France in 1587, he was told by Thomas Philips in Walsingham's name to watch Stafford, and copies of some of his letters came into the latter's hands when he was arrested in Paris in December that year. Unfortunately, the copies in which we are interested are missing, but they were, to use Stafford's own words, 'the most villainous against me and mine that could be'. Among other charges that Stafford instances are these: 'that Charles Arundel, that haunted me, was the rankest traitor that was on this side the seas; that he haunted me by the Spanish ambassador's appointment; that God knew what practice was between him and me'. Stafford poured his soul out in a letter to Burghley. The charges are such, he wrote, 'as both I and mine are in worse predicament than the confessed traitors that are on this side the sea.... And upon these practices and such-like are come all the good offices done with her Majesty of me and all mine'. To Walsingham he wrote a vigorous protest and announced his intention of seeking leave to withdraw from his post as soon as he decently could. It is tantalizing that again, when our perplexities might have vanished, the all-important document is missing. We only have Stafford's acknowledgment of Walsingham's reply. Whether the explanation which he gave of Gifford's instructions and behaviour was a genuine one or only a lame excuse which Stafford perforce accepted — I 'am contented to swallow anything for the time', Stafford had told Burghley — is not clear. What is clear is that Walsingham was anxious to assure Stafford that there was not the slightest smirch on his fame. It was a complete exoneration.[1]

[1] *Foreign Cal. Eliz.* XXI, i, 485, 548, 662 seqq.

How far, if at all, Stafford went in informing the authorities at home of his relations with Guise and Mendoza is not an easy question to answer. The review that I have given of his schemes of deception suggests that he was generally careful to secure approval of his plans, even though he was apt to enter upon them before writing home and consequently found himself compelled to withdraw as tactfully as he could when the Queen vetoed his proposals. It was dangerous enough, he thought, to enter into relations with the Queen's opponents even with authority: I have a lesson, he told Burghley, 'to take the less care to break my head by accepting so dangerous a course as that would have been to me' – the course being, I think, that pretence of friendship with Mary Stuart's adherents which Elizabeth would not let him pursue.[1] And the caution against acting without warrant, which the Queen's repeated chidings must have conveyed, was reinforced by his conviction that Walsingham was constantly on the look-out for an excuse to disgrace him:

> Yf I had nott so badd frendes att home [runs one of his plaints to Burghley] and mought followe thatt course thatt I kowlde best fynde expedient heere withowte danger of false interpretation, your lordship showld finde I wolde knowe more of theire [i.e. the Queen's opponents'] secretes then I doe; butt to hazarde the perill of evyll disposed parsons' power to have thinges misconstered [i.e. misconstrued] and to have thinges well ment evyll taken, I had rather then [i.e. than] to venter to doe well and have no thankes, nott hazarde so mutche and sleepe in a whole skinne.[2]

It is clear that Stafford felt a constraint upon the liberty of action to which he thought an ambassador had a right in organizing his secret service; but that is not to say that he did

[1] *Foreign Cal. Eliz.* XIX, 653.
[2] Cotton MS. Galba E. VI, fol. 219, Stafford to Burghley, April 6th, 1584.

not think a measure of liberty was left. In using an intermediary (Charles Arundel) in his relations with Guise, he avoided direct relations and met what I take to have been the principle of Elizabeth's objection to his earlier Guise scheme. Moreover, since being told of that objection Alençon had died, the League had been formed in France, the Throckmorton plot had been discovered, and it had therefore become much more incumbent upon him to watch the Duke of Guise. The veto which had been placed on consorting with Charles Arundel had been lifted, and Walsingham, as we have seen, knew that Stafford was 'dallying with' him. Perhaps that is the extent of the authority Stafford had for his dealings with Guise. Perhaps – though I am inclined to doubt it – some allusion to these dealings was made in cipher letters of his about new schemes for which he wanted Elizabeth's approval in December 1585.[1] If the latter is true, then before his letters reached home the report had been received in which his name was linked with Arundel's and Arundel's with Guise. At any rate, Stafford had warrant for using Arundel and, since the latter frequented Guise's house, Stafford naturally used him there.

Much the same is to be said of Stafford's relations with Mendoza. Arundel was a pensioner of Spain and haunted Mendoza's house. Walsingham almost certainly knew that Stafford's Spanish news came through him: 'As for Arundel', Stafford wrote when inveighing against Gifford's accusations, 'you know that in the beginning I writ to you of it and you advised it.'[2] The actual device that Stafford adopted both with Guise and Mendoza may strike us as suspicious. We have seen, however, that it was not alien to his genius, nor was it alien to the genius of his age. That is not all. Stafford had to provide a cloak for his dealings with Arundel, since in a society honeycombed with spies few things could be kept secret for

[1] *Foreign Cal. Eliz.* XIX, 211, 222.

[2] Ibid. XXI, i, 664; for the pressure on Stafford to secure Spanish news cf. ibid. XX, 314, 361-2, 550.

long; and, by pretending to play his country false, he left Guise and Mendoza perfectly content to learn that Arundel haunted his house. In other words, Stafford's money difficulties made feasible a form of deception which other reasons prompted.

Dr Read is inclined to think that Arundel played both sides false. That was not Stafford's opinion, and for my part I would find it extremely difficult to square with my reading of the *Spanish Calendar*. 'No man of this side', Stafford told Walsingham after Arundel's death,

> served my turn as he did for her Majesty's service, and never Spanish ambassador nor his master were better handled.... I have had a great loss of him, for the certainest and quickest advertisements out of Spain I had of him; for the Spanish ambassador had that credit in him as he hid nothing that was reasonable from him. He had continually letters from Sir Francis Inglefield and Pridieux, whose letters I ever saw afore he deciphered them; and ... the advertisements that he gave me first were ever confirmed ... by those letters that came to the Venice ambassador, and the advertisements that Pinard sent me as they came from their agent.[1]

If a critic were still to cling to a belief in Stafford's treason he would have to imagine that the man was monstrously foolhardy, for even after Gifford's, the second, betrayal of Stafford's dealings, Julio or the new friend or the new confidant continued to pour his news into Mendoza's ear. In fact, the most palpable acts of treason, according to Dr Read, were yet to come. But the truth is that Julio went on, not until the defeat of the Armada shook his faith in Philip as the next sovereign of England – an idea Dr Read advances – but until 'the new confidant' told a tale about Don Antonio's agent in Paris who, unknown to him, was in Mendoza's pay, and Mendoza

[1] *Foreign Cal. Eliz.* XXI, i, 663, and cf. p. 664: 'In the end I think Philippes himself is not so honest a man as I made Arundel, nor did not the Queen so good service.'

took the trouble to test it.[1] In other words, the gull became suspicious and Julio gradually vanishes, as he might have vanished before if Mendoza had been more sceptical.[2]

One task remains, and that is to explain Stafford's relations with Walsingham. The explanation turns, I think, on a division in Elizabeth's Council which Dr Read himself has made clear. There were two parties, the one a war party with Leicester and Walsingham at the head, the other a peace — though not a pacifist — party led by Burghley. Stafford quite definitely aligned himself with Burghley. He sent him regularly copies of his letters to Walsingham and the Queen,[3] and added personal letters, sometimes unimportant, being merely covering notes, sometimes so confidential that he asked Burghley, perhaps to divulge their contents to no one unless to the Queen, perhaps to burn them. It is one of our misfortunes that the greater part of this correspondence is missing, and the injunction to burn some of the letters leaves one speculating about the nature and fate of the rest. He poured out his complaints against Walsingham, while Burghley in return warned Stafford of criticism against him at home and occasionally confided his own grievances, though it seems in a manner more measured.

Now one must distinguish between the mere rancour of party-feeling and the clash of policies from which it largely sprang. The former will explain much in the relations of Walsingham and Stafford. I think it not incautious to assume that Walsingham would have been glad to see Stafford withdrawn from his embassy and replaced by a friendly or neutral ambassador, who would be less the agent of Burghley than of

[1] *Spanish Cal. Eliz.* iv, 416.

[2] It seems to me striking evidence of Mendoza's credulity that he swallowed the excuse Stafford advanced for entering on his relations with him. It was surely the most inartistic move in Stafford's game (ibid. iv, 7, and quoted by Dr Read, pp. 302-3).

[3] A notable example is in *Foreign Cal. Eliz.* XXI, i, 568, where Stafford discloses to Burghley the nature of a letter from Elizabeth which Walsingham said was known only to Elizabeth and himself.

himself. After all, a vigorous foreign secretary must have fretted at that division of authority which was at once a cause of faction and the secret of Elizabeth's personal control of affairs. We may give credence then to Stafford's belief, which was shared by Burghley, that the Walsingham party seized upon chances of discrediting him. But Stafford's view of the situation was a jaundiced one. He attributed practically all his rebuffs to Walsingham. When told to write fewer official dispatches and cut his postal expenses, which were too high for Elizabeth's liking, he jumped to the conclusion that here was a device of Walsingham's to make him appear slack in his duty and so have him disgraced. And the latter's suggestion that, notwithstanding Elizabeth's orders, he should send accounts of the daily occurrences in France, which Walsingham would keep to himself lest Elizabeth should fret at the expense, aroused his suspicions: 'I stand somewhat jealous of his meaning toward me by it,' he told Burghley,

> because I have been served but very evil touches since I came hither.... I know that by his means the Queen has had false advertisements of preparations here from his factors and has been incensed that news of importance should come from others, and some have come from me and he has kept them a day and delivered his first.[1]

He also complained to Burghley — this in November 1584 — that Walsingham kept him ignorant of news:

> I never heere lyghtlye of anie thinge from him, yf ytt be nott matter to be delivered by me heere, and yf att anie time I heere anye thinge, which is butt syldomme from him, ytt is so late as I heere ytt from them heere afore I heere ytt owte of Ingland.[2]

Possibly there was more than party rancour to strain their

[1] Cotton MS. Galba E. VI, fols. 218b seq., Stafford to Burghley, April 6th, 1584; *Foreign Cal. 1583-4*, p. 459. Also cf. complaint, ibid. p. 475, last paragraph.
[2] Cotton MS. Galba E. VI, fol. 271, Stafford to Burghley, November 7th, 1584. These are a few examples only of Stafford's complaints.

relations. Elizabeth did not conduct her foreign policy solely through Walsingham. She kept information from him and sometimes acted without his knowledge, though probably with the knowledge of Burghley, who more nearly shared her outlook. But it is easy to exaggerate any difference of policy, and Walsingham after all had to obey the Queen's commands. Let us put the difference at this time — that is, after the intervention in the Netherlands — at a difference between faith and disbelief in the overtures for peace, and therefore between caution on the one hand and on the other a thorough-going enthusiasm for the rebel cause in the Netherlands and the Huguenot-Navarre cause in France. Temperamentally Stafford would have fitted better into the Walsingham party, but he was Burghley's man and there was undoubtedly a relationship between the Queen, Burghley, and himself which excluded Walsingham. How far this went it would be rash to guess in the absence of most of the documents; but even assuming that it amounted to little, Walsingham knew of Stafford's correspondence with Burghley and knew that Elizabeth did not divulge all that was written to her, and he must have desired to know what was kept from him. If his spies pried into Stafford's activities without any other apparent reason, here at any rate is a possible reason.

Certain incidents were hardly likely to make Walsingham trust Stafford. According to the latter, Walsingham instructed him, 'by word of mouth, but never by writing', that he should and might deal in anything Leicester sent him as in her Majesty's own affairs, because now she had entered into open action of government in the Netherlands. Stafford refused to take knowledge of these verbal instructions and so be a party to what he regarded as an attempt to overreach the Queen: 'There was nothing they desired more', he told Burghley, 'than to have her Majesty so far engage herself in name and effect in those matters, as no way she should get out of them again.'[1]

[1] *Foreign Cal. Eliz.* XXI, i, 126.

Also, he probably worked for an alliance between Henry III and Elizabeth with a zeal that did not please Walsingham as much as the Queen. Certainly it did not please the Navarre party. Stafford says that they attempted to prevail upon him to bring about a breach between Henry III and Elizabeth, taking advantage especially of Mary Stuart's execution: in this way they hoped to force Elizabeth to help them more. Stafford's refusal, and other actions of his, led Navarre's agent in Paris to write a long, abusive, and scandalous letter against him — containing, *inter alia*, the charge of misappropriating money — to the agent in London who, according to Stafford, was an intimate of Walsingham's.[1] Stafford got hold of the letter and sent it to Walsingham, asking him to show it to the Queen. At the same time he wrote to Burghley. Not only did Walsingham say nothing to Elizabeth, but he intercepted the letter to Burghley and wrote to Stafford telling him what he had done, begging Stafford, as he loved him and had confidence in him, to keep the incident an absolute secret.[2] Walsingham's action is understandable. He was bent on avoiding harm to the King of Navarre's cause, and Stafford's action must have displeased him.

The brushes between Walsingham and Stafford were intermittent and were sometimes followed by friendly explanations from Walsingham and protestations of friendship from Stafford. But beneath reconciliation there no doubt slumbered distrust. Whether this continued until Walsingham's death I cannot say, as I have not seen the documents beyond the close of the new volume of the *Foreign Calendar* in June 1588. It is possible that the Gifford incident acted as a cathartic, or that the coming of the Armada sank all rancour. However it be, I cannot more appropriately close this article than by quoting a postscript

[1] This was Paul Choart, Seigneur de Buzenval, from whom, so Stafford says, Walsingham hid nothing (cf. *Foreign Cal. Eliz.* XXI, i, 132, 133, 485); and it is worth noting that Stafford seemed to be able to tap Buzenval's correspondence with the agent in Paris, the Abbé del Bene (cf. ibid. pp. 125-6, 484).

[2] Ibid.pp. 374 seqq., 483-4, 485.

added in Walsingham's hand to a letter written to Stafford shortly before his return home:

> Her majestye dothe acknowledge with most gracyowse speeches your good servyce don unto her. I praye god, put in her harte to proportyon her recompence of your servyce according[ly].[1]

[1] Cotton MS. Galba E. VI, fol. 397, Walsingham to Stafford, December 24th, 1588. Stafford returned to England in April 1589. He was sent back to France in the autumn of that year (cf. *Am. Hist. Rev.* xx, 312).

ELIZABETH AND THE NETHERLANDS, 1586-7[1]

With the two latest volumes of the *Foreign Calendar*[2] we begin that separation of the foreign papers, Holland and Flanders, from the general series of *State Papers, Foreign*, which was announced in the last volume of the Calendar and was necessitated by the great increase in these papers after Elizabeth's open intervention in the Low Countries in 1585. The volumes cover the period June 1586-December 1587, roughly coinciding with the period of the Earl of Leicester's rule, who was in the Netherlands from December 1585 to November 1586 and again from June to December 1587, retaining his authority, at least nominally, in the interval between the two seasons of active leadership. The story of these two years has been told by Motley, with such liberal quotations from the English state papers as make the more striking passages in the Calendar familiar; and in recent years the documents have again been surveyed in the scholarly work on Sir Francis Walsingham written by Dr Conyers Read. A reviewer might despair of finding much to say that is new and especially of upsetting any leading judgment; but while I cannot imagine anyone wanting to rehabilitate the principal actor in the story, Leicester, there is one reputation, that of the Queen, which has suffered without an adequate examination of the evidence.

That Elizabeth was parsimonious seems too familiar to be doubted. That her niggardliness was responsible for the chronic poverty of her army in the Netherlands and the sufferings of her soldiers, appears to be placed beyond question both by the complaints of her officers and officials, and the

[1] Published in the *English Historical Review* (July 1930), xlv, 373-96.

[2] *Calendar of State Papers, Foreign Series, of the Reign of Elizabeth*, vol. XXI, parts ii and iii, ed. by Sophie Crawford Lomas and A. B. Hinds (London: H.M. Stationery Office, 1927, 1929).

undoubted reluctance of Elizabeth to supply them with the money they demanded. However, the story has another side to it, which has so impressed itself upon me in reading these new volumes of the *Foreign Calendar* that I have ventured to turn my review of them into a study of Elizabeth's army finance. It will, I hope, prompt similar investigations of other Elizabethan campaigns. Parsimony may be a misleading word without facts to explain it. I propose to present those facts, so far as I can collect them from the Calendar, for the first two years of the Netherlands campaign.

We must start with the treaty obligations which Elizabeth undertook when in 1585 she agreed to send an army to the Netherlands.[1] They were heavier than any reasonably optimistic person could have anticipated in the first stages of the negotiations. Beginning with a relatively scanty offer, the Queen was at length drawn in the preliminary agreement of August 12th to maintain a force in the Netherlands of 4000 foot, 400 horse, and 700 men for garrison duty. She had apparently conceded her utmost. Antwerp fell, and, stirred by the loss, she increased her obligations to 5000 foot and 1000 horse. Here she intended to stop, but pressure from the Dutch and from her own Councillors wrung a final concession from her: she agreed to make this force additional to the English garrisons in the cautionary towns, thus adding the cost of 450 foot for Brill and 700 foot for Flushing and making her total commitments amount to 6150 foot — there were actually 6400 — and 1000 horse.[2] In addition she was saddled with the payment of the English general and the chief officers of the field. This charge she believed that the Dutch had agreed to bear; but their story was that, when under discussion, they had neither allowed nor disallowed it; hence by their subtlety they postponed the

[1] Cf. Read, *Sir Francis Walsingham*, iii, 107 seq.

[2] Cf. *Cabala* (1691 ed.), ii, 54-5. The garrisons in the cautionary towns were increased to 1400, making the total 6400 (S.P. Holland, Eliz. xvi, 40, xix, fol. 211 seqq.). Ibid. vi, 17, calculates 43 companies of 150 each, and ix, 36 seems to suggest that the total was 6750. The latter I think wrong and 6400 right.

issue until Elizabeth was fully engaged in the war, when they flatly refused to pay.[1] Perforce Elizabeth paid; she insisted, however, on regarding the States as responsible for the money and excluded it from her commitments. She had been driven step by step to the utmost limits of the help that she felt she could afford. If after this she expected to keep to her commitments and resisted with singular tenacity being dragged into an abyss of extraordinary expenses, we can at least appreciate her conduct.

She translated her commitments into a money charge of £126,180 10s. per annum, calculated from an establishment list and rates of pay.[2] It is well to remember that the charge equalled about two-thirds of the ordinary expenditure of her government at the time and about one-half of the ordinary receipts.[3] She kept the sum constantly in mind and allowed no one the slightest excuse for imagining that it would be or could be increased.

What, then, did she actually pay? I will trace individual payments later. For the moment I confine myself to a general financial statement for the first two years.

Down to October 11th, 1586, she paid out £154,620.[4] To arrive at a figure which will approximately represent what the cost ought to have been to that date, we must separate the first four months to December 11th, 1585, during which the full burden of the Queen's rate did not fall upon her and ought not to have done. It is extremely difficult to name a sum for these months. Elizabeth's view was that the full treaty obligations did not begin until November 12th and therefore to that date the cost of 4000 foot only ought to have been borne. Actually, an extra thousand foot was taken into her pay on

[1] *Foreign Cal.* XXI, ii, 40, 109.

[2] S.P. Holland, Eliz. ix, 37.

[3] Cf. Scott, *Joint Stock Companies*, iii, 485 seqq.

[4] I arrive at this figure by taking £153,000 paid out by privy seal to October 3rd, 1586 (S.P. Holland, Eliz. xiv, 106) and adding a sum of £1620 defalked for armour and credited to the treasurer (cf. ibid. ix, 36). I suspect that this latter figure really ought to be larger (cf. ibid. v, 98). The monthly reckonings began on the 12th of one month and ended on the 11th of the next.

September 27th; and I include them in my calculation. We must also include the cost of coat, conduct, and transportation money. I think an estimate of £29,000[1] to December 11th would have been regarded by Elizabeth as excessive, and that in adopting it I am therefore erring on the right side. To this we must add the cost of ten months at £126,000 per annum, which equals £105,000, thus bringing my estimate of what the cost ought to have been down to October 11th, 1586, to the sum of £134,000.

From that date to December 11th, 1587, a sum of £144,140 was paid out,[2] making a total to date, including the period already discussed, of £298,760.[3] The total charges from August 1585 to December 1587 ought to have been £134,000 plus £147,000 or £281,000 in all, to which we may add £15,000 promised as an additional contribution for the year to 1587.[4] Thus payments equalled £298,760 and charges ought to have amounted to £296,000.

[1] I arrive at this figure by taking the under-treasurer's statement of £25,019 for the payments to December 11th (ibid. v, 98) and adding a figure of £3875 for coat, conduct, and transportation found in the treasurer's account (*Foreign Cal.* XXI, ii, 351). The former figure includes three items, amounting to £290, which Elizabeth would probably have challenged. I have checked the items of pay, and they equal full pay at the rate of £170 per month per company, with no deductions for wastage in numbers. Consequently I regard the figure as on the high side when we are merely considering what the cost theoretically ought to have been. Actually, the treasurer's account (ibid.) shows a total of £29,025 for this period as against the figure of £25,019 taken by me; but his item of infantry's wages, to cite one example only, equals the pay of 37 companies for four months, which certainly was not a legitimate charge. The figure for coat, conduct, and transportation is the only one in the treasurer's account, except the immediately preceding item for pioneers who were in the States' pay. The £3875 may include money paid for troops in the States' pay, but I think not. Its error, for our purpose, if error there be, is on the high side.

[2] I arrive at this figure by adding to the money paid out (£143,703 in all) two sums, totalling £439, for armour, munition, and powder to be defalked from the companies' pay (S.P. Holland, Eliz. xix, 211 seqq.).

[3] This total does not include sums totalling £15,600, of which £13,000 was for the levy of horse (ibid. xix, 222). If any of this was defalcable on the pay of the horse it should show as an addition to my total. Nor does my total represent the whole amount really laid out by Elizabeth, as a result of the war: it does not, for example, include the charge of ships kept upon the narrow seas towards Flanders, which by December 11th, 1587, had amounted to £47,695 (ibid. fol. 230).

[4] Cf. below, p. 178.

The charges, however, exceeded that sum, and the pay of Elizabeth's troops was badly in arrears in December 1587. I cannot give the amount owing at that date, but over £40,000 was owing on July 11th, 1587,[1] and an idea of the situation may be gained from an estimate by the Privy Council in that month — too conservative, I fear, in its figure — which puts the charge for the two years November 1585-November 1587 at £313,000.[2] Consequently, in the two years or so with which we are dealing we can say that Elizabeth paid out rather more than she had undertaken to do, and yet her charges were far from met. Why was this?

I begin the answer by noting the financial provisions of the States for the troops in their pay. For 1586 they undertook to furnish an ordinary contribution of £20,000 per month, and an extraordinary one of £10,000 per month for the four months March-June to meet the expenses of the summer campaign.[3] In all, the provision for 1586 was £280,000, which with Elizabeth's £126,000 brought the total to £406,000. I am not considering delays in payment of the contributions. Delays were natural, if not inevitable, in that age; and Dutch easily outdid English. They merely intensified a problem, bad enough without them. The cost of the whole army, Dutch and English, in a month of maximum expenses, namely September, was estimated at £65,136 per month.[4] For the whole year the cost in money and debts was said by Wilkes to have been over £560,000, while Norris, separating the States' and Elizabeth's charges, put the former at £432,473 and the latter at passing £150,000.[5] Thus the cost of the whole army that year exceeded the provision by at least £150,000.

Since Elizabeth's liability was limited, there can be no question that all extra charges ought by right to have fallen

[1] Cf. below, p. 197.
[2] Dasent, *Acts of Privy Council*, xv, 176.
[3] *Foreign Cal.* XX, 347; Bruce, *Leycester Correspondence*, p. 426.
[4] *Foreign Cal.* XXI, ii, 176.
[5] Ibid. p. 315; XXI, iii, 14.

on the States. They had therefore failed to cut thir coat according to their cloth, for though the charges were probably not beyond the wealth of a country with many war profiteers, they were certainly beyond its taxing powers. It matters little to my argument whether the States were right in imputing the blame to Leicester, or the latter in denying that he raised troops without their authority, or indeed whether both were responsible for the muddle.[1] Leicester showed himself singularly optimistic, stupid, or dishonest. In February 1586 he wrote to Burghley expressing the hope that the £20,000 per month from the States would suffice for their ordinary garrisons and present men of war, and vowed that he would not 'press or move her Majesty for one penny more than she hath promised and contracted with these States'. Davison, by no means lukewarm in the cause, writing home only a few weeks later, remarked that the States' troops could hardly be paid by their government's contributions were it not that 'they think they have done well if they pay 6 months out of twelve'.[2]

The mere fact that Elizabeth was intimately linked to insolvency through the dual position of Leicester as general of her troops and governor of the Netherlands, put her finances in danger; and the danger became desperate owing to the further confusion that there were English troops in the States' pay. At the height of their numbers, in September 1586, these troops totalled 7512 foot and some 550 horse.[3] A month earlier Wilkes had written home a warning: Dutch means, he remarked, were 'so weak, as not able to maintain the third part of their numbers here in pay; and yet there come daily now hither forces, as well from England as from Scotland, whom they are not onely not able to pay, but not in case to feed'.[4] The inevitable happened. Money meant for the companies in Elizabeth's pay was diverted to save the English troops in the States' pay—and

[1] Cf. Leicester's defence, *Foreign Cal.* XXI, ii, 191.
[2] Ibid. XX, 347, 394.
[3] Ibid. XXI, ii, 176.
[4] *Cabala*, ii, 7.

even on one occasion at least, Dutch troops[1] — from mutiny and starvation.

This, however, was not the only way in which Elizabeth's money was diverted. The cost of levying the English companies in the States' pay was borne in England and credited to the treasurer-at-war, to whom it was repayable by the States in the Netherlands. Hence it was nominally available for the pay of Elizabeth's troops. In fact, it was not repaid, or was repaid after intolerable delay and with infinite pains.[2] By October 11th, 1586, according to English reckonings a sum of £25,740, which included the pay of the chief officers of the field as well as the diversions of money just mentioned, was due from the States.[3] It is not an adequate measure of the harm done by parasitic Dutch finance, for it does not include the sums which were advanced and repaid and which while unpaid increased the confusion of the English accounts and the hardships of Elizabeth's soldiers.

The £25,740 due from the States remained due. When pressure was put upon them in the summer of 1587 to repay, they replied that they — by which they meant chiefly their towns and possibly even individual merchants — had advanced more than that sum in money and victuals to Elizabeth's troops. Assuming that the States were taking credit for debts contracted by Elizabeth's captains with towns and burghers, the contention was no doubt sound, especially by June 1587. It reminds us that there was a Dutch side to this business of credit, of which we shall obtain a glimpse later. But it was no satisfaction to Elizabeth; for if this sum was to be debited against her treasurer's account and not against her captains' private accounts — in other words if she was to be responsible for her captains' debts — then it should also have been credited

[1] Cf. below, p. 187.
[2] Cf. *Foreign Cal.* XXI, ii, 140.
[3] Ibid. XXI, iii, 486. The sum seems to vary, but the £20,804 noted, ibid. XXI, ii, 351, does not include the pay of the chief officers (cf. the original document). Also cf. *Acts of Privy Council*, xv, 177, and *Foreign Cal.* XXI, iii, 166.

in the treasurer's account by way of deductions from the pay of the companies which had received the money and victuals. This will explain itself when I discuss the army system of pay. In fact, it had not been so credited, nor had a list or account of the advances been presented to Elizabeth's officials, nor could one be obtained from the States, press as these officials and the Privy Council would. It was an impossible situation, for with the passing of time any figures produced by the States would be less capable of verification and the recovery of the money from captains and soldiers less feasible.[1]

The year 1586 wrecked all hope of moderately straight accounts. It hardened Elizabeth in her efforts to keep within commitments, and taught the States a lesson. During the winter the States cassed or dismissed most of their English companies; but such had been the wastage from desertion and other causes — a normal occurrence in those days — that the discharged men could be drafted into Elizabeth's companies without even bringing these to full strength.[2]

In June 1587 the States had a nominal force of 1800 English foot in their pay. Actually the number was 1400. They were determined to limit their obligations, and no doubt their experience with English troops in 1586 and the fear of false play aroused by various incidents — by Stanley's betrayal of Deventer in January and the peace negotiations maintained by Elizabeth — strengthened other reasons which led them to refuse flatly to entertain more than 1800-2000 Englishmen. Their plans for 1587 were arranged with Lord Buckhurst, who went out as ambassador during Leicester's absence in England. An army for garrison and field, including a force of German horse and foot, was to be raised, which it was calculated would involve an extraordinary expenditure of £150,000 over and above their ordinary contribution of £20,000 per month. Of this sum they agreed to raise £100,000 themselves and asked

[1] *Cabala*, ii, 43; *Foreign Cal.* XXI, iii, 244, 256-7, 312.
[2] Ibid. XXI, ii, 244, 261, 265.

Elizabeth to contribute the other third.[1] An earlier attempt to persuade the Queen to increase her contribution, inspired by Leicester, had been met with scorn and indignation: reasonably enough, Elizabeth expected straighter financial dealings before being asked to subsidize a bankrupt concern still further.[2] On this later occasion she seems to have been advised by someone that a smaller army would be equally efficient, if only less men were immured in garrisons, and that consequently the £100,000 promised by the States was adequate. She offered to contribute an extra £15,000, but no more. What the Dutch did in fact raise by way of extraordinary contribution, the Calendar does not indicate. In September Leicester was writing of it as still a promise, but a promise now converted from £100,000 into £80,000.[3]

In these circumstances Elizabeth was asking for trouble when she dispatched a new force of 4650 foot[4] to the Netherlands in June-July 1587, expecting the States to take them into their pay. She had succumbed to pressure from Leicester, who was still, we must remember, governor of the Netherlands, even while resident in England. There is this to be said for Leicester, that it was obvious from reports he received – and events when he reached the country substantiated them – that he would have to depend upon his own resources for the relief of besieged Sluys; while he hoped to be able to substitute the English

[1] *Cabala*, ii, 15, 17, 45-6.

[2] *Foreign Cal.* XXI, ii, 174, 229, 357.

[3] Ibid. XXI, iii, 181-2, 325.

[4] The question of the number is a little puzzling, and Dr Read has a note on it (op. cit. iii, 245, n. 3). The numbers he cites can be reconciled in the following way. Elizabeth arranged to levy 6000 more men. Her plan was that 1500 were to supply wastages in her own companies; 1500 to supply ten new companies in the States' pay, which by a misunderstanding of Buckhurst's letters she thought they had agreed to; and 3000 to be the extraordinary foot-bands. She learnt from Buckhurst that wastages in her own companies required only 1000 and that at most 600 could be sent to bring the States' English foot to 2000. If we assume that 6000 men were levied and that the States finally limited their numbers to 1800, then 1400 men represented replacements, leaving 4600 for the new companies. The actual figure of the latter was 4650, or 31 companies (*Cabala*, ii, 25, 45-6, 48; *Acts of Privy Council*, xv, 128; *Foreign Cal.* XXI, iii, 116).

troops for the German mercenaries, counting from experience on the latter refusing to fulfil their engagement. The Germans did in fact finally refuse to march without a guarantee of their wages from Elizabeth, so strong was her credit and so weak that of the States; but Leicester's other assumption, that he could substitute his English for the Germans, was a false hope.[1]

When the order was given for raising this new English army it was not known that the States would refuse to entertain them. A letter from Buckhurst, however, made this clear, and Elizabeth in consequence wanted to stop the levy. Leicester, as we have seen, persuaded her to let the troops go over, but he was ordered to send them back if the States refused to take them into their pay. To all appearance Elizabeth had safeguarded herself against a repetition of last year's extraordinary expenses, for not only was there this order; the extra £15,000 which she had agreed to furnish was in Leicester's hands to be spent on these troops,[2] and should have sufficed to see them paid and home again if after a month or so the States persisted in their attitude. It was a sound plan, except that Leicester had to execute it. The money disappeared, and from talk on July 27th of returning the men as fast as he could, Leicester took to pleading that he could not send them back unpaid; and so they remained in the Netherlands until October 14th, when the treasurer was busy paying and dispatching them.[3]

Thus in the summer of 1587, over and above Elizabeth's ordinary forces, there were 1800 to 2000 — probably 1800 — Englishmen nominally in the States' pay, and 4650 nominally in no one's pay. The former, in addition to the latter, became a burden on English finances, diverting money that was meant for the ordinary forces; and here also Elizabeth tried to stop the drain and confusion by ordering Leicester in August to discharge all Englishmen in the States' pay who could not be

[1] *Foreign Cal.* XXI, iii, 128, 322.
[2] Ibid. p. 116.
[3] Ibid. pp. 200, 307, 317, 370.

drafted into her own companies, unless relief for them was speedily forthcoming from the Dutch.[1] Whether her order was obeyed, I cannot say. The year 1587 consequently repeated the year 1586, and this despite all Elizabeth's precautions. We can express the burden in figures. Elizabeth claimed the pay of the 4650 foot from the Dutch, and a sum of £26,151 appears as the money disbursed to the use of the States in that year.[2]

Our story is as yet only half told, and as sorry a tale of confusion remains to be unfolded in the financing of Elizabeth's own troops. From many points of view the army was like an aggregate of mercenary companies, hiring themselves through their captains. The captain stood between the Queen's officials and his men, in some respects the exploiter of their labour, in others their representative and defender. He was to a certain extent responsible for arming, clothing, and feeding them, all of which were expenses covered by their pay; and if provision of these necessities was made by royal officials — which was not necessarily the case — the sums expended were charged against the company and settled between the treasurer-at-war and the captain when payment was made. The captain was also responsible, so far as the supply of men allowed, for maintaining his company at its proper strength; his clerk kept muster rolls to record changes in numbers, and accounts to show how the company stood with the treasurer. When money was not forthcoming from the treasurer, or victuals from the victualler — that is to say, from royal officials — the captain pledged his credit with city, merchant, or anyone he could, to keep his men going; and when money was forthcoming, he redeemed his credit so far as he could or would, and from the residue paid to his men, not necessarily their due, but what he thought fit.

Payment therefore involved a settling of accounts with the Crown and also a settling of what we may call the private debts of the company; and it was natural for the captain, who

[1] *Foreign Cal.* XXI, iii, 223, 289.

[2] Ibid. p. 348.

controlled the company's accounts, to be left to settle with his men at his own discretion, even though the Queen's instructions were for the treasurer to pay by poll. It was the captain's prerogative over his soldiers, as one of them put it, and when the experience of its abuses in 1586 made Elizabeth insist peremptorily on payment by poll, her orders were only carried out in the face of strong opposition and were soon being neglected as of old. The whole system put a premium on corruption, offering the captain a double chance of fraud, at the expense of his men and the expense of the Queen. And where fraud was so easy, it flourished. There were captains whose one idea was to get rich quick and others, dubbed 'Court captains', who left their companies in the trying winter season, when money was short and their personal credit most needed, to flaunt themselves at Court in England.[1]

The key to understanding this army system is a distinction between the word 'pay' and the words 'imprest' or 'lendings'. Strictly speaking pay was the final payment of wages for a given period. The full pay of a company of 150 men was at first £170 and after Leicester's arrival £176 5s. per month.[2] If, in the intervals between pay, money was forthcoming, then imprests were made from time to time or the troops were paid a weekly imprest known as lendings — really a subsistence allowance, differing in amount but generally £20 per week for each company or half a crown per man. If money was not forthcoming, the victualler might be able to supply food. If this failed, then the company was left to its own resources and went through the gambit of the captain's credit, threats, mutiny, desertion, and starvation. There were few soldiers, English, Dutch, or Spanish, in the Netherlands who did not know that gambit.

Ideally 'payments' should have been monthly, but it will

[1] Cf. *inter alia, Foreign Cal.* XXI, ii, 314, 324; XXI, iii, 14, 22, 84; *Leycester Correspondence*, pp. 357-8; *Cabala*, ii, 13.
[2] Cf. below, p. 185.

be readily understood, in view of the system of imprests, that they might drift hopelessly into arrears without disaster; and such an entry as the following in the Calendar under September 26th, 1587[1] — 'this garrison ... in October will have been twelve months without pay' — is much less startling than one who does not know the technical meaning of the word 'pay' could suspect. Arrears of pay, in fact, are a much surer measure of the confusion of accounts than of the misery of troops.

Payment was a complicated process. The muster-master mustered each company — examining the men's 'furniture, arming and training' —saw the muster rolls or 'books of poll' kept by the captain's clerk, and on the basis of these and his own muster made a statement of the 'checks' to be deducted for soldiers 'dead, discharged or departed'. Defalcations or deductions were also made for armour, clothing, or victuals supplied by the Queen's officials and for advances in money for which the treasurer was directly or indirectly responsible; and all deductions being subtracted, the residue that was outstanding, to the date to which payment was being made — which might not, of course, even approximate to the day on which the money was disbursed — was paid to the captain by the treasurer.[2]

Obviously it was essential in Elizabeth's interests to have frequent musters in order to control the captains' muster rolls and make proper checks for shortages. But there were many obstacles in the way. In the first place a muster to the soldier meant pay — at least it did in 1586[3] — and without pay was likely to lead to mutiny. 'Without pay', wrote Leicester on

[1] *Foreign Cal.* XXI, iii, 334.

[2] Cf. *inter alia*, ibid. XX, 198, 278.

[3] No 'pay' was made in 1586-7 to a date later than October 11th, 1586; at least for Elizabeth's ordinary troops. Apparently musters ceased to denote 'pay' and Leicester issued orders — one cannot believe they were obeyed — for monthly or, 'at the farthest', quarterly musters (cf. *Acts of Privy Council*, xv, 412; *Foreign Cal.* XXI, iii, 324). In December 1586 the muster-master wrote: 'The musters are already taken of all the forces, but not one penny ready to pay them ... so what will follow thereof, God knoweth' (ibid. XXI, ii, 254). This probably is the point at which the wrath from afar — Elizabeth's — overcame the fear at hand; and represents the end of the doctrine, muster equals 'pay'.

March 15th, 1586, 'there can be no muster, and till pay the old rolls come on, be the bands never so weak. And it is the thing the captain desireth, never to have full pay, but to run on with imprests, for so shall his bands be never looked into.' The captains were to have a surfeit of this Elysium. Their frauds, however, continued, and in October Leicester was telling the same tale: for lack of money and a true muster roll 'there will be whole bands demanded for half bands, and all the world cannot help it, do what man can'.[1] We can understand that, when in July 1586 the muster-master was mustering companies and checking accounts to make a pay for the period December 1585 to April 1586, his chance of controlling the captains' figures was remote. Against adequate checks the whole army was in conspiracy, from the general, who had his own troop of horse, down to the meanest captain of foot, and even including the treasurer who took his hundredth penny as fee and profited the more the more he paid. The muster-master, who, with the Queen, alone benefited from checks, taking a percentage for his fee, was outwitted and overborne.

There were other obstacles in the way of musters. The English companies were scattered in garrison over the country, and the muster-master's task was peripatetic and very uncertain when he had to cope with obstinate captains or captains whose muster rolls and accounts were not ready. Elizabeth made provision for this in June 1586 by allowing him to appoint substitutes in every province.[2] But this eased one obstacle only. Another was the treaty right of the States to be represented by their commissioners at musters, the reason for this being that Elizabeth's payments, according to the treaty, were no more than loans, to be repaid after the war was ended. After the first general muster in 1585 this provision of the treaty was ignored, until the States protested in July 1586 and questioned their liability for payments over which they had had no

[1] *Foreign Cal.* XX, 285, 447; XXI, ii, 191; *Leycester Correspondence*, p. 325.
[2] *Foreign Cal.* XXI, ii, 41.

supervision. Consequently the muster-master was compelled to support another hindrance to his duties, and if his complaints are true it was no slight one, what with the accustomed dilatoriness of Dutch official action and their deliberate delay when fresh troops arrived from England, a delay made in the sure hope that by the time musters were taken wastage would have diminished the number of men, and they would consequently be able to challenge the English figures.[1]

We are now in command of sufficient knowledge to follow in detail the financing of Elizabeth's army and appreciate the problems with which she was struggling. Financial provision was made for the launching and first payments of Elizabeth's forces by a privy seal for £5000 to John Norris, who was in command till Leicester's arrival, and one for £17,000 to the treasurer-at-war. The former was dated June 21st, 1585, the latter July 30th. A further privy seal for £10,000 was issued to the treasurer on October 10th.[2] The preliminary expenses consisted of coat and conduct money and cost of transportation, and an imprest of approximately half a month's pay.[3] This was the cost of levy. The imprest was supposed to be defalked from the troops' 'pay', as also was the cost of armour which the treasurer had not borne himself and which therefore ranked as an additional credit to him, available for payments. Monthly payments were contemplated, and according to calculations at home the money in the Netherlands was sufficient to meet them. But after one month's pay had been made, the officials got into difficulties and were only able to keep the men from starving by raising loans from English merchants. The reason for this was that money disbursed by the treasurer in England for the levy of voluntary troops serving in the States' pay, and repayable promptly in the Netherlands by the States, was not repaid. Also, the defalcations from Elizabeth's own troops

[1] *Foreign Cal.* XXI, ii, 90-1, 231; iii, 312.
[2] S.P. Holland, Eliz. xiv, 106.
[3] Cf. *Foreign Cal.* XIX, 647.

were not recovered rapidly enough. And finally, additional troops were taken over from the States' pay into Elizabeth's before November 12th, when by treaty, according to her view, her full obligations began.

This was the situation when Leicester arrived in the Netherlands. A privy seal for £20,000, dated November 14th, 1585, had been issued, and most of the money arrived with him.[1] Part was used to make a full payment to December 11th, from which day Leicester's regime may be said to commence. The new regime was signalized by an increase in the rates of pay, which instantly converted Elizabeth's calculation of £126,180 10s. per annum into £133,994 10s. or more.[2] After consultation with the captains, who naturally did not say no, Leicester arranged an increase of £6 per company monthly, and a reduction of six men,[3] in doing which he broke the treaty terms as well as the Queen's orders, and gave the States further reason for objecting to English accounts. The increase almost certainly was in the pay of the officers. In fact, an all-round increase for gentlemen was effected. For himself, Leicester raised the Queen's rate of £6 per day to £10 13s. 4d., an increase of £1715 per annum.

The treasurer was helpless. He could only write home to Walsingham: 'The disbursements are grown great since his Excellency's coming, by extraordinaries crept in, outside the rate which you gave me at my coming away, so that a more speedy supply is required.'[4] There is, I think, an explanation of Leicester's action — leaving aside the raising of his own allowance — but it is not a very satisfactory one. Apparently, the

[1] Cf. S.P. Holland, Eliz. xiv, 106.

[2] The old and new rates are given ibid. ix, 37, whence I take my figures. The monthly cost is given as £9679 old, £10,279 new. This is the lunar month. *Foreign Cal.* XX, 338 and elsewhere, gives the new monthly charge as £11,334. It is the calendar month, but all the same exceeds the annual charge quoted by me.

[3] Ibid. 218. The increase was from £170 to £176 5s. This is the figure in the detailed statement of the monthly charge (totalling £11,334) given in S.P. Holland, Eliz. vi, 17. The muster-master, in *Foreign Cal.* XXI, ii, 262, puts the increase at £3 5s. only, but I think it better to take £6 5s.

[4] Ibid. XX, 308.

English Council thought — erroneously — that the rates paid to the army in Ireland worked out at a lower figure than Dutch rates, which the treaty contemplated.[1] Consequently, they authorized a change to Irish rates. That Leicester was in prudence, if not in duty, bound to notify the Council of its error before embarking upon a scale of expenditure in excess of what the Queen had repeatedly named, and was in the future repeatedly to name, as the limit of her charge, there can be no doubt.[2] But Leicester was loftily indifferent to prudence and not too nice about duty: 'extraordinaries' crept in wherever he moved.

After the £20,000 of November no more money reached the Netherlands until the first week in April 1586. At the end of January only £5017 was left in the treasurer's hands, and to complete payment till January 11th an extra £3214, or perhaps less, would seem to have been needed.[3] The troops were in desperate straits before treasure arrived. I am not at all sure about the reason for the delay. I fancy that, if one had figures showing the ebb and flow of money in the exchequer, a convincing explanation of the periodic dispatch of treasure to the Netherlands would be found. But it is also true that from now on Elizabeth was putting pressure on her officials abroad to keep them from playing ducks and drakes with her money. Already the money had evaporated in a way that was incomprehensible in England, and no accounts were forthcoming, later than December 11th, to explain the new prodigality.

[1] Cf. *Foreign Cal.* XX, 308 and XXI, ii, 262. By Dutch rates the pay of a company of 150 was 1700 guilders = £170. It is calculated as £184 3s. 4d., ibid. p. 129, which may explain the mistake of the Council.

[2] Norris discovered that Irish rates exceeded Dutch and wrote to the Council rather than increase the charge. This on December 8th, 1585 (ibid. XX, 203). Cf. ibid. p. 656, where on May 23rd, 1586, Elizabeth says she 'will not assent to any extraordinary charges above the sum of £125,000'.

[3] Ibid. p. 338. Only £3102 is shown as imprested for the month to January 11th. In S.P. Holland, Eliz. vi, 18 (cf. *Cal.* XX, 291), £9432 is shown spent on Leicester's warrant. The two documents are the same date roughly, because the balance in hand is the same. Probably £9432 includes imprests for January-February, but even so £3102 seems a low figure.

'My lord,' wrote Burghley to Leicester on March 31st, 'untill the state of the Queenes army by muster book, and hir monthly charges, may appear more clear, here will be no further meanes for any more monney. At this present ther is paid £24,000 and that, added to hir Majestyes former chardg of £52,000 maketh £76,000, which some hir majesty doth often repeat, with gret offence.'[1]

It so happens that we can at this moment present the difference between theoretical calculations in England and actuality in the Netherlands, in striking fashion. Evidently in March 1586, when £24,000 was sent, Walsingham jotted down an estimate calculating how far the money would go, adding to it the surplus in the treasurer's hands on January 24th and sums due from the States, from the soldiers for armour, and from the profit on gold. His figures, which seem erroneously to assume that full pay had been made to January 24th, show provision for three months' pay from that date to April 24th, and a surplus of £6690. They were, however, based upon a monthly cost of £9680 which was according to the old rates.[2] Turning to realities, what happened was that the infantry — I cannot give the cavalry figures — received only two-thirds of their pay to April 11th, leaving £8875 to be paid to complete their wages to that date, when more treasure was sent in July.[3] Thus the money sent in March 1586 left the general settlement still at December 11th, where it remained until July-August.

Can one wonder at Elizabeth's growing alarm? It was not lessened by the information that part of the money had been advanced to companies in the States' pay. Unlike a similar occasion, within a month of Leicester's arrival in the Netherlands, when he advanced £600 to some Dutch troops and paid and imprested three English companies in the States' pay,[4] the

[1] *Leycester Correspondence*, p. 199.
[2] *Foreign Cal.* XX, 319. The document is wrongly put under January 24th. It should also be noted that 'A note of such sums of money', ibid. p. 291, includes the £24,500 sent in March, and consequently is wrongly dated in the Calendar.
[3] Ibid. XXI, ii, 199. [4] Ibid. XX, 310.

responsibility this time was the treasurer's. Leicester, who behaved despicably, protesting with a great oath to the treasurer that he never wrote against him either to Queen or councillor, used the incident to try and oust him from his office: the treasurer had evidently not been amenable enough. He accused him of paying this money in order to enrich himself, and made other charges against him.[1] Nothing could better Elizabeth's reply. She refused to dismiss the treasurer without proof of his ill-doings: 'you know my old wont', she wrote, 'that love not to discharge from office without desert; God forbid.' But pending inquiry, she took precautions by joining Sir Thomas Shirley in the office and concentrated responsibility on Leicester by ordering that no money should be paid out without his warrant.[2]

In July-August 1586 more money was sent. The sum paid out of the exchequer was £45,000; but £5000 of this was money borrowed by Leicester from the Merchant Adventurers in May and now charged against the treasurer, £2000 was a further loan from the merchants which I can only think had been borrowed to make advances to troops in the States' pay,[3] and £2660 or a sum thereabouts represented money paid in England in levying more troops for the States and recoverable in the Netherlands, but not recovered by October 29th.[4] Consequently the actual sum handed over to the treasurer was about £35,000. At home it was calculated that, if the States refunded what was due from them, there was enough money to make a full pay till August 11th.[5] Actually, the infantry were fully paid only till April 11th, while the cavalry, save for Sir Thomas Cecil's cornet of horse, were left unmustered and unpaid.[6] The rest of the money went in

[1] *Foreign Cal.* XXI, ii, 11-12, 26, 134; *Leycester Correspondence*, pp. 299-300, 324 seqq. The treasurer's explanation is in *Foreign Cal.* XX, 587.

[2] Ibid. XXI, ii, 94.

[3] Ibid. p. 199. This money comes under 'payments extraordinary' and was imprested to certain companies; hence my inference.

[4] Ibid. XXI, ii, 83, 84, 199, 209.

[5] Ibid. p. 98.

[6] Ibid. pp. 133-4, 164, 199, 209.

impresss, those to the cavalry being on a lavish scale. The excuse for impresting instead of paying the cavalry was that it was on campaign. Whether in view of the financial importance of musters this year the excuse was adequate, I do not know; but the treasurer and muster-master certainly viewed the situation with misgiving and disapproval.[1] To make matters worse, Leicester diverted part of the money to the States' troops. The muster-master on hearsay put the sum at £16,000, in all probability an exaggeration. The treasurer mentioned £3300 in a letter dated October 29th, by which time it had been repaid; but it is quite possible that the sum temporarily diverted was more.[2]

The total result was that the largest amount yet sent by Elizabeth to the Netherlands had failed hopelessly to straighten finances out, and the prospect of obtaining proper accounts by which to discover what was actually happening, check frauds, and recover her due, became more desperate. 'God knows by whose default', she wrote, but she could never receive any just account. Her treasure was still sent, and yet she heard that all want; her chief garrisons — the Brill and Flushing troops appear not to have had a penny of the last money — were unpaid and those in the field bare enough furnished. 'It is a sieve', she exclaimed, 'that spends as it receives to little purpose.' Leicester washed his hands in self-righteousness, blaming everyone but himself of incompetence and corruption.[3]

At the end of October 1586 a further £30,000 was received. It was used to bring payments as far as possible down to October 11th; but Leicester took more for himself when he left to come home than the treasurer anticipated, and some of the 'Holland captains' — whatever the phrase means — going over with him were paid, so that the treasure did not suffice.[4] £15,609 of the next issue of money in March 1587 was needed to complete payments to October 11th and settle debts incurred to that

[1] Ibid. pp. 152, 172.
[2] Ibid. pp. 172, 209.
[3] Ibid. pp. 188, 195.
[4] Ibid. pp. 199, 243.

date.[1] Adding this amount to the sum of £119,837 paid by the retiring treasurer for the period December 12th to October 11th,[2] we arrive at a total of approximately £135,000 as the charge borne by Elizabeth for ten months of Leicester's leadership. It represents an excess of two-sevenths over the rate which she had never ceased to affirm that she would not exceed.

The year 1586 taught Elizabeth that she could trust no one in the Netherlands to keep proper watch over her finances. Innuendo or open accusation of slackness and fraud touched everyone. Leicester's extravagance at her expense was obvious and was more than once covertly hinted at by subordinate officials. The treasurer, interested because of his percentage in the total of imprests and payments, was accused by the muster-master of excusing 'checks' in order to increase payments; while the muster-master, dependent on checks, was accused of writing down Norris's troop of horse at fifty in excess of its proper number in order to deduct their pay in the form of checks. The captains accused the treasurer of defrauding them, and the victualler and baker of defrauding their soldiers; while the captains' own frauds were on the lips of everyone.[3] Only the common soldier shared with the Queen the honour of being a mere victim; and we shall see that Elizabeth did her best for him as she did for herself.

It was obvious that there was slackness and fraud. Elizabeth's £126,000 per annum was based upon a calculation of full companies and bands. Wastages, which were very great in such armies as Elizabeth's, should have resulted in 'checks'; and even if the higher rates at which Leicester paid the troops must be set against the saving effected by checks, one might have expected the £126,000 not to be appreciably, if at all, exceeded. At least, that was Elizabeth's expectation. But checks and defalcations were unpopular. There were inadequate

[1] S.P. Holland, Eliz. xix, 211 seq.
[2] *Foreign Cal.* XXI, ii, 351-2.
[3] Ibid. pp. 75, 78, 385; iii, 33, 198.

defalcations and no checks at all for the period August to December 1585. Leicester wiped the latter out by ordering pay to be made to December 11th on the first muster rolls.[1] His reason was to enable the captains to bring their companies to full strength again without charge to the Queen; and apparently this was a permissible policy.[2] But it was permissible only in moderation. For the period December 1585 to October 1586 the checks amounted to £2642, about 2 per cent of the charges, but this was reduced to £1157 by the muster-master's fees, sums for levying cornets of horse, etc.[3] I can give no estimate of what the sum ought to have been, except to record that the States, in an apostil to the treasurer's accounts commenting on the absence of checks from the payments for November and December 1585, claimed that at least one-third of the pay ought to have been defalked.[4] Little doubt their estimate was a high one. There can be even less doubt, from the fuss made about checks at home, that the actual figure of £2642 gross for December-October was ridiculous.

It is this question of checks that largely explains Elizabeth's behaviour in 1587. What the real state of her troops was in the winter of 1586-7, it is very difficult to say. Norris reported that they never numbered more than 3000 foot — an estimate which excludes the garrisons in the cautionary towns and therefore equals a shortage of 2000 — and scarce 500 horse. Wilkes appears to have shared this view, and the States naturally upheld it: in March 1587 they alleged that Elizabeth's troops were not complete by almost one-half, and in transmitting their complaint to Leicester Wilkes did not say that it was a lie. On the other hand, the muster-master later on vigorously denied Norris's statement and asserted that 'there were never near 1000 wanting', which may perhaps mean little more than that the captains' returns, under too easy

[1] Ibid. XX, 343, 414.
[2] Ibid. XXI, iii, 33.
[3] S.P. Holland, Eliz. xvi, 186 (*Foreign Cal.* XXI, iii, 215).
[4] S.P. Holland, Eliz. xii, 59, apostil to first account, cap. 2.

supervision, accounted for no more.[1] Naturally, Elizabeth seized upon Norris's report and anticipated substantial checks. For our part we must leave the contradiction standing; but it seems safe to assume that the checks from October 1586 to June 1587 ought at the very least to have equalled the pay of 1000 foot – this number was short in June[2] – and 500 horse for six months, or approximately £13,000.[3] What sum they ought to have reached for the whole year down to October 11th, I cannot guess. In fact, they yielded a net sum of just over £3000! Why this was, the muster-master explained. After he and his commissaries, he wrote, had by great travail discovered many frauds and abuses, the captains, complaining of his severe dealings with them, joined together in appealing to Leicester. Leicester,

> finding indeed that it was not possible for them to maintain their bands without certain allowances, did mitigate or pardon the checks, and also, upon testimonies shown by the captains of horse, of horses slain and lost in service, remitted between three and four thousand pounds in the checks of the horse bands, besides his own and the Lord Marshal's band, which in consideration of their losses and charges in making them strong again, his Excellency passed without checks.[4]

Between captains' frauds and Leicester's generosity it looks as though nearer £20,000 than £10,000 due to Elizabeth vanished.

Without accounts the Queen was helpless. She could only know that her money invariably disappeared long before it ought to have done, and listen for explanation to one official blaming the other. With accounts it was possible to focus inquiries, as the list of questions compiled on the account ending December 11th, 1585, indicates.[5] But demand as she

[1] *Foreign Cal.* XXI, ii, 298, 419; iii, 256; *Cabala*, ii, 6.
[2] Ibid. 45-6.
[3] For the sum cf. *Foreign Cal.* XXI, iii, 472.
[4] Ibid. 441.
[5] Ibid. XX, 343; *Cabala*, ii, 84.

would and threaten as she could, months passed and the accounts did not arrive. The checks for the winter 1586-7, asked for throughout the following summer, were sent only in December. Small wonder that she refused to forward enough money to pay her captains in full until a detailed statement of what was owing was sent her and she could examine the figures herself. She asserted peremptorily in October 1587 that she would send no more money until she had been answered about the money paid to the States, and until her treasurer had made a particular declaration of the payment of the great sums he had had. She paid a muster-master and an auditor, she said, yet could get no perfect report. She demanded to know what checks had been certified since last October: the treasurer and auditor had told her that the muster-master gave them no knowledge thereof. She was never duly advertised what her monthly charge was, nor how far the treasure she sent extended; and, she complained, 'though it be continually alleged that great sums are due, yet why such sums are due, or to whom they are due, and who are paid and who not paid ... is never certified'.[1] All were responsible but the common soldier, and her effort in 1587 was to see the common soldier fed and the rest left to suffer for their sins, if sin they would.

Let us see how the financial history of 1587 fits in with this explanation. After Leicester's return to England in November 1586, no more money was sent over to the Netherlands until February-March; but arrangements had been made which freed the garrisons in the cautionary towns of Flushing and Brill from the more dismal consequences of intermittent supplies. At Flushing the Merchant Adventurers of Middelburg, from November 12th until the following September, were under order to supply the garrison with weekly lendings of £20 per company.[2] At Brill similar lendings were advanced by the burghers of the town.[3] The rest of the troops, however,

[1] *Foreign Cal.* XXI, iii, 396. [2] Ibid. XXI, ii, 286; iii, 13, 338.
[3] Ibid. XXI, iii, 141, 160; *Cabala*, ii, 43.

were in hard straits when money arrived. The sum issued from the exchequer in February 1587 was £39,154, but of this only £30,000 was at the disposal of the treasurer, £1500 going to the victualler — and therefore indirectly benefiting the treasurer — the rest being allocated to the sectional financing of the cautionary towns.[1] Out of the £30,000, the treasurer had to pay £15,609 to meet charges down to October 11th last.[2] The rest was distributed in imprests, part, paid to the horsemen, being allocated on the basis of a fictitious strength.[3] The main portion of the treasure, however, was paid out by poll.[4] I have already remarked on the opposition that this method of impresting aroused. No doubt one indignant captain was more or less right, and, when a victualler was set to make imprests, the wretched soldiers merely fell out of one wolf's clutches into another's: he bought their reckonings for half their worth and paid them in nothing but drink. But when the captains got back their prerogative, which by reason of official slackness they seem to have done by July, most of them — if we are to believe our tale-tellers — kept back a third of the weekly lendings of half a crown that they were given for their men.[5]

By April 20th, 1587, desperate cries for money were again going out, and on May 7th a further £30,000 was sent, an additional sum of £4549 being paid to the Merchant Adventurers of Middelburgh, by the same privy seal, to cover lendings to the Flushing garrison till October 12th.[6] According to the computations of the Privy Council, £42,000 would have been needed to make a full pay to April 12th, but the Queen was determined, before paying in full, to see what she owed and how the sum was arrived at, and so could not be induced to send more than £30,000.[7] Her thoughts were no doubt set

[1] S.P. Holland, Eliz. xix, 211. [2] Ibid.
[3] *Foreign Cal.* XXI, ii, 384. The £3000 refers to a portion of £5000 sent in advance (cf. ibid. p. 372). [4] Ibid. XXI, iii, 56-7.
[5] Ibid. XXI, iii, 22, 145. [6] Ibid. p. 24; S.P. Holland, Eliz. xix, 211.
[7] *Acts of Privy Council*, xv, 68. The editor's marginal note is 'The Queen's parsimony'!

on 'checks'. How deliberately she was trying to restore financial order in her army can be seen from the Council's instructions. Instead of leaving the money to disappear like water poured upon a parched land, Buckhurst was ordered to allot part of it to pay weekly lendings and part for imprests to the captains, and to determine the division and arrange details in conference between himself and certain specified people. Also, accounts were to be made with the captains to May 11th, showing how much was due to them after all defalcations had been made: this would enable full payment to be made under control from home.[1]

Buckhurst and the rest duly took order for the division of the money. First, so much was to be set aside as would make weekly lendings till September 11th, for horse, foot, and the garrisons of the cautionary towns. The lendings might have continued even longer, so a later comment on the scheme stated, for the companies were incomplete and the garrison at Brill got its lendings from the town; and the commentator might have added that provision for the lendings at Flushing had already been made, apart from the £30,000. The second provision was for an imprest amounting to a month's pay to each company, half to pay debts, half for present relief. The third was a sum of £2000 appointed for raising up the decayed companies of horse.[2]

It was an admirable scheme, on paper. But Elizabeth proposed, and Leicester and others disposed. 'I hear', wrote the commentator on the second provision, 'that these imprests not being paid upon my lord of Leicester's arrival, there was stay made for paying the said month's imprest to the garrisons of Flushing, Bergen and others.' The £2000 of the third provision was diverted to other uses.[3] As for the weekly lendings fund, it collapsed. Not a penny of the whole £30,000 was left by July 15th, according to Leicester. Probably he lied, to make

[1] *Foreign Cal.* XXI, iii, 57.

[2] Ibid. pp. 141-2.

[3] Ibid. pp. 141-2.

his demand for more money plausible; but it is unlikely that the remnant at that date totalled £3000.[1] The evidence does not enable us to apportion the blame between Leicester and his predecessors. I do not think that he was entirely responsible, but certainly he was not as innocent as his letters home suggest, for part of the money was used to pay lendings to the new companies,[2] which was wholly inexcusable, since Leicester himself brought money to finance them.

There is good reason to think that Leicester was plotting at this time, in collusion with Walsingham, to over-reach Elizabeth and defy his instructions. £30,000 had been issued to him, to be at his disposal. His instructions bound him to reserve at least half to pay the Queen's ordinary forces.[3] The other half was an extraordinary contribution and should have been used for financing the extraordinary bands that went over with him. He spent £4000 in England on the levy of these bands, thus leaving £11,000 in his hands to finance them in the Netherlands and £15,000 for the ordinary English forces. What he had in mind is revealed in a letter to Walsingham, dated July 20th: 'When I last came out of England', he wrote, 'I had with me but twenty-six thousand pounds, which by your project was to serve for the pay of 3000 English for four months, for a levy of 2000 Walloons and the charges of transportation, which I might make good shift to do.'[4] Possibly we ought not to construe this as meaning that he intended to spend the whole £26,000 on extraordinary forces; but on £11,000 he certainly

[1] *Foreign Cal.* XXI, iii, 175. On July 4th Leicester told Walsingham that not above £4000 was then left (ibid. p. 149, and cf. p. 188); on July 13th he told Burghley that there was not £3000 left when he arrived on June 26th (ibid. p. 171); somewhere between July 12th and 24th he told Needham that there was then not above £3000 left (ibid. p. 196). Actually the treasurer had £8777 in hand on July 1st (S.P. Holland, Eliz. xvi, 40).

[2] Ibid. fol. 175.

[3] *Foreign Cal.* XXI, iii, 122. Beale's remark on p. 173 shows that this point in the instructions was not altered. It is interesting to note that Stafford charged Walsingham and Leicester with trying to over-reach the Queen. Cf. above, p. 167.

[4] *Foreign Cal.* XXI, iii, 188.

could not pay 3000 foot for four months and meet the bill for the levy, and the levy only, of 2000 Walloons. Moreover, the number of extra English foot was 4650, not 3000, and if he contemplated paying the Walloons as well as levying them, then he might just have made shift to do all this on £26,000, but not a penny would have been left for Elizabeth's ordinary forces. It looks as if it was in an effort to preserve his own fund for his own purposes that he raided the treasurer-at-war's money, and finally ruined Buckhurst's scheme for its disposition by making lendings from it to the new English bands. Probably he raised his Walloons: at any rate, in a rough estimate that he sent home of the spending of his £30,000, there is an item of £1060 for levying and reinforcing certain bands 'as Mr Secretary Walsingham knoweth'.[1]

As for the reckoning to May 11th which Elizabeth had asked for in order to know what a full pay required, it had not been prepared, and a statement was only forthcoming in July when Leicester sent, first the auditor and under-treasurer to England, and later the treasurer, to speed over more money. And what a statement it was that the auditor produced! First, the cost of the army at full strength from October 12th to July 11th was given, then the amount paid out; and the difference, less £8777 left in the treasurer's hands on July 1st, was shown as the amount owing by Elizabeth, a sum of £44,725.[2] Not a word of checks, except that the captains' muster-rolls had not been brought in in time and so no report of them could be made. Moreover, the statement took no account of money paid to the new companies. At the time it was presented, Leicester's letter must have been received announcing that the treasurer had no money left and that he himself had tried, but failed, to raise money from the English merchants; and within a week or two came a rough statement from him – whether true or not, we need not inquire – showing that by August 12th only

[1] S.P. Holland, Eliz. xvii, 236.
[2] Ibid. xvi, 40 (*Cal.* XXI, iii, 160, and cf. p. 215).

£6500 of his own £30,000 would be left.[1] No wonder that on August 8th the Council had to announce that they could not prevail upon Elizabeth to send more treasure; that she desired first to see the muster-master's books of the checks.[2]

However, the Queen was better than her word. On August 17th, 1587, a further £30,000 was issued and arrived in the Netherlands with the treasurer early in September.[3] Despite Leicester's estimate, showing only £6500 of his £30,000 left on August 12th, Burghley expected the treasurer to find a balance of £7000 in the hands of Leicester's secretary when he returned, and to receive it from him. In fact he found not a penny.[4] The treasurer came with orders to liquidate the situation. The principal officers of the field, the lord marshal and others, were cassed, much to Leicester's disgust, who felt himself shorn of his dignity; and at last, early in October, that season's new companies, which had been rejected by the States, were shipped home.[5] It is worth noting that, in contrast with the States, who cassed last year on the basis of a month's pay and met claims for arrears by saying that there was no money for them,[6] the captains of these companies were paid in full to October 11th.[7]

The captains were paid, but, true to their traditions, they defrauded their men. 'Great numbers of private soldiers', it was reported from England, 'come over in lamentable case, alleging for their defence, when they are charged as vagabonds and threatened to be punished ... that their captains have paid them neither wages nor lendings, but have also disarmed them, and sent them away without any food, money or passport.' Thirty made their way to the Court gate. Hearing they were there, the Queen ordered the Council to examine two

[1] S.P. Holland, Eliz. xvii, 236. [2] *Foreign Cal.* XXI, iii, 227.
[3] S.P. Holland, Eliz. xix, 211; *Acts of Privy Council*, xv, 221; *Foreign Cal.* XXI, iii, 425. [4] Ibid. p. 369.
[5] Ibid. pp. 317-18, 369, 370.
[6] On the States as bad payers see *inter alia*, ibid. XXI, ii, 288, 289, 340, 369; iii, 31, 32, 110, 136, 173.
[7] S.P. Holland, Eliz. xix, 211 seq.

of them, and was seriously concerned at the effect which the ill-usage they had received was likely to have on future recruitment for foreign service. She commanded that Leicester should be informed, and that inquiry should be made how the captains had been paid and how they had treated their soldiers.[1] After receiving word from the Netherlands that the captains had been paid in full,[2] the Council on December 16th directed letters to the lords lieutenant and others in the various counties ordering them to send up to the Court 'all suche souldiers as uppon the last levyes were sent and served in the Lowe Countryes ... to th'ende that yf they could duly claime and shewe manyfest proofe for any wages behinde and unpaied for their service and entertainement in those countryes, they should upon their repaier to the Court be fullye satysfied thereof'. After examining the statements and accounts of certain men and their captains, the Council remitted the detailed examination and judgment to two prominent gentlemen in the shire, and by means of a circular letter set up a local committee of appeal and award, to see justice done to the common soldier in each county. In this way did Elizabeth continue her struggle with laxity and corruption.[3]

The cashiering of these companies depleted the treasurer's funds, and the cry for more money was set up as early as October 14th, 1587. The treasurer told Burghley that only £1000 was left on that day, but as £1400 was still unspent early in December and we may well surmise that in the interval Leicester and those who accompanied him home took their pay out of the balance, the treasurer was obviously crying 'Wolf', as Leicester had done, before the wolf was at his gate.[4] Both he and Leicester recognized at last that the receipt of more money was dependent on the presentation of proper accounts; but they called for money all the same. When Elizabeth sent

[1] *Foreign Cal.* XXI, iii, 396-7. [2] Ibid. p. 441.
[3] *Acts of Privy Council*, xv, 303, 334, 337, 338, 339, 343-4.
[4] *Foreign Cal.* XXI, iii, 369, 447.

Herbert over at the beginning of November, she stated her decision with final emphasis: money they would not get till the accounts were to hand.[1] The accounts were not dispatched till early in December. On November 14th £10,000 was issued for the garrisons of Flushing and Brill,[2] but so far as the main army was concerned Elizabeth kept her word, and our Calendar ends at the close of the year 1587 with the need for money once more desperate, and no money sent. Pay was nearly fifteen months in arrears, the last settlement still remaining at October 11th, 1586.

No doubt there is a quixotic element in this picture of Elizabeth tilting against corruption. When the history of official probity is written, the Elizabethan age will not make pleasant reading, and here in an army free rein was given to that laxity and corruption which made it cheaper to farm out business than perform it by officials. But the slacker the control at home the greater the orgy of corruption would have been abroad, and it is no condemnation of Elizabeth that to some extent she kicked against the pricks. She was betrayed in her efforts by Leicester, just as I suspect that similar studies to this will show that she was later betrayed by Essex. Had Leicester possessed the wit and desire to keep finances straight the story would have been very different, on the Dutch side no less than the English; and military achievements would not, indeed scarcely could, have suffered. As it was, he could spend but not save. I can see no trace of financial or organizing ability in his actions, as there is no trace of statesmanship. And duty sat lightly upon him. Rank he possessed, but no other quality for his office. Even honesty, in the sense of straight dealing with his mistress, was absent. His reputation is deservedly low.

It is otherwise with the Queen. After all, her advisers had estimated the cost of the army. Her financial principles were those of sound business: to pay what she owed and spend what she could afford; and in an age with no funded debt and very

[1] *Foreign Cal.* XXI, iii, 384, 396, 406-7. [2] S.P. Holland, Eliz. xix, 211.

restricted credit, they were sound for war as well as peace. They were principles rare among princes in her day and explain that miracle of her age, the solvency of her government. The story that I have traced is merely these principles in action. Even her peace negotiations take on a milder hue. The years 1585-7 saw expenditure far beyond the resources of the Netherlands and beyond what Elizabeth thought it prudent to spend of English money; and the military achievements were worse than negligible. If such efforts resulted in no gains comparable to losses, what but disaster did the future seem to hold? It is a facile answer to say that Elizabeth ought to have increased her help substantially and forced Spain to a quick, decisive issue. It assumes that a concentrated military effort on modern lines was possible, which would drive the Spaniards out of the Low Countries or force them to peace – an assumption which borders on the absurd when one thinks of the military conditions for its achievement; and a sane memorandum in our Calendar shows that at least one of Elizabeth's advisers was aware of it.[1] The answer also ignores the fact that no historian has possessed the necessary financial and other knowledge to pronounce on its financial wisdom. Leicester and his kin are not sound guides to follow.

Despite the ultimate issue of the revolt, a reasonable peace – and Elizabeth was not so accommodating in her negotiations as to suggest that she would have accepted any other – was not a pusillanimous or even imprudent policy to pursue in the light of events in 1585-7. Naturally, official Dutch and English views conflicted. English trade suffered severely from the war. Dutch trade flourished, for their merchants victualled the Dutch, English, and Spanish armies, and profited by war prices; and controlling Dutch politics through the States General, they naturally opposed peace. The future justified them, but it is false logic to argue that it therefore condemned Elizabeth.

[1] *Foreign Cal.* XXI, ii, 247-9.

ENGLISH LOCAL GOVERNMENT

A HISTORICAL RETROSPECT[1]

ONE hundred years ago Parliament passed the Municipal Corporations Act. The modern history of English local government had commenced; a long chapter of our institutional history had come to an inglorious end. In reading the final pages of that chapter a tidy mind of today is inevitably filled with disgust – disgust that reform was so tardy in coming, and perhaps that it was so incomplete when it did come. But that disgust is itself a tribute to the tenacity of the constitutional and legal principles in which the old decrepit system was set. Those principles in their turn are the clue to our political and individual liberty.

Put it another way. A recent critic of our local government wrote: 'If one feature characterizes local administration in England more than another, it is the utter want of symmetry or system under which it is carried on.' Fifty years ago another critic was making much the same comment, though with far more justification: 'A chaos of authorities, a chaos of jurisdictions, a chaos of rates, a chaos of franchises, a chaos worst of all of areas.' And a hundred years ago, the commissioners charged with reporting on the municipal corporations of England might well, among less charitable expressions of feeling, have echoed a great seventeenth-century antiquary: 'Whoso desireth to discourse concerning corporate towns must be allowed a great deal of time and preparation.'

This society of ours is set in its history. Revolution looks enviously upon it but passes it by. We may quake at the spectacle of root-and-branch changes in other countries, but we

[1] The Centenary Lecture on Local Government, delivered at the Annual Conference of the National Association of Local Government Officers, held at Cheltenham, Whitsuntide, 1935.

seize firmly hold of the past when adventuring into the future. 'In what we improve', wrote Edmund Burke, 'we are never wholly new; in what we retain we are never wholly obsolete.' In some moods this gospel of conservatism seems merely obstructive. At other times, and particularly in these times of dictatorship abroad, we may thank God that we are not as other men are and share the ecstasy of Burke: 'Our political system is placed in a just correspondence and symmetry with the order of the world and with the mode of existence decreed to a permanent body composed of transitory parts; wherein, by the disposition of a stupendous wisdom, moulding together the great mysterious incorporation of the human race, the whole at one time is never old or middle-aged or young, but, in a condition of changeable constancy, moves on through the varied tenor of perpetual decay, fall, renovation, and progression.'

'The happy effect of following nature, which is wisdom without reflection', so Burke termed it. Fortunately a historian is not called upon to pronounce with or against him. History perhaps is wise in the way old people are wise, who know that the hopes of youth are illusions. It perhaps is foolish in being a collection of cautionary tales. But it does answer our desire to know how we have arrived at where we are; and in this humble mood I wish to glance back over the history of our local government. If perchance a little wisdom creeps in, take it for an unexpected bonus.

Let us set ourselves in the sixteenth century. A great tidying-up was then taking place in England and in western Europe generally, much like the tidying-up that took place a century ago and that many think is due again today. We might apply to the period Raleigh's description of Queen Elizabeth in old age: 'a lady whom Time had surprised'. The institutions of a primitive age had survived into an age that was broadening its mind, bringing new-found lands into the compass of a rapidly expanding commerce, and trying to adjust its social and political life to the growing demands made upon it. They were the institutions of a society in which central government had been weak and poor and in which a great part of history had been local history because the monarch had not the means to plan and maintain a centralized and uniform system of institutions. The localities had been left largely to themselves, to their old folk-institutions and the feudal institutions grafted on to them. Shire and Hundred and Manor, each with its court or courts, blending what we today would separate as administration and justice: that is the picture of medieval England, and with some change of nomenclature, of medieval Europe. Law was custom, custom law. It varied from court to court, from local community to local community. Institutions were primitive: that is, they were the reverse of simple. They stagnated.

These were the institutions 'surprised by Time'. The new age needed, among much else, a common system of law, a common regulation of economic life, a common solution of some of the problems of modern life – that of poverty, for example. This systematizing activity had to come from the central government, in other words from the monarchy. Hence the sixteenth century was the age of the New Monarchy. In its womb lay the absolute monarchies of the seventeenth and eighteenth centuries. The question for us is, what happened to local government? In the Middle Ages local government had been self-government because no other had been possible; but whether the old system would continue or not depended upon its sophistication, whether it was flexible enough to provide the minimum of efficiency and uniformity that the new nation-state demanded.

It was here that England differed from the continent, and in consequence the parting of the ways came which led to the conservation and development of parliamentary institutions and self-government in England while abroad the New Monarchy gave birth to absolutism. By a paradox the reason for this was that in the Middle Ages the monarchy had been stronger in England than elsewhere and our government the most centralized in Europe. The symbol and instrument of this centralization was the King's law. It had penetrated through the length and breadth of the land until it had become common to all men: it had become the Common Law of England. Leaving aside the law of the Church, this quality of universality was unique in medieval Europe. Unique also were the gilds or trade-unions – the Inns of Court – which the lawyers set up, with their system of apprenticeship or legal education, ending in the call to the Bar. The trade of the law was organized. It was also taught; and taught, not by professional teachers prone to let their teaching wilt into a dead scholasticism, but by practising lawyers, among whom were some of the finest intellects of their time. The Common Law was therefore both sophisticated and practical. In its formative youth it had drawn largely from the law of a much more advanced and intricate civilization – that of the old Roman Empire; and though it became excessively formal and marred by many grave flaws, it was a fit instrument to regulate the more complicated life of modern times. Moreover, by another dispensation peculiar to England, it could be amended and extended by parliamentary statute.

Now this law had its roots in the feudal age, the essence of which was that all rights were private rights. Even the King's rights, though more extensive than others, were private not public. The law necessarily reflected the structure of society. It consequently became the palladium of individual rights and of that most obvious of rights in an agricultural society, private property. It was no accident that an English philosopher, Locke, placed the right to property not only beyond the challenge of the King but even of the community: it was, he argued, the end for which Civil Society came into existence. A great medieval legal writer had enunciated the principle of English law: 'The King ought not to be under man but under God and under the law' – that is, under a law that was a strait-waistcoat on the monarchy. Judges, said Francis Bacon, should be lions under the throne. They have been; but *rampant*, not *couchant*.

The permeation of the whole country by the King's law was accomplished by the device of itinerant judges – our Justices of Assize. Once more let us remind ourselves that this legal system was developed before there was any strongly marked differentiation between the functions of government and when administration and justice were naturally merged together. Consequently the Justices of Assize not only tried criminals when twice a year they perambulated through the counties, but also they had before them local officials and a great number of the inhabitants and instituted a searching inquiry into the way local government was being carried on.

Local and central government were therefore linked together. This in itself was a great help in making the transition from medieval to modern times without an institutional revolution – a revolution which in the sixteenth century could only have resulted in bureaucracy. But the Justices of Assize were no more than occasional visitors. The fate of local government depended on the quality and adaptability of the normal local institutions. If these had remained none other than the Shire Court, the Hundred Court, and the Manorial Court, courts where the body of freeholders present – at any rate, in Shire and Hundred – constituted the deciding authority and immemorial custom was the guiding principle of action, how could the monarchy have failed to override such a custom-bound, inefficient organization by a system of professional officials? But it is here that another feature of medieval development in England came to the rescue. I refer to the Justice of the Peace. Sixteenth-century writers on our constitution were loud in their praise of him: 'There was never in any commonwealth devised a more wise, a more dulce and gentle, nor a more certain way to rule the people, whereby they are kept always as it were in a bridle of good order.'

These Justices, as their name implies, were primarily officials of the law: they presided over local criminal courts. But they, too, had their beginnings when administration and justice were undifferentiated, and from early times administrative duties accompanied legal. In the J.P. the sixteenth-century monarch had an official whom he could make his local man-of-all work, and whom he could saddle with the licensing of alehouses, the control of vagabonds, restraint of extravagance in dress – 'a pestilent canker in the commonwealth' – the fixing of wages for farm labourers and artisans, supervision of the poor-law, and, indeed, the hundred and one jobs that the central government wanted doing in the locality. In addition the Justices of the Peace had to supervise the conduct of the other local officials: in the words of their commission they were 'to enquire by oath of good and lawful men of the county' concerning 'such sheriffs, bailiffs, stewards, constables, keepers of gaols and other officers as are lukewarm, remiss, or negligent in the performance of their offices'. Their duties were legion, the flexibility of their office astounding.

Let us note the variety of their work in a few extracts from the Quarter Sessions Records of the West Riding of Yorkshire in 1598:

> For that information is given unto this Court by the High Constables of Staincross that Adam Hutchinson and Thomas Hodgson of Barnsley, alehouse keepers, are men of bad behaviour and do maintain ill rule in their houses. It is therefore ordered that a warrant shall be made against them to discharge them from keeping any alehouse until reformation be had.

> Whereas there is a poor infant child left within the town of Southowrom, who are so sore charged with their own poor that they are scarce able to relieve them, and therefore hath required aid of this Court. It is therefore ordered that the said child shall not only be relieved within the same town, but also through the whole parish of Halifax.

Ordered that no brewsters within this division shall brew any ale or beer of greater price to be sold, or sell any for any greater price than only of a penny the quart, except they shall have a special licence from some Justice of Peace.

Whereas the highway leading from Leeds to Wikebridge hath been heretofore presented by jury to be in great decay.... Therefore the foresaid jurors by the consent of the Justices here present do lay a pain that every person occupying a plough tilth of land within any the parishes of Leeds ... shall send their draughts and sufficient labourers and repair the same before August 25 upon pain of 20s.

Forasmuch as Thomas Stringer was brought here in Court for suspicion of sheep stealing and did confess himself guilty thereof. It is therefore ordered that he shall be conveyed to Wentbridge from whence he came and there by the Constable whipped, being stripped naked from the middle upwards.

The J.P. was a local gentleman, whose pay of 4s. per day when he sat in Quarter Sessions was far from making a professional official of him. And even that modest payment died out, like the wages of Members of Parliament, in the seventeenth century. Here again the age in which his office originated determined its character. A monarch who found it a necessary economy to reward central officials with ecclesiastical benefices, could not afford an army of local officials. Moreover, the baronage and gentry were too independent to be controlled by such a system. Set a thief to catch a thief; set the gentry to keep peace among the gentry. Consequently, local government became merged with the interests of the gentry. It also became merged with the interests of the Common Law, for it was this law that the Justices administered and they became imbued with its spirit. Moreover, in the sixteenth and seventeenth centuries many country gentlemen, who then went to the universities very young, finished their education at the Inns of Court. You will remember that in Shakespeare's *Henry IV*, Justice Silence told Justice Shallow that his boy, William, was at Oxford. 'A' must, then, to the Inns o' Court shortly,' said Shallow. 'I was once of Clement's Inn; where I think they will talk of mad Shallow yet.... By the mass, I was called any thing; and I would have done any thing indeed too, and roundly too. There was I, and Little John Doit of Staffordshire, and Black George Barnes, and Francis Pickbone, and Will Squele a Cotswold man; you had not four such swinge-bucklers in all the Inns of Court again.'

Further, by the close of the sixteenth century these same country gentlemen had got themselves in overwhelming numbers into the House of Commons. And so Parliament, which as the great amending organ of the law was already bound up with the legal system, was also linked with it through the personnel of the House of Commons. In sixteenth-century Europe the tide set in favour of monarchy, but what could it do in England save pound ineffectively on the rock of our Common Law? The future of England as a constitutional monarchy under a rule of law was already determined, and determined in no small measure by the survival of our medieval system of local government.

On the continent the story was different. In the fifteenth and sixteenth centuries the countries of western Europe underwent what is known as the Reception of Roman Civil Law. That is to say, the royal courts took over the law of the old Roman Empire, and it was this law which, as the monarch's power developed, became the common law of France, the German states, and other countries. Its sophistication commended it. There were no Inns of Court to foster any rival, and the only secular law taught at continental universities was the Roman Civil Law; as, indeed, it was the only secular law taught at the two English universities until the eighteenth century. Its roots lay not in a feudal society but in a despotic empire. Its fundamental principle was the famous dictum, 'What pleases the Prince has the force of law.' The stage was thus set for the emergence of absolute monarchy. Nothing from the past could stand permanently in its way. Representative assemblies, the sisters of our Parliament, were not set immovably in the structure of society. They were not law-making bodies. They were out of harmony with Roman Law. They went. Local institutions, too, were merely primitive and feudal institutions, as unfitted to survive into modern times as our Shire and Hundred and Manorial Courts would have been without the saving grace of the J.P. Royal officials overrode them. Even the cities, those oases of advanced self-government, were brought under royal control.

The medieval system of local government survived in England because of its relative efficiency and remarkable flexibility. Let us see how it worked at what, before the reforms of last century, was in some ways its period of maximum satisfaction — the end of the sixteenth century. England was then an agricultural country of some four million people. It had its towns, of which I will speak in a minute or two; but primarily it was a land of thousands of villages, seldom containing more than one or two hundred inhabitants and often much less. Standards of human welfare were simple, and to leave each community to look after itself, with the requisite jogs from the central government, was the easiest and best policy.

In the feudal age the village had been organized as an association of producers through the manorial system. The Manor was now dying, but it left the Village organized. Its place was taken by the community in another aspect — grouped round its church. This was the Parish, and when the Reformation turned the Church into a department of State, the Parish offered itself as the basic unit of local government. It was already a self-governing community, ordering the religious welfare of its members in an age when membership of the Church and attendance at it were compulsory on everyone. It was also a financial unit, for it had to maintain its church and to look after its poor even before the State turned this work of charity into a statutory obligation. Often it had endowments, lands or houses; or maybe cows and sheep left by pious parishioners, the exploitation of which caused anxious thought: was it better to sell outright, or to let on hire and risk losing capital and income if the wretched beasts died? The Parish might even turn money-lender or pawnbroker, tempering its activities by a spirit of charity strange to such callings. It also had an ever-present help in time of financial trouble, the sixteenth-century prototype of our church bazaar; only it was a Church-ale, a Gargantuan feast and even more Gargantuan drinking, to which people streamed from far and wide. Finally, when other resources failed, there was the Parish rate. What was all this — Church-ale excepted — but an embryonic unit of local government?

The ecclesiastical Parish bequeathed to the secular Parish an official, the Churchwarden, who was treasurer and executive officer for the community and was elected annually by the parishioners assembled in the vestry of the church. He was unpaid, and when elected had no option but to serve. The State joined other men with the Churchwardens and created the Overseers of the Poor, using parish finances to carry out its Poor Law. Another official, this time bequeathed by the Manor, was the Constable, the village policeman, also appointed annually and unpaid. In a small community the human material from which to select officials was limited, and simple mind and simple heart had often to cope with a simple job. You probably know the inimitable Dogberry and Verges in Shakespeare's *Much Ado About Nothing*. Dogberry of course was constable of a borough, but we'll risk his wrath and make him sit for our portrait of a parish constable. 'I am a wise fellow,' he said; 'and which is more, an officer; and which is more, as pretty a piece of flesh as any in Messina; and one that knows the law, go to; and a rich fellow enough, go to; and a fellow that hath had losses; and one that hath two gowns, and everything handsome about him.' As you will remember, he also said, 'Write me down an ass!' And I am afraid we must, though a very lovable ass. We complete our principal parish officials with the Surveyor of the Highways. Like everything else — and for the same reason, namely that no other expedient was practicable — the care of the roads was a local responsibility. Every householder was under obligation to go road-mending. Bad roads! But there were no motor cars and practically no carriages.

Parish government needed supervision by a higher authority; the Parish too might prove an inappropriate area for its work. Machinery was required to meet these needs, and the answer was the County. Not the ancient County Court, which was practically moribund, but the County J.P.s in their Court of Quarter Sessions or exercising powers as single Justices or in groups of two or more. They sometimes appointed parish officials; in any case the officials were answerable to them for performing their duties. When a particular Parish was overburdened with its poor, the Justices could spread the cost beyond its bounds. They could levy rates to repair the county highways — bridges in particular — when the Parish failed as an appropriate area for the work. They could levy county rates for many other purposes; for example, to enable poor prisoners to pay their gaoler's fees, since imprisonment in those days was not at the expense of the Crown but the prisoner. The distribution through the County of these charges and of certain central taxation was facilitated by the divisions known as Hundreds into which the County had for centuries been divided. At one time the Hundred with its folk Court had been an important unit of self-government. By the Elizabethan period it had become little more than an extremely useful subdivision of the County, with two officials known as High

Constables — usually gentlemen — through whom financial and other county burdens could be conveniently apportioned and passed on to the Parish.

Thus — if once more we exclude the Borough — English local government was based upon the Parish, a real social unit, and upon the County, a geographical area with little rhyme or reason in its boundaries save this, that centuries of history had transformed a geographical expression into a self-conscious community. Add the invaluable distributive area, the Hundred, and I think you will agree with me that in relation to its time this system of local government was sound.

The propulsion to keep the pendulum swinging came from the central government. As we have seen, the Justices of Assize paid periodic visits to the Counties and reported to the government when they returned to London. But there was also an unsleeping watch kept by the Privy Council, and in the Star Chamber there was a disciplinary court which did not hesitate to bring to his senses any J.P. or local official who tried to play the tyrant or villain in his locality. Whitehall today may scourge with whips. Elizabeth's Privy Council employed scorpions. An eminent American historian, reading the chidings and threatenings that descended on the Elizabethan J.P. from Westminster, was shocked. But, in truth, this strong discipline was the secret of successful local self-government.

Queen Elizabeth herself took a hand in the job. Towards the end of her reign the J.P. was under fire from critics, and as the Lord Keeper of the Great Seal explained, 'For that the number of Justices of the Peace was grown almost infinite, to the hindrance of justice, the one trusting so much unto another that there are more justices than justice ... and of these many insufficient, unlearned, negligent, or undiscreet, Her Majesty therefore, like a good housewife looking unto all her household stuff, took the book — the list of J.P.s — in her own hands, and in the sight of us, the Lord Keeper and Treasurer, went through and noted those Justices she would have continue in commission, and [those] whom she thought not meet, and willed us to consider of the rest.' The incident reminds us that Elizabethan England was not unlike an enormous family, the gentry for the most part being known at Court as Debrett was known last century.

So far I have excluded the Borough from my narrative. Not inappropriately, for what is its history but a story of exclusion from the normal institutional life of the country? Its life was a broadening out from charter to charter. It bought franchises from the King. If it could – and it generally could – it bought out, partially or wholly, the lord who owned it, whether king or subject. During the centuries when group personality found natural acceptance in the current body of ideas it assumed a corporate character. When in the fifteenth and sixteenth centuries royal judges were taking over from the Roman Civil Law the concept that a non-natural, a fictitious person – in other words, a corporation – could only be created by the Prince, it secured a charter of incorporation from the Crown, permitting it to sue and be sued in its corporate capacity.

The Borough was a community withdrawn, in varying degree, from the normal system of local government and governing itself through its own institutions by virtue of the privileges it had acquired. You can see the Manor absorbed into it, with its control of the town fields, its picturesque – or rather, its picturesquely entitled – officials, such as Aleconner, Bread-weigher, or Dog-muzzler; also with its general right to cope with nuisances and formulate obligations for the common good – a right out of which much of modern municipal activity, including what we now call Public Health, could be made to grow if the authorities had the wit, honesty, and drive to develop their opportunities. It was an association of producers in the spheres of commerce and manufacture. You can see this in the control of its market and its trade regulations. It had civil jurisdiction in cases of debt and trespass. In the past this had cut it out from the old folk-court of the Hundred. In some instances – notably London, York, and Bristol – it had become a county in itself and excluded the sheriff. It even sought exclusiveness within the system of Justices of the Peace. If wholly successful, its own officials held Quarter Sessions for the Borough. If partially successful, they might be on the County Commission, while, if unsuccessful, the Borough was subject to the jurisdiction of the County Justices like the Parish. It is all a story of incredible variety, which is merely to say that it is medieval: like Topsy, it 'grow'd'.

These urban communities at the end of the sixteenth century were with few exceptions tiny societies. Norwich, one of the largest, had a population of about 17,000, Coventry 6500, Cambridge, excluding the University, 5000, Leicester 4000. These were on the large side. Liverpool had about 750 inhabitants. Their finances were correspondingly modest. The balance sheet for the year 1599 of the small Suffolk borough of Dunwich, which sent two representatives to Parliament and had criminal jurisdiction extending to all felonies, was: receipts £41 12s. 10d. plus £5 still owing; expenditure £41 10s. 3d.; result, as Mr Micawber would have said, happiness.

There was no single system of government. Very much the contrary. But in the fifteenth and sixteenth centuries there was a tendency towards a normal system of Mayor or Bailiff assisted by a group of twelve or twenty-four brethren usually called Aldermen, and a second group twice the number, known as the Common Council or The Twenty-four or Forty-eight: in other words, our modern Mayor, Aldermen, and Councillors. It was once thought that the story of Borough government was that of a decline from democracy to oligarchy. Rather, it is a story of oligarchy – or maybe we should say aristocracy – harassed or tempered by occasional 'democratic' agitations. The Common Council, which was really a second Council grafted on to the Council of Mayor's Brethren or Aldermen, was the result of democratic agitation in the late Middle Ages.

But it too tended to decline into oligarchy. The fact is that few people were competent to rule, and, as the fines imposed for refusing office show, fewer still were willing.

The Corporation in the late sixteenth century was a close body, co-opting new members; though it was carrying out its task with relative efficiency. Like the Parish it drew its income from property and rates, but property included more than land: market-tolls, fines from courts and for refusal to accept office, also the occasional sale of the status of Burgess, a valuable privilege exempting its holders from various tolls and entitling them to trade within the Borough. If the income was small, so in those days was the possible scope of government, while the range of obligation on the individual resident was wide. The resident was obliged, for example, to repair and clean the street in front of his house. During this century, Boroughs were busy paving their streets. Power was needed to compel each resident to pave his particular patch, and for this and other reasons private acts of Parliament were obtained. The Private Act was an important sign of the way municipal government was to expand in the future. So was the occasional appearance of a borough pavior. Again, the connection between dirt and disease was not unknown. The authorities compelled each resident to clean his area of the street once or maybe twice a week and ordered street and house refuse to be dumped in certain places. Then they took to employing a common carter, who, however, was paid by the individual resident whose obligation he was fulfilling. The public scavenger thus arrived. From time to time a rate was levied or a fund was raised for some common action. By these means most towns in the sixteenth century brought a water supply through conduits from springs outside the town, to supplement the inadequate wells within. No doubt we would shudder at the primitive and insanitary character of Elizabethan towns; but standards have altered enormously since those days and towns have become devastatingly urban which then were semi-rural. On the whole the impression is one of active communities whose authorities were not asleep, nor grossly corrupt, nor, be it added, blessed with much chance of gross corruption.

We have finished our survey of local government at the close of the sixteenth century. What is the sequel? In the first place, the inherent weaknesses of the system grew as the demands on it increased. Take the J.P. An Elizabethan statesman complained that many people sought inordinately for the office 'not of any mind to bring good to their county, but of a desire either to bear rule and sway or to be exempted from inferior services or to find immunity from common charges or to be avenged'. A member of Parliament in 1601 added another criticism. 'A Justice of Peace', he said, 'is a living creature that for half a dozen of chickens will dispense with a whole dozen of penal statutes. These be the Basket-Justices of whom the tale may be verified of a Justice that I know, to whom one of his poor neighbours coming, said, "Sir, I am very highly rated in the Subsidy Book; I beseech you to help me." To whom he answered, "I know thee not." "Not me, sir?" quoth the countryman. "Why, your Worship had my team and my oxen such a day, and I have ever been at your Worship's service." "Have you so, sir?" quoth the Justice. "I never remember I had any such matter, no not a sheep's tail." So unless you offer sacrifices to these Idol-Justices, of sheep and oxen, they know you not.... They be like the wise men of Chaldee, that could never give judgment till they saw the entrails of beasts.'

Indolence, tyranny, corruption were the vices apt to show themselves in the J.P. They are common human failings. Indolence was rampant owing to the motives that led many of the gentry to be Justices. The office was becoming a point of dignity with them. You remember the dialogue of Justice Shallow and his cousin, Slender?

SHALLOW: If he were twenty Sir John Falstaffs he shall not abuse Robert Shallow, esquire.

SLENDER: In the county of Gloster, justice of peace, and *coram*.
SHALLOW: Ay, cousin Slender, and *cust-alorum*.
SLENDER: Ay, and *rato-lorum* too; and a gentleman born, Master Parson; who writes himself *armigero*, in any bill, warrant, quittance, or obligation – *armigero*.
SHALLOW: Ay, that I do; and have done any time these three hundred years.

What the father had been, the son naturally expected to be. Moreover, to be a Justice kept some neighbour on the Commission from interfering in the village over which one lorded it as squire. The number of J.P.s therefore grew, not in relation to the needs of local government but to the desires of the gentry. Queen Elizabeth complained of the numbers, but they apparently continued growing, and growing rapidly, in the decades following her reign. There were about 2500 in 1650. The number increased steadily. So did indolence.

There was one means of keeping these vices within bounds: vigilance and firm control by the central government. Star Chamber documents of Queen Elizabeth's reign abound with cases against local officials, and any victim of their tyranny could, to quote friend Shallow, 'make a Star-Chamber matter of it'. But the Tudor disciplinary system fell with King Charles's head. The Star Chamber was abolished in 1641, and the Restoration monarchy limped after the accident of January 1649. It had the boldness under Charles II and James II to interfere with the autonomy of municipal government. The Glorious Revolution put an end to that folly. Consequently, from 1689 until the great reforming activity of the nineteenth century local government grew like an untended garden, without plan, choked with weeds, here some order, there riotous disorder.

Grow it had to do, for trade and population and social needs were expanding. In the County the Justices ruled the roost. There was no longer any means of challenging their decrees except by a troublesome and costly process in the High Courts. Such was the reign of law. By issuing general orders or pronouncing something to be a public nuisance they developed quasi-legislative powers; for were they not the tribunal before which breaches of their orders would be tried? It was like the old practice of Privy Council Proclamations, breaches of which were punished by Councillors sitting in the Star Chamber. The country gentry had seen this mote in the monarch's eye, but being now the rulers of the country they did not see the beam in their own eye. The most famous instance of this legislative activity occurred in May 1795, when the Justices of Berkshire met at the Pelican Inn, Speenhamland, and passed resolutions to deal with the problem of poverty — resolutions which were subsequently adopted also by the Justices of other counties. They were made in good faith and are more understandable today when we too have an exceptional problem; but they revolutionized the statutory Poor Law, pauperized the community and were socially disastrous. The name these resolutions obtained — 'The Speenhamland Act of Parliament' — and the heading — 'According to Act of Parliament' — printed on one of the scales of income which they assured to each family, form the pithiest comment on their constitutional significance. Of course, like the Borough the County as a community needed local legislation, local administration, and local justice; and these functions were inherent in the system of J.P.s from early times. The one important change was that by various devices the Justices got rid of juries in their legislative-administrative functions. They dropped the democratic element. They became close bodies, like borough corporations, like Parliament.

However, I must not convey the impression of a wholly rotten state of things. A great deal of solid, unremunerative, and more or less enlightened work was done by the J.P.s. Speaking generally, the system worked well where the community remained rural; that is, in its proper setting. It worked well for those, the majority, who acquiesced in the social order:

> The rich man in his castle, the poor man at his gate,
> God made them high or lowly and ordered their estate.

The system failed where the J.P. controlled growing urban centres. The duties here were particularly onerous and disagreeable. There were not enough gentlemen qualified by status or willing to undertake the office, and either there was a deplorable lack of magistrates or the qualification was lowered and the magistrates were deplorable. The Justices of Middlesex, who controlled Westminster and much of London, 'were generally', said Burke in 1780, 'the scum of the earth – carpenters, brickmakers, and shoemakers; some of whom were notoriously men of such infamous character that they were unworthy of any employ whatever, and others so ignorant that they could scarcely write their own names'. They were the notorious Trading or Basket Justices, availing themselves of the powers vested in one or two Justices. They set up offices and competed for business, since the small fees and fines incident to the judicial process could be made remunerative when multiplied in an urban centre. Extortion, blackmail, injustice were the inevitable outcome of the trade.

> So sorely did the trading harpies waste us
> We suffered less from Spanish guarda costas.

This dreadful scandal was suppressed in 1792 and a system of stipendiary magistrates took the place of the Middlesex Trading Justices. The more respectable Middlesex Quarter Sessions remained, under the chairmanship of a banker of reputed piety, to show in the next decades that corruption was not a monopoly of the small man. It merely became insidious and colossal in respectable hands.

And now what of the Boroughs? We left them as close corporations. We also left them wedded to the country gentlemen in

Parliament, for by the close of Elizabeth's reign the gentry monopolized the representation of the Boroughs in the House of Commons. As yet this meant little or no corruption, but merely persuasion or coercion by local magnates. Corruption began in the seventeenth century and reached the lengths with which we are familiar in the eighteenth century. The consequences are significant. The monarchy made its last attempts to interfere with the government of Boroughs in Charles II and James II's reigns. With the Glorious Revolution Parliament was in the saddle and the only chance of reform from without lay in its will. But the majority of the House of Commons sat for these close Boroughs, while the Lords were equally interested in maintaining them, either because they owned Pocket Boroughs or for other reasons.

This is not all. In the eighteenth century the English constitution reached equilibrium. It reflected society in reflecting the dominance of the territorial class. The country lived under a rule of law, the rule of a law which was the palladium of property. In the early seventeenth century the Common Law had produced its prophet in Sir Edward Coke who boldly denounced the royal prerogative. 'Magna Carta', he declared, 'is such a fellow that he will have no sovereign.' In the eighteenth century it found its prophet in Sir William Blackstone who extolled the constitution and declared the Common Law to be beyond the skill of earthly law-givers seriously to improve. Its faults could not be eradicated without grave harm to the subject. It was a perfection of imperfections. The conservatism and somnolence of old age were upon the constitution. Medievalists will tell you, with some exaggeration, that nothing was abolished in medieval government. New methods took the place of old, but the old continued alongside the new. Vested interests is the explanation. It is the explanation in the eighteenth century. Government was riddled with corruption and abounded in sinecures; but the spoils went into the right hands. The details are incredible. The office of Tally Cutter was not abolished until 1783, and even then abolition was not to be effective until the then holder retired or died. This medieval Dodo lingered until 1826, and his useless wooden tallies went up with such a fine roar when they were being burned in 1834 that they destroyed the old Palace of Westminster. A symbolic bonfire! Take a look some time at *The Extraordinary Black Book*, a propagandist publication of the early nineteenth century, and marvel at the anomalies of the *ancien régime* in England.

Obviously, national planning was not to be expected from the eighteenth century. Non-intervention was its philosophy and policy. But development there had to be. At the end of the century towns were expanding prodigiously and villages becoming prodigious towns. We saw the sixteenth-century Borough coping with its problems of paving, water-supply, and scavenging. They were child's play compared with problems two centuries later. Towns had expanded beyond the old circle of borough authority; moreover, there was the occasional indifference and more general incompetence of the borough corporations and the lack of moral authority which their close and often grossly corrupt character gave them. In default of national planning, local initiative remained: that is to say, private Acts of Parliament conferring on local commissioners the necessary powers to supply one or other of the services that an urban community required. There were hundreds of such Acts, and in this way sewers, paving, lighting, water-supply, police and other services were provided and maintained by commissioners authorized to levy rates. Unfortunately, these Improvement Commissioners, as they were called, were not the borough Corporation, although they might sometimes include its members. This was the price paid for the close Corporation. It meant the disintegration of the Borough and a multiplicity and confusion of authorities. The Borough, like the other organs of local government, only to a greater degree, called for reform. The need was urgent for national planning.

One of Blackstone's pupils at Oxford was Jeremy Bentham.

He had the impertinence to publish a *Fragment on Government*, revealing the absurdity of his professor's classical work on English law. It was a portent: David slinging his stone at Goliath. Bentham brought the *ancien régime* to the test of his principle that the authority of the State must be founded on the general utility of its constitution. He was speaking the language of the nineteenth century, and it is to him and the disciples whom he influenced that the major reforms of the century owe most. Reform indeed was in the air. The greatest institution of all, Parliament, had been under attack from the middle of the eighteenth century, and when in 1832 the Great Reform Bill was carried, it was only a question of time before the close Municipal Corporations, with which the unreformed House of Commons had been so closely connected, should in turn undergo reform.

The Municipal Corporations Act of 1835 was, all things considered, a bold and drastic Act. The elective principle for Councillors, which it established, was sound. So was the separation of justice from administration and the appointment of a professional Recorder. It conferred unlimited authority to levy rates, and by making the Corporation responsible for 'the good rule and government of the Borough' gave scope for new developments and for the absorption of services still left in the hands of *ad hoc* bodies. The Act applied only to existing Corporations, and of these only to a proportion. Consequently, towns like Manchester, which had never been incorporated, were left in their old state; but provision was made for them to petition for incorporation.

The Act emphasized one principle in the history of English local government: that of local autonomy. And the greatest tribute to its success is that when later — lamentably late — in the century, the County at last came to be reorganized, Parliament — to use the familiar phrase — municipalized it. But there was a second principle that the Act utterly ignored. This was central control. As a matter of fact, the principle had been applied in the previous year in the Poor Law Reform Act of 1834. The need for a common standard of public health was later to extend it. Thus our local government developed during the nineteenth century through local autonomy, gradually and increasingly tempered by government supervision.

I referred earlier in this lecture to the late sixteenth century as in some ways the period of maximum satisfaction before the reforms of the last century. I had in mind the blending of the two principles in local government. But central control then came from the monarchy, and now it is from Parliament. Or rather, for I know that you will hasten to correct me, it is from bureaucrats in Whitehall. Maybe you think that the wheel has come full circle back to the sixteenth century, only today it is a Leviathan with which you have to contend. I offer no comment, remembering Raleigh's words, 'Whosoever in writing a modern history shall follow Truth too near the heels, it may haply strike out his teeth.' I have made my perambulation and am back in the Elizabethan period; and so, like the medieval scribe, I end with

Laus Deo.

THE BIOGRAPHICAL APPROACH TO HISTORY[1]

FIRST, a word about the title of this paper. I am not going to discuss the merits or demerits of biography as a form of historical writing. In other words, I am not speaking as the author of *Queen Elizabeth.* I was told that at a Thursday-evening conference at the Institute of Historical Research, devoted to the question of a new edition of the *Dictionary of National Biography*, some speakers were inclined to regard biography as outmoded: to be classed with the Dodo or Queen Anne. If that view was taken, I should have liked to join issue on it: I am a staunch friend of the *D.N.B.*, though whether the time has arrived to rewrite the *Dictionary* is an arguable question, and I think I should argue 'No.'

My old master, A. F. Pollard, who did his best work as a biographer, was opposed to biographies as research theses — I mean biographies in the conventional sense. So, if I remember aright, were Tout and others of that generation. It is a prejudice that I have inherited and retained. If I examine my prejudice, I find that it is not against biography itself, which in any case we must have, and which can be as exacting and searching a discipline as most types of history. It is against young people writing of life before they have gathered sufficient experience to interpret it.

This leads me to a reflection — a provocative one, maybe — with which to end an irrelevant prologue. Between the two world-wars, biography had a remarkable vogue. *Littérateurs* and their publishers scanned history for interesting persons, hitherto unsung or uncursed, or insufficiently cursed. I doubt

[1] A paper read at the Anglo-American Historical Conference held at the Institute of Historical Research on July 14th, 1950, and published in *History* (Oct. 1951), n.s. xxxvi, 193-203.

if there has been anything quite like the craze. Even Jane Shore, to cite one of the most conspicuous examples which came my way as a reviewer, found her biographer. And when an author's sources failed him, we had monologue and dialogue, and much else into the bargain, invented to liven up the story. I remember how in one book Wolsey communed at night with his soul in a remarkable monologue, unknown to the *Letters and Papers of Henry VIII* or any other historical source. The vogue began with Lytton Strachey, who caught or created – something of both, I think – the post-war mood for 'debunking'. His imitators were legion. None equalled the master in quality; some – perhaps most – were pitiable flounderers. Nevertheless, I think that history may have gained rather than lost by this prostitution of the subject. Although Lytton Strachey, through inability to judge sound historical scholarship, based his *Elizabeth and Essex* on a naive, if learned-looking book on Queen Elizabeth's health, and though he did not always know how to interpret his sources, I am an admirer as well as a critic of his work. He and the abler of his imitators were expert in interpreting human beings: they took psychology seriously, as the literary critic, indeed, must. Their historical portraits may have been partly or largely fictional, but they lived. For our part, as professional historians, our traditions and scholarship ensure that our portraits are factual. May we not learn something from the literary experts and make them also live?

But this prologue has gone on too long, and I must turn to my subject. I toyed with the idea of calling my paper, 'The demographical approach to history'. Two or three considerations deterred me. I am not sure that I know what 'demographical' means, and in any case it is a loathsome word. 'The biographical approach to history' it therefore is, though I hope you will not mind if I become surreptitiously 'demographical'.

I do not know how old this type of historical approach may be. The first modern book in my range of reading to apply it was Charles Beard's *Economic Interpretation of the American*

Constitution, the basis of which was a series of biographical studies of the framers of the constitution, keyed into the two rival economic interests of creditor and debtor in the United States. How much of Beard's thesis has survived subsequent critical examination, I am unaware; but clearly, within properly controlled limits his method was a great and promising advance upon what we may call the conventional approach to constitutional history, just as the latter was upon the legal-minded approach of still earlier generations. In England, I remember when we used to see reviews in the weeklies signed 'L. B. Namier' and heard of a formidable and mysterious biographical card-index. We pitied the *littérateur* and the weaker brethren who strayed into his field: we also enjoyed the reviews. And at last came the two volumes on *The Structure of Politics at the Accession of George III.* It is a book which in retrospect must be regarded in this country as one of the supremely influential historical works. Pollard's *Evolution of Parliament* stimulated a remarkable amount of research, but Namier's book began a new historical method.

I suppose that indirectly Marx has had something to do with this new approach, just as Darwin influenced the earlier generation of institutional historians – as witness the title of Pollard's *Evolution of Parliament.* Pollard himself in his last years started what I may call the Namier method in dealing with the Reformation Parliament. He got far with the biographical foundations, but the synthesis never came; and I often wonder whether this was owing to physical or to psychological causes. Was he too much a Darwinian to change over to new methods? Of course we must not press the ideological explanation too far. After a period of frontal attacks on institutional history, a new generation of scholars was bound to try a flank attack, if only in the hope of fresh victories. And I do not doubt that Professor Namier would argue, as I should in my own case, that all he was doing was getting at the facts.

Human beings are the stuff of history. Their social activities, whether political or otherwise, are the result of environment and personal qualities, in which I include personal interests. And to these two I would add that third, strange factor, group behaviour, which almost justifies the personification of abstractions like the State. For as Rousseau has taught us – and we have only to look around to see it justified in a way that would have horrified him, as it horrifies us – the general will is not the arithmetical sum of individual wills. I mention this third factor, not because I propose to dwell on it, but because the biographical approach to history, with which I am concerned, is essentially the method of discovering the 'arithmetical sum of individual wills'; and if we allow ourselves to become mere mathematicians, ignoring the elusive forces that enter into group behaviour, we shall err as surely as our predecessors did in confining themselves to a frontal approach to institutional history.

I state the obvious when I say that we cannot fully understand the nature and functioning of any human group without knowing about the individuals who compose it. This knowledge must come from a series of biographies. But that is not all. We must first know what questions we hope to answer from the biographies, and if at all possible the necessary information must be got. This is a very different proposition from writing ordinary biographies. Indeed, we may have very little interest in the usual contents of a biography. Some of the facts we seek may be difficult to come by; they may seem insignificant and in themselves dull. Once more I may be stating the obvious; but not without provocation. The historians on Colonel Wedgwood's committee dealing with a biographical study of parliament could never get this fundamental thesis home, and he went on compiling biographies without the preliminary enunciation of questions. Such procedure prevents the vital, broad questions being answered; and the answering of these is in my view the principal – I would almost say the sole – justification for the prodigal labour of compiling hundreds of biographies. All facts are not born free and equal. They may be to the antiquary, but not to the historian.

When the same questions are asked and – if possible – answered in each biography, the results can and should be summarized and given in tabular form as statistics (if a mere historian, without the pale, may use that word). It is from these tables, plus the biographies and all the direct evidence commanded by previous scholars, that we can hope to fashion a new and illuminating interpretation of our subject.

For my own part, I am gradually having the parliaments of Elizabeth's reign – and before quitting I hope to add the two preceding reigns – studied in this way. Facts which can be expressed in tabular form include: the social class to which members belonged; their occupation—for example central or local officials, lawyers, etc.; their education; their age; their religious affinities, if ascertainable; their previous and subsequent parliamentary experience; their family relationships; the location of their residence or estates in relation to the constituency. I need not linger to point out the supreme importance of such information for parliamentary history. If only we had similar studies over a long range of time we should be able to trace the infiltration of the gentry into borough seats; changes in the educational quality of the House of Commons and the sort of experience found there; the balance of political, economic, class, and religious interests; and so on. And we could relate these to the parliamentary story and to the legislation that was passed. Nor must I forget to add that for the sixteenth century, and doubtless other centuries, it is only through biographies that one can obtain much of the evidence for an electoral history of the House of Commons. There is direct evidence for a number of elections in the Elizabethan period: for a surprising number, one might perhaps say. But this simply sets the pattern. More often than not the story comes by inference from facts in the biographies. When I wrote my recent book, *The Elizabethan House of Commons*, though I had a shrewd idea of the truth about that notorious problem, the Cornish boroughs and their connection, if any, with packed parliaments, I lacked the evidence to deal with it in detail. So far as the sixteenth century is concerned, the secret will yield itself only through deliberately designed biographical studies of all the Cornish members over a long period of time. A student of mine is tackling the problem along these lines; and I am confident that we shall at last crack this doughty nut.

A study of the members of one parliament makes an almost ideal subject for a research student. The biographical work introduces him to an extraordinarily wide range of sources and secondary material; and what is more, links the material for local history with that for national history. There are no immature disquisitions on character. The results are matter-of-fact; but the pursuit of them has plenty of human interest and gives an admirably broad sense of the structure of society. There is also synthesis, which I regard as highly desirable for the research student. In the hands of the second-class student — and let me add in parenthesis that we should not depreciate such people, who can render great help in extending the frontiers of history and who may, as teachers, carry into the schools the inspiration and enthusiasm, as well as the knowledge, that comes from creative, scholarly work: as I was saying, in the hands of the second-class student the synthesis may be jejune and faulty; but the tables and biographies remain, and if compiled with accuracy — and their factual character helps to induce this — they are invaluable. On the other hand, the finest mind can be stretched by the work to the limits of its ingenuity, critical capacity, and imagination.

Biographies — compiled, shall I say? in the mass, and on this plan — when they come to be studied reveal many facts that can be correlated; many social similarities and differences which in themselves are worth pursuing. They suggest fresh studies, though they may not supply the complete answer. For example, I feel the urge, as a result of my parliamentary work, to probe into the social affinities and implications of university and legal education in the sixteenth century. I should like to trace the invasion of the universities by the country gentry and to establish the facts about what I regard as one of the most important developments in English life – the use of the Inns of Court as finishing schools for the gentry, divorced from any intention of legal practice. Such a study might seem formidable, for it involves biographies on a wholesale scale, though in this particular instance there are Wood and Cooper and Venn to help us. But the archaeologist, with his system of sample trenches, shows us how to tackle the over-large job. We can take our samples at intervals of time, though the sample must always be a complete unit – for example, in the instance I have cited, we must include everyone at the universities and Inns of Court in a particular year.

My work has been the application of the biographical method to parliamentary history – the obvious field of inquiry for an Englishman. But, as my previous remarks indicate, there is a great area of history where the method is also applicable. One could, with great profit, study the Church, especially its higher dignitaries, along these lines. One of my American students this year has been applying the biographical method, as well as the more conventional one, to a study of the episcopacy during the great Reformation divide. He thought that he saw a correlation between the reactions of the bishops to the Reformation and training in the Roman civil law. Whether his facts will ultimately justify such a thesis, I do not know. All that I am concerned with is that here is an approach which may contribute to our understanding of a significant historical theme. Then again, how much I should like to see the information in Miss Garrett's valuable biographical census of Marian exiles supplemented by the necessary facts and thrown into tables showing the social class to which each exile belonged, his vocation, his residence – whether it was in town or country and its geographical location – etc. etc. I imagine that the result would cast a great deal of light upon the political and religious history of the time and in particular on the Elizabethan Puritan movement. One could also study in this way the legal profession, from judges down to barristers, the justices of the peace, the royal household – either in the form of the Court or one or more of its administrative organs – and so on. The essence of the game – if I may use its jargon – is to 'biograph' everyone, ask the right questions, and assemble the facts in tables where their significance may be readily grasped.

In a different way, the biographical approach (by which I mean the compilation of a number of biographies) can be amazingly effective in solving many otherwise insoluble problems in ordinary biography. This of course is particularly true in periods when relatively little direct evidence can be found about many important people. The underlying facts are that men have friends and enemies, and that their activities, in one way or another, are so often related to those of a group. Biographical studies of a man's acquaintances may shed invaluable light on the life of the individual; or it may prove profitable to study someone as a member of a group rather than in isolation. Professor A. W. Reed's *Early Tudor Drama*, which deals with a group round Sir Thomas More, is a conspicuous example of the interaction of several biographical studies. Indeed, it is literary historians, and particularly those interested in Shakespeare, who, for very obvious reasons, make most use of this method. Dr Leslie Hotson's work proceeds along these lines, and in the course of long years of research he has compiled a card-index which deserves, in the best sense of the word, to become fabulous. Historians – or at any rate, modern historians – who usually are concerned with men who have left more ample records of their careers, are not often driven to multiple biographies in order to write one biography; and after all, life is finite and a sense of proportion in research is essential. But it is worth noting that a young American scholar, Mr Zeeveld, has recently thrown interesting and fresh light on Henry VIII and Wolsey, Pole, and Cromwell by a group study of a number of humanists. Others, no doubt, will follow his example.

And now I come to that horrid thing whose name must be whispered – 'demography'. I think there is immense scope for studying people in their social units and classes. I do not mean conventional social history, but something that I might describe as a mixture of institutional history, sociology, and social history. Let me explain. In the Elizabethan period the social and administrative unit *par exellence* was the county, and the politically significant class the country gentry. I should like to see one county taken (with others to follow), each family planted on its land, each family made the subject of a biography, with the same questions asked – all the questions that one could imagine as being interesting when generalized. I should like to elicit information about wealth and movement, social, political, and administrative activities, social, political, and geographical antecedents, size and sex of family, education, marriage, length of life; to ask many of the questions that the peripatetic takers of the census in America seem to be asking just now. I should like, in my own period, to extract through these biographies all that can be obtained about clientage – the political and social relationship of patron and dependant, which prevailed in the sixteenth century – and to investigate the nature and extent of local faction, its influence on local affairs and its connections, if any, with national politics. In that stimulating essay called *A Room of One's Own*, you may remember that Virginia Woolf asked questions about women in the past – and waited for an answer. I should ask them, and ask more of them; and I should obtain the answers, or most of them. I should have this information tabulated and probe into all the conceivable correlations.

What a task! you will say. But each county will make an admirable subject for a research student. The first thesis will face all the difficulties and bear all the blemishes of pioneer work. But improvement will come. And if the teacher is, as we are in London, happily situated in having sufficient students to form a seminar, and if two or more such theses can be constantly under way, then the students will develop a special technique which they will hand on from one to another, encouraging and helping one another. This is co-operative work of the kind achieved when the *D.N.B.* was being written; and I well remember how often A. F. Pollard used to talk of the skill so gained and preserved in the *D.N.B.* office and of the loss to scholarship when that organization was dispersed. Since 1945 I have secured this continuity in the study of Elizabethan members of parliament. There have been two or more students at work each year, overlapping one another. They find confidence and happiness working together; they certainly do better work than they would in isolation; and yet all are stretched to the limits of their varying ability.

Of course, what really interests me is the pattern that emerges when the results of these individual pieces of work are put together; when the synthesis is made of answers to identical questions, asked over a period of time or over a series of separate counties or communities. And I look beyond my Elizabethan period. If we could have similar syntheses arising from similar studies throughout the range of a nation's history, what a remarkable master-study would ultimately be possible! Naturally, some of the questions one would need to ask would change in the course of the centuries, as would their relative importance. Such changes would in themselves throw into relief points of supreme significance. I hasten to add that I am not urging the organization of historical research on a vast scale. I am essentially an individualist and am as hostile to making sociological historians of us all as I am to converting us into bibliographers. Let the spirit blow where it listeth, and example, not committees, guide our interests.

I came to this type of investigation as an institutional historian; and in these latter years the repercussion of the contemporary world has made me more and more want to get behind the formal architecture of constitutions to the men who worked them; to the way politically significant people lived, to the nature of their interests and the conflicts they provoked, to the reflection of all these facts in the social and institutional structure of society; shall I say, to realities? Asking myself, as I constantly do, how far a Hitler or a Stalin is master of his political system or becomes merely another victim of inherent, unplanned, and perhaps unforeseen tendencies in it, I want to look at the past in the same way. And I think that if historians can by this type of inquiry elicit and explain the inherent tendencies in various political or even social and economic systems, they may be adding to the available wisdom of mankind: which, after all, is their supreme function.

For example, I am not satisfied, as my predecessors might have been in rosier days, with describing the personal monarchy of the sixteenth century in terms of what the monarch could and could not do according to the law and custom of the constitution, plus a factual account of what was done. I see the monarch as the principal dispenser of patronage in society, and I want to discover the effect of the competition for this patronage on the structure of Court life, of politics, and of national life in general. My attention, in consequence, is directed to what I have ventured to call clientage, which in the sixteenth century might be regarded as a vestige of feudal days, but can also be viewed as a response to the system of personal monarchy. And let me here interpolate that in my post-war reading about the Hitler regime, I was struck by its resemblance to personal monarchy in the sixteenth century, with many of the stresses and strains familiar to me in Elizabethan history. If it be possible — and I imagine that the biographical approach would alone make it possible — I should like to discover through whose influence every Elizabethan official got his job; to find out in which great courtier's orbit he moved. And I should expect in this way to reach a new understanding of Court politics. Certainly, I should be able to explain much that has seemed very puzzling and unconvincing when tackled along old, conventional lines.

Let me cite another illustration. I am interested in the payment of officials. Pursuing the older approach to constitutional history, Pollard, with his mind always alert for details – and, incidentally, what a privilege it was to be trained by that great scholar, who, though concerned with the large picture, never missed the detail! – noted the wages paid to officials by the Crown. But it is not simply formal wages that interest me. These were supplemented by a system of fees and gratuities which often – perhaps usually – made the total income many times the amount of the formal wage. Now it is the effect of such a system upon society that awakens my curiosity: the tendency towards corruption, the means and effectiveness of controlling this, the result on the efficiency of the service, the danger of corruption getting out of hand. One can see this last danger clearly in the closing years of Elizabeth, and corruption was rampant under James I. Would a series of such studies, analysing the weaknesses of society at various periods, show – as one might expect – a tendency in human affairs for increasing pressure to be exerted on the flaws of any system, distorting its purpose and in the end breaking it down? If so, knowledge of this is valuable. If not – well, there is at any rate virtue in asking the question.

It will be noticed that my questions are always concerned with individuals – with individuals in groups, in the mass. I do not deny that many of the questions could be pursued by direct attack – by seeking directly for the items of evidence, instead of obtaining them through the medium of biography. Nor do I deny that the direct attack must be employed. But the merits of the biographical approach are several. As we construct these group biographies significant points emerge as common elements in the evidence; points which were not likely to reveal their significance in a non-biographical approach. This has certainly been my experience – to a degree that I can hardly exaggerate. My second point is that very many questions in their nature presuppose biographies: the facts are unobtainable without at least skeleton biographies. Then again, the tables showing the prevalence of the phenomena in which one is interested postulate a biographical basis.

Admittedly there is danger in the method. I well remember a convulsive review by the late Professor Hearnshaw of a book which reduced to statistical form a study of aids to the teaching of history in American schools: 'So many per cent used maps, and so many per cent used intelligence!' But folly will out whatever the approach to a subject. Perhaps it shows itself in stark nakedness in this particular approach. But is that a disadvantage?

Let me conclude by assuring you that I am not advancing the proposition that all history is biography. Some history – very fruitful history – is biography.

PROFESSOR A. F. POLLARD[1]

ALBERT FREDERICK POLLARD died on August 3rd, 1948, at the age of 78. He was a product of Oxford, where he obtained a first class in Modern History in 1891, won the Lothian prize in 1982, and the Arnold prize in 1898. In those days the way of a young scholar was hazardous, and it was not as a university teacher but as an assistant editor of the *Dictionary of National Biography* that he began his career in January 1893. He retained this post until the completion of the Dictionary in 1901, contributing the equivalent of a whole volume in signed articles, in addition to his considerable editorial duties.

It would be difficult to exaggerate the significance of this period in his career. These were his formative years. Working under the pressure of an inflexible time-table, he became a master of his craft. His articles — especially those on the Tudor period — remain models of scholarly precision and critical insight; and the range of knowledge and wide acquaintance with historical sources that he thus acquired were an invaluable background for his later writing and teaching. But there was far more to it than that. Pollard's outstanding achievement was to be the organization of historical research, and in the great co-operative enterprise with which his youth was associated the future academic statesman found much of his inspiration. The Dictionary office, with its team of workers mastering a technique that they handed on to new recruits, and with its well-equipped, specialized library, gave him the idea from which ultimately was to come his conception of a postgraduate seminar as a group of scholars, young and old, meeting in a library, as

[1] Published in the *English Historical Review* (April 1949), lxiv, 198-205.

scientists in a laboratory, to discuss their work and aid each other by the incidental dissemination of both method and knowledge. A seminar was neither a class nor a lecture; nor was there any necessary time-limit to membership except that imposed by satiety or death. In his Dictionary experience we may also perceive the germ of the Institute of Historical Research and of the weekly Thursday-evening conference of historians and archivists with which it was associated. Pollard attached much importance to this conference, and in its heyday it accomplished all and more than he expected of it. Those who knew it at its best are not likely to doubt its social value, nor its subtle influence in creating high standards of historical scholarship. The interplay of expert minds in more or less casual 'shop' talk had a worth quite distinct from that of lectures or papers. And though the quality of the conference declined, that was due to accidental causes: life became too full for weekly meetings, and perhaps Pollard was too dominant a personality to preside continuously over this type of meeting. But his gospel remains true, and deserves preaching anew.

Pollard never ceased, on cultural grounds, to deplore the extinction of the Dictionary office. On the material side, he was left with his livelihood to make. He was busy writing at this time. His study of *Protector Somerset* had appeared in 1900; in 1902 he published a biography of *Henry VIII*, and in 1904 a life of *Thomas Cranmer*, as well as five chapters in *The Cambridge Modern History*. The three biographical studies, which still remain standard works, foretold their author's place as the future master of Tudor history in this country. If they had been published today, they might have produced a modest income; but in those days, as Pollard himself wrote, 'the first requisite for an historian in England' was 'neither skill nor industry, neither knowledge of documents nor a faculty for turning them into literature, but the command of financial resources, independent of those which can be derived from the writing of history'.[1] He had to earn a living by teaching at Wren's coaching establishment.

The opportunity for which he had been preparing himself came in 1903 when the chair of Constitutional Law and History fell vacant at University College, London. It is a droll story. The names of both Pollard and W. S. Holdsworth were before the electors, and, embarrassed by such a choice, they had the happy idea of splitting the chair into two, thus taking both. ' "Why not?" said the presiding genius, "there is no stipend for either".'[2] The professor merely received a portion of his students' fees; and in fact Pollard's emoluments for his first year as Professor of Constitutional History amounted to £25 14s. 6d. For the time being he had to continue his outside coaching; but to a young man of vision, drive, and exceptional vigour, the prospect was the reverse of depressing.

In 1903, though Oxford possessed a flourishing undergraduate school of history, there was nothing remotely worthy of the name in London. In the seven previous years the various institutions that made up the teaching University of London had produced six candidates between them for the B.A. Honours degree. No doubt a London school of history would have developed in the course of time, even without Pollard. But he was its architect. It owed everything to him in quality and, above all, in form. In October 1904 – some weeks, it is worth noting, before Firth's plea for historical research in his inaugural lecture at Oxford – he delivered a striking lecture on the subject. In retrospect it seems strangely pessimistic about undergraduates; but for the rest, what vision! Seizing on London's unique advantage as the repository of national records, he promulgated the idea of exploiting fortune by creating 'a postgraduate school of Historical Research in London'. 'A dream does sometimes come true',[3] he added; and though its

[1] Pollard's *Factors in Modern History* (1948 edn, p. 238). The third edition of this book contains comments on the state and development of historical studies in London, written in 1904, 1926 and 1931.

[2] Ibid. p. viii. [3] Ibid. pp. 245, 253.

realization proved more dependent on the growth of an undergraduate school of history than he anticipated, he accomplished his purpose, not by waiting on events but by forcing the pace. He drew the London County Council and its teachers of history into his plans, thus being led into founding the Historical Association in 1906 and acquiring for it, ten years later, a journal, *History*, the exemplary standard of which he set as its first editor. In 1910 he began a twelve years' chairmanship of the University Board of Studies in History, from which position and from his membership of the Senate in 1910-15 he was able to shape the policy of the University in historical studies and to fight a triangular duel with the forces of disruption. Since his goal was a postgraduate school of history, which could only be achieved on a university basis, he was critical of a situation in which the Colleges were all-powerful, while the University, impotent through internal rivalries, remained less than a geographical expression.

As Pollard's vigour was felt in College and University, so his academic position improved. The story, which is drawn from College records, is worth telling because its interest is more than personal. Already in his second year as professor a modest 'stipend' of £50 had been added to his exiguous income from fees. By 1906-7 the 'stipend' had become £200; the fees remained little better than in his first year. Then in 1907 came the first significant change. In order to free him from the necessity of coaching at Wren's and claim his whole time for university work, the 'stipend' was doubled and his 'salary', from 'stipend' and fees, was guaranteed to reach a minimum of £500. This arrangement, which seems strange in our university world of today, was then a normal method of solving the financial problems at University College. The title of Pollard's chair was at the same time changed to Professor of English History, with the obvious purpose of extending both his lectures and his fees. The change was significant in another way. Pollard was, and indeed remained, the junior of the two professors of history.

To leave the senior professor a part-time teacher while preferring the junior was a delicate step. But the decision was wise. If the History Department had not been built round Pollard, the character of historical studies in London – nay more, the shape of the University itself – would surely have been very different today.

In 1908 Pollard was elected to a research fellowship at All Souls College, Oxford, 'on condition', as he states in the preface to his *Evolution of Parliament*, 'of pursuing researches suggested by the late F. W. Maitland'. In this way began a long association which brought him much pleasure and intellectual stimulus. Week-end conversations with men eminent in public life developed that 'academic interest in politics' which revealed itself in much of his writing and teaching. At University College, London, his financial position continued to improve; and another significant stage was reached when in 1912 the practice of paying partly from fees – the professor's share being usually five shillings in each guinea – was abolished. Pollard had been a keen critic of the convention, pointing out – as his own experience showed – that it was more profitable to do elementary than advanced teaching. Curiously enough, there is still a tradition at the College that professors should lecture to Intermediate students. The reason has been idealized, and few are aware of its profane origin.

The war of 1914-18 broadened Pollard's activities. The postgraduate seminar that he had established at University College inevitably dwindled in size, as did his undergraduate school: the realization of his dream might seem to have receded. But in 1914 he began a weekly Thursday-evening conference of historians, archivists, and others, which in many ways proved to be a step forward in his plans and remained a permanent feature of them. He lectured weekly to very large audiences on the course of the war – an enterprise which he regarded as the attempt of a scholar to write strictly contemporary history and out of which came a number of ephemeral though able writings, including *The Commonwealth at War* and his *Short History* of the war. These activities and the stimulus of the times brought out the publicist in him. He was appointed a member of the Government Committee on the League of Nations, set up in 1918, and later sat on two other Departmental Committees. He even stood for parliament, contesting the University seat in 1922, 1923, and 1924, fortunately without success.

He had become a public figure; and this perhaps was essential for his greatest act of academic statesmanship – the creation of the Institute of Historical Research. In retrospect this can be seen as the logical outcome of his lecture in 1904. It was also implicit in his Thursday-evening conference. The scheme was launched in 1920 on the post-war renaissance of historical interest; and Pollard himself found the wealthy donor whose beneficence was needed to supplement the humbler donations of others. By a happy coincidence a site became available on the proposed new University area in Bloomsbury, and though dissensions in the University momentarily forfeited the site and threatened to extinguish the new-born Institute, in the end all turned out well. The Institute was opened in 1921, an event timed to coincide with the first Anglo-American Historical Conference held under its auspices. It was typical of Pollard's vision that from the beginning he saw the Institute, not simply as a London but also as a national and international institution. It has indeed been of incalculable service to Anglo-American cultural relations, and its oecumenical character has never ceased to develop.

Judged either by his ideas or by what he accomplished, Pollard must be accounted one of the outstanding statesmen of the University of London. Imitation is the sincerest form of flattery, and recent developments in the University, such as the Institutes of Archaeology and of Advanced Legal Studies, as well as other schemes now in prospect, spring from the example set by the Institute of Historical Research. True, his opportunity was unique. He found a non-existent school of history at the heart of the Empire, where there was an unparalleled concentration of historical documents. But if the opportunity was unique, so were the obstacles. They would have daunted most men. Combined with the pace at which he drove himself, they nourished the combative instincts in a born fighter. He did not suffer fools gladly, nor did he, like his contemporary, T. F. Tout, allow his heart to soften a somewhat gruff exterior. He won respect, deep respect; rarely affection.

Pollard could never have been the great statesman and teacher that he was, had he not also been a great scholar. His articles in the *Dictionary of National Biography*, his early biographies, and finally his fine volume on the period 1547-1603 in *The Political History of England* established him as one without rival in the field of Tudor history. In 1912 he published his admirable little *History of England* in the Home University Library, which revealed the constitutional trend of his mind, and in 1913-14 three source-volumes on *The Reign of Henry VII*. These last were designed for the growing undergraduate history school in London. They illustrated his insistence on the virtue of training students in the use of original sources, and were the first of a number of volumes inspired by him, either for 'Special Subject' work at the final degree examination, or to introduce students to source material at the Intermediate B.A. stage. In time their pioneer purpose was accomplished, and fashion, becoming critical, let the two series fade out; but the volumes have retained a value quite apart from examination purposes.

In 1920 Pollard published his *Evolution of Parliament*, the most debatable of his serious writings. The book possessed all its author's qualities: careful, minute work on the printed sources, a wide range of apt knowledge, imagination, and a lucid, arresting style, adorned with antithesis and epigram. But medievalists were critical, and Pollard, who was apt to become a controversialist once he had committed himself to writing, did not mend matters by his elaborate attempt to retain untenable positions. However, if it be the mark of an outstanding book to stimulate further research – and no more ambitious claim was advanced in its preface – then this book abundantly merits the distinction. Pollard wrote only one more major work, his biography of *Wolsey*, published in 1929, the product, as so many other notable books have been, of the Ford Lectures. Here the techniques of the biographer and the constitutional historian were blended in one cumulative argument. So fresh was the interpretation that nothing previously written on the subject retained much value. Perhaps it is his finest work. Certainly this, together with his more sober volume in *The Political History*, and his biography of Henry VIII are masterpieces of the historian's craft, and remain unsurpassed in their several fields.

Though more than enough to dignify any normal man's life both in the labour involved and in their quality, his books far from exhaust Pollard's literary output. The articles that he contributed to *The English Historical Review*, to *History*, and to *The Times Literary Supplement*, among which may be mentioned the three on 'The Council, the Star Chamber, and the Privy Council' printed in this Review, would in themselves make a very substantial corpus. They range from detailed pieces of research to scholarly journalism. Nor should we forget his reviews in these periodicals. For some years he reviewed most of the works on Tudor history noticed in this Review, and thereafter performed a similar service in *The Times Literary Supplement*, where the rule of anonymity rarely concealed his identity, for no one else could have written with the same critical ability and authority. His reviews were usually trenchant; maybe too much so on occasions. But they extended to the sixteenth century the field in which shoddy work was almost certain of exposure, and were of untold service to the standards of English historical scholarship.

Pollard did very little work among manuscripts: indeed, his activities as an academic statesman, and perhaps his temperament, made such painfully slow research impossible. He was fortunate in having at his service the matchless calendar of the *Letters and Papers of Henry VIII*, his knowledge of which was unique and may long remain so. In his latter years he began to work on the Reformation Parliament, along biographical lines. He had returned, so far as the basic research was concerned, to his Dictionary days. The biographical work that he did was masterly; but alas! the synthesis never came. In these years he published a number of extremely detailed articles, resting on the biographical technique. They are almost antiquarian in character, but anyone working over them would be moved to pay tribute to the extraordinarily acute quality of the scholarship. It is a quality that underlies all his work in Tudor history. He never hesitated to pursue his facts with the utmost patience and skill.

In 1921, when he founded the Institute of Historical Research, Pollard had retained his chair and work at University College, and had run the Institute as Chairman of its Committee. The two functions proved too heavy a burden, and therefore in 1927 a part-time Directorship was established, coupled with a part-time chair at his College. He reverted to his old title of Professor of Constitutional History, and was in fact virtually free to concentrate his energies on the Institute. In 1931, when he went to live in Hampshire, he resigned the chair and became Honorary Director of the Institute; a generous action which at a time of financial stringency preserved the principle of having a great scholar at the head of the Institute, though oddly enough this was a principle to which later his Committee proved to be more strongly attached than he. In 1939 he resigned the Directorship. In view of the outbreak of war, it was perhaps as well that he retired when he did; but the dispersal of the University for so many years prevented adequate tribute being paid to him. Tribute had indeed been paid in the volume *Tudor Studies*, presented to him in 1924 after retirement from the chairmanship of the History Board. There still remained an epilogue to be spoken on fifteen years of further activity and service. In the end, his powers failed. He had worn himself out.

Pollard was his work. Essentially a moralist, he was hard with himself, and frequently with others. 'What a man does, depends on what he does without', he often said: and this stern creed, along with his tireless energy, explains his astonishing literary output and the miracle of the London history school. He regulated his life to a time-table, and was at his best working under pressure. For many years sheer necessity did not permit him to relax, and subsequently character maintained the habit. There was little time for the graces: some may have thought there was little inclination, though shyness and a Victorian fear of emotion also enter into the explanation. He was perhaps most at ease with American scholars, whose country he twice visited, and for whom the Institute and its conferences did much to transform the old life of isolation when visiting London. But few of his contemporaries or even of the younger generation achieved intimacy with him. He was not a good listener in conversation that ranged outside his interests. The urge to lead was too strong and his nature too stubborn to be appreciably mellowed by age and success. Here his first wife, a constant companion in all his work, more than made amends; and there are many British and American scholars who remember that kindly lady with gratitude. Nor would it be fitting to write of Pollard's achievements without reference to Miss Jeffries Davis, whose learning earned her a niche of her own, but who toiled selflessly at the many tasks created by his activity. How true it is that great men rarely accomplish their missions without the devotion of others. Such a figure as Pollard's belongs to pioneer days, and we who are the beneficiaries must revere the qualities of character and intellect that shaped our inheritance.

INDEX

INDEX

INDEX

INDEX